Resaying the Human

Levinas Beyond Humanism and Antihumanism

Carl Cederberg

Södertörns högskola

PREVIOUSLY PUBLISHED TITLES

Hermeneutik och tradition: Gadamer och den grekiska filosofin (2003)
Hans Ruin & Nicholas Smith (eds.)

Kommentar till Heideggers Varat och tiden (2005)
Hans Ruin

Rethinking Time: Essays on History, Memory, and Representation (2011)
Hans Ruin & Andrus Ers (eds.)

Phenomenology of Eros (2012)
Jonna Bornemark & Marcia Sá Cavalcante Schuback (eds.)

Ambiguity of the Sacred (2012)
Jonna Bornemark & Hans Ruin (eds.)

Translating Hegel (2012)
Brian Manning Delaney & Sven-Olov Wallentein (eds.)

Foucault, Biopolitics, and Governmentality (2013)
Sven-Olov Wallenstein & Jakob Nilsson (eds.)

Madness, Religion, and the Limits of Reason (2015)
Jonna Bornemark & Sven-Olov Wallenstein (eds.)

Phenomenology of Pregnancy (2016)
Jonna Bornemark & Nicholas Smith (eds.)

Södertörns högskola
SE-141 89 Huddinge
2010

www.sh.se/publications

Cover & Cover Image: Rafael B. Garrida
Graphic Design: Per Lindblom & Jonathan Robson

Stockholm 2010

Södertörn Doctoral Dissertations 52
ISSN 1652-7399
ISBN 978-91-86069-21-6

For Silas

Contents

Acknowledgments

First I want to thank my colleagues in the Philosophy Department at Södertörn University. I am especially indebted to my supervisors: Marcia Sá Cavalcante Schuback and Hans Ruin, not only for their patient and insightful supervision, but also for being the two persons who most of all are responsible for the formation of the philosophical environment in which I have been learning and working as a Ph.D. student. Without them I could not have conceived and developed the thoughts presented in this book. For this I am deeply grateful.

Södertörn's higher seminar of philosophy was the main forum in which I presented my work as it progressed. I want to thank all the participants in these seminars for fruitful discussions, and particularly mention Anders Bartonek, Jonna Bornemark, Krystof Kasprzak, Christian Nilsson, David Payne, Ramona Rat, Anna-Karin Selberg, Fredrika Spindler, Fredrik Svenaeus, and Sven-Olov Wallenstein, all of whom gave important comments and remarks in the process of this thesis' production.

As a Ph.D. student, however, I had more than one institutional affiliation. My studies could not have been conducted had I not been accepted at the Baltic and East European Graduate School (BEEGS). There I enjoyed a warm and inspiring atmosphere and I am very thankful to my fellow Ph.D. students, to the direction and administrative staff of BEEGS and CBEES (Centre for Baltic and East European Studies) for this time together. Rebecka Lettevall, Research Leader at CBEES, receives my heartfelt thanks for putting me in touch with Robert Bernasconi and arranging so that he could come as a Guest Professor to Södertörn. Moreover, even if BEEGS and the Philosophy Department at Södertörn was my home environment for work and study, Södertörn had still not received their rights to examine doctorates while I was a Ph.D. student. Therefore, I was inscribed in the Philosophy Department at Stockholm University. I want to express my gratitude to them for agreeing to be the host department for my dissertation. My sincere thanks go to Staffan Carlshamre who, not only acted as my formal supervisor but read my text and gave helpful comments.

When my project was still in the process of being worked out, I was invited by Werner Stegmaier to present my thesis in Greifswald. He supported my endeavour from the start and gave me good advice. Moreover, he introduced me to Silvio Pfeiffer, to whom I am also grateful for his early feedback.

I spent a lovely year 2005–2006 in Copenhagen at the Center for Subjectivity Research. I am very thankful to Dan Zahavi for inviting me to stay there for that year, and have all my colleagues there as a warm reminder.

I also want to express my thanks to the institutions that made my research financially possible. Firstly, the Baltic Sea Foundation generously provided the funding for my research. Later, when my financing as a Ph.D. student had reached its time limit, I was employed part time by the Department of Teacher Training and Education Studies (Lärarutbildningen) at Södertörn University, while putting the finishing touches to my thesis. Apart from allowing me the opportunity to finish the thesis, it has shown me an avenue down which this research can be taken further.

In close vicinity to the academic institutions, the Levinas reading group (Anna Holmström, Christian Nilsson, Ramona Rat, Gustav Sjöberg, Björn Sjöstrand and Ynon Wygoda) was an excellent environment for trying out some of the ideas presented in the dissertation.

Warm thanks must go to Robert Bernasconi. Firstly, his work has shown me (and many, many other people) how to read Levinas. In addition to this, Robert generously read and offered an extensive commentary on the dissertation in two different stages of its production.

Probably the singularly most important intervention came from David Payne. He worked as a proof-reader and language consultant in the final stage of the thesis, and his comments helped me to see many of the weaknesses and obscurities of my text. Moreover, his almost uncanny understanding for the mechanics of my argument as well as his expertise in political philosophy made him valuable to the dissertation far beyond the expectations of a proof-reader. Any remaining mistakes and obscurities are due only to my stubbornness.

For the ingenious book cover I thank Rafael Benito Garrida.

There are many others whose contributions have left their mark during the course of this project. I would therefore like to extend my warmest gratitude to Tandi Agrell, Ulrika Björk, Agnes Ers, Johannes Flink, Jonna Hjertström Lappalainen, Stine Holte, Lars-Erik Lappalainen Hjertström, Kate Larson and Søren Overgaard. Each provided valuable comments on ideas eventually presented in this book.

Working on a philosophical thesis for more than five years is an adventure and an incredibly inspiring challenge. But it is also a long and lonely endeavour. Philosophy aspires for the highest of meanings and can at the same time seem utterly void. Without the horizon of philosophically inspired friendship outside the "academic philosophy" it would be difficult to uphold the sentiment of its meaningfulness. I want to mention three friends in particular who have contributed in this way: Daniel Fäldt, Lari Honkanen and Paul Maslov Karlsson.

Finally, I thank Eva Schwarz. We work and love was das Zeug hält. And my son, Silas, to whom this book is dedicated. With the two of you, life is sweet.

C.C.
Stockholm, 1 November, 2010

Introduction

Is there a place for the notion of the human in contemporary philosophy? It might seem that, ever since the 1960s, the concept has become so tainted by ideology one wonders how it can once more gain philosophical traction. Yet, at the same time, how could philosophy possibly relinquish this notion? Has not philosophy always revolved around some idea of the human? Arguably, it has always occupied a position from which other central philosophemes have gained their structural consistency. The most radical changes in the history of philosophy have had to pass through an understanding of the human, either by maintaining its central place but transforming its elemental structure, or more radical still, by questioning its pivotal position, seeking to remove the idea of the human from the centre through an act of displacement.

In this book, I would like to show how the philosophy of Emmanuel Levinas can be read as an attempt not only to partake in this debate, as if he were only offering just another understanding of the human. Rather, a rethinking the notion of the human makes possible a new understanding of the moment of critique, which for Levinas is constitutive of philosophy. In the reading of Levinas that I wish to advance, the notion of the human is the very condition of possibility for critique. By highlighting the notion of the human rather than that of the other, my aim is to show how the ethics of difference, often associated with Levinas, is unjustified, and how this dominant reading risks pushing him into an apolitical cul-de-sac. Rather, what makes his philosophy all the more pertinent is its mobilisation of a universalist project from within the categories of difference and alterity.

In this study, comprised of two parts, I intend to present and argue for the relevance of Levinas's notion of the human for contemporary thought. In the first part, I will show how his notion of the human developed throughout his philosophical itinerary, through an engagement with other thinkers and movements. In the second part, I present and discuss the position Levinas arrives at in his later work. Using this, more fully articulated position, I show him to be a political thinker of contemporary relevance.

In this introduction to the study, three significant steps will be made. First, in order to provide a background against which the force of Levinas's intervention appears, it is necessary to give a brief account of how the human has been understood in the history of philosophy. Second, the status of the present political and intellectual discursive situation regarding the notion of the human and humanism will be investigated. Finally, a brief outline of the main argument and structure of the book will be provided.

A Genealogy of the Concept

Classically, defining the essence of the human meant setting a moral standard for oneself and for others. The human was in this sense a task to be fulfilled; one must prove oneself human. This is clearly evident in the Roman virtue of *humanitas*—the virtue of the cultured citizen constructed in contrast to the figure of the barbarian. The idea has a longer genealogy, however; even if *humanitas* as a virtue was a Roman invention, the path had been prepared by the Greeks long before. The notion of the human had, from the beginning of what can be called the history of Western philosophy, a particular relation to the Good, *to agathon*. Heraclitus said that only the best (*aristoi*, plural comparative of *agathon*), who "prefer immortal fame to mortal things", are more than beasts.[1] This greatness was proven by deeds. With Plato, this story took a distinct twist. To be truly human was now to live a life devoted to reason, to fulfil the movement of *paideia*, the education of the soul. Not to do so would be to live on the level of a "mollusc"—or hardly to live at all, since the acts of perceiving, experiencing and remembering one's life are all associated with Reason, *nous* (Phil. 21a-c). For Plato, the fulfilment of humanity proceeds by way of the advance of *paideia*: the movement out of the limits of the merely sensible world, grasping one's situation from the universal perspective of the Ideas. This is the essential meaning of the cave allegory. The access to the human performs what we would now call *critique*: the notion of the human is connected to an emancipatory function, allowing one to transcend the present state of affairs with the help of the Ideas. This movement is stated in metaphysical terms, and must be performed with the help of dialectics, in which one is forced to justify one's conceptions of the good life, and in the process of this justification find oneself to be dependent on the Ideas, and ultimately, on the Good. The one who does not do this, will not elevate his eye of the soul from the barbaric dirt (*borboros barbarikos* (Rep. 531d)). The "eye of the soul" is of course the image of reason, understood as giving access to the noetic dimension of life. Being is understood to have its essence in its understandability (i.e. in the Ideas) and the soul of the human being is "related to" the Ideas; it is defined by this relation. According to this view, therefore, to be human is to understand being. This is not just a question of placing the soul in a free relation with the Ideas. For Plato, what counts is the most felicitous relation between the soul and the realm of Ideas. In its relation to the ideas, the soul is ultimately related to the Good. In this way the Ideas are themselves hierarchised, with the human soul turning towards the Good as that which ultimately gives meaning and orientation to the Ideas and to human existence. The perfection of

[1] Fragment B29 in Hermann Alexander Diels, *Die Fragmente der Vorsokratiker*, rev. by Walther Kranz, Weidmann, 1952.

the human being therefore lies in expanding the noetic capacity, in understanding the Good, thereby becoming good. This, for Plato, is the movement of philosophy.

This logical entailment of the Human, Reason and the Good has been reiterated in different versions throughout the history of Western philosophy by thinkers as different as Aristotle, Seneca, Pico della Mirandola and Descartes. In each case we witness the forging of a connection between the notion of the human and the exercise of reason as the ability to perceive the truth of being. This practice of the eye of the soul is also its liberation, becoming free from determination from the outside. Rationality has, at least since Plato, been articulated with a notion of autarchy (in modern thought: autonomy), understood as the mastery of one's own thought and actions. To be human is to be free, in the sense of not being defined from what is other (heteronomy). This claim might seem to run counter to the fact that Plato's model for the liberation of the human soul was the exposition to the elenctic reasoning of a master dialectician. Moreover, to say that for Plato reason is distinctly linked to autonomy appears at variance with his subordination of man under the Ideas. Does not the cave allegory start by the person having his head turned towards the opening by an external force a force coming of course from the Ideas? Doubtless, this is the case. Nonetheless, we should take caution not to understand the Ideas as alien; the soul is "related to" (Phaid. 79d) the Ideas. Submitting to the force of universal reason is necessary for autonomy; the true self is the rational self.

This ideal of autonomy has an indelible presence in the history of philosophy, finding particular perspicuity in the age of Enlightenment. Kant's "Answer to the question: What is Enlightenment?" has, in this regard, canonical status.[2] There, Kant defines enlightenment as "man's emergence from his self-incurred immaturity".[3] This is in its turn defined as the incapacity to make use of one's reason without the guidance of others. When Kant formulates his ideal of an autonomous reason it is very much directed against the authority of religion. As a strong advocate of freedom of religion, Kant places his faith in the liberatory role that such a freedom would have in the movement towards an enlightened conscience (p. 60). Not to allow every human being to make use of their own reason would be tantamount to "trampling underfoot the sacred rights of man" (p. 58). With Kant, the holiness of the clergy makes its descent to encompass the individuality of the human being as such. His call for enlightenment is in this sense an invocation for Human Rights by means of secularisation. The implications of Enlightenment in this sense go further than the freedom of religion. At root is a

---

[2] "Beantwortung der Frage: Was ist Aufklärung?" in Immanuel Kant, *Schriften zu Anthropologie, Geschichtsphilosophie, Politik und Pädagogik 1*, Werkausgabe Band XI, edited by Wilhelm Weischedel, Suhrkamp, 1996 [1783], pp. 53-61, translated by H.B. Nisbet as "Answer to the question. What is Enlightenment?" in Immanuel Kant, *Political Writings*, Cambridge University Press, 1991, pp. 54-60.

[3] "Beantwortung der Frage: Was ist Aufklärung?", p. 53; "Answer to the question. What is Enlightenment?", p. 54.

sanctification of individual liberty, a recognition of the inalienable Rights of Man, of human rights (as formalised in the aftermath of the French Revolution). The Enlightenment is in this sense the progenitor of Humanism as a fully integrated world-view.

With Feuerbach,[4] this movement in (or away from) German Idealism is taken to an extreme: a deification of man; the attributes of perfection given to God as the Supreme Being are now understood to be externalisations of the belief in the highest destiny of man. The young Marx, in his *Critique of Hegel's Philosophy of Right,* summarises what he calls "German Theory" as follows: "The critique of religion ends with the teaching that *man is the highest essence for man*—hence, with the *categorical imperative to overthrow all relations* in which man is a debased, enslaved, abandoned, despicable essence".[5] Even if this has taken very many different forms and understandings, a constant running through this movement, from Plato to Marx, is the belief that there lies in the notion of man the possibility to see beyond one's situation and change it. In this way, the history of this movement—freeing man from the bounds of necessity, from social and religious destiny—is inextricably tied to another tendency, the possibility of critique. However, the relation between these two tendencies, between humanism and critique, has been far from smooth and uncomplicated.

Certainly, the concept of critique has since Kant been a pretendant to the philosopher's throne. Critique has been understood as circumscribing both the possibility and the limit of the task of philosophy. Defined by Kant as the "science of the mere examination of pure reason, its sources and limits"[6], the role of critique is to reign in the excesses of speculative reason, so as to think the very condition of possibility for knowledge.

But while Kantian critique is consistent with a positive thematisation of the human, establishing a co-belonging between philosophy and man, the history of critical thought contains within it a counter-tendency. Such is the case with Nietzsche, with the later Marx, and with what later in France during the 1960s became known as "antihumanism". Here, the tables are turned against the idea of the human. Since the notion is associated with humanist discourses that are unwilling or unable to question the predominant system of powers, a true critique carried out in the name of humanism has become impossible. The political consequences of the various critiques of humanism can vary, but common to all

[4] *Das Wesen des Christentums*, Akademie Verlag, 1984 [1841].

[5] *Marx-Engels-Werke*, Bd. I, *Kritik der Hegelschen Rechtsphilosophie*, Dietz Verlag, p. 385; "Contribution to the Critique of Hegel's Philosophy of Right" in Marx, Karl and Engels, Friedrich, *On Religion*, (ed. Reinhold Niehbuhr), Scholars, 1982, p. 50.

[6] *Kritik der reinen Vernunft*, Felix Meiner Verlag, 1998 [1781], A 11 / B 25, translated by Norman Kemp Smith, Palgrave Macmillan, 2003.

is that each holds humanism to be an attitude unable to question fundamentally the hegemony of Western power and reason.

With Nietzsche, the notion of critique is turned against philosophy and science. "Science itself now *needs* a justification", he writes.[7] Nietzsche sees it as a deficiency of every contemporary philosophy that one has failed to realise this. This ignorance is caused by the inability of philosophers to see truth itself as a problem. Accordingly, Nietzsche claims: "The will to truth requires a critique—let us thus define our own task—the value of truth must for once be experimentally called into question."[8] For Nietzsche, this critique will show that science and philosophy are still inextricably bound up with a Christian-Platonist morality, suppressing life to the benefit of transcendent values. The focus philosophers and others have placed on these "human, all too human" values has imposed a too strict limitation on philosophical thought. Accordingly, the notion of the human stands for a philosophical myopia, a view unable to criticise the Christian-Platonist values, deeply rooted in Western thinking.

In retaining the emphasis on the notion of critique, Nietzsche places himself in the tradition of Kant. Here, however, critique undergoes a radical twist; it is brought to bear on an entirely different task. Rather than freeing human reason from its self-inflicted immaturity, Nietzsche believes that critique must serve life in freeing itself from the remains of the Christian moralism in which he saw it implicated. For Kant, critique meant divorcing illegitimate claims of knowledge (about the thing-in-itself) from legitimate truth claims (about the condition of possibilities). For Nietzsche, even the legitimate truth claims must be critiqued. Truth is seen as a value, as one value among others, and the task of philosophical critique is the examination of values.[9]

A somewhat different rejection of humanism was put forward by Martin Heidegger, who reacted against his contemporary, Jean-Paul Sartre and his attempt to formulate existentialism as a humanism. For Heidegger, humanism in its different hues has always been ensnared within a metaphysical interpretation of being, not sufficiently open to the historical event of Being. Unlike Nietzsche, though, Heidegger does not formulate this in terms of a critique of values, reducible to a value for life; for Heidegger, this would still be a concession to metaphysical thought.

Besides its Nietzschean variant, the idea of critique played an important role within Marxist theory, again taking on an altogether different inflection from its Kantian forebear. The subtitle of *Capital* reads: "critique of political economy",

---

[7] *Zur Genealogie der Moral* III.24; KSA 5, p. 401, my translation.

[8] Ibid.

[9] Gilles Deleuze writes: "One of the main forces behind Nietzsche's work was to demonstrate that Kant had not performed a genuine critique, because he had not asked the question of critique in the form of value", *Nietzsche and Philosophy*, Continuum, 2006, p. 1-2, Cf. Ibid, 66ff.

performing a materialist critique of the economical terms of society. The critique of ideology unearths the system of values that are used in order to prop up a certain power regime. Philosophical discourse was as ideological—and ripe thereby for critical examination—as any putative political discourse. Speaking of philosophy's 'critical death', Louis Althusser saw Marx, in his later writings, pronouncing the death of humanist philosophy, ushering in the birth of ideology critique.[10] In a similar vein, the Frankfurt school coined their own mode of critique. Max Horkheimer pronounced Critical Theory as a critique of society in explicit opposition to a critique of the faculty of pure reason.[11] It is a critique of the irrationalities of a putatively rational bourgeois society, for the purpose of a *truly* rational determination of events in a future society.[12] His erstwhile collaborator Theodor Adorno distanced himself a little more from the Marxist subordination of philosophy to theoretical critique, working on a truly dialectical relation between the materialist critique of society and the idealist critique of reason: "Social critique is critique of knowledge and vice versa".[13]

Later, in what is commonly referred to as the era of postmodern philosophy, critique has itself become an object for problematisation. Foucault writes:

> There is no longer any orientation [...] We must start over again from the beginning and ask ourselves what we can base the critique of our society on in a situation, in which the previously implicit or explicit foundation of our critique has broken away. We must start again… start the analysis, the critique all over again."[14]

But whereas Foucault still identifies his own philosophy with the notion of critique,[15] for Derrida the idea of critique is itself part of the metaphysical heritage that is in need of deconstruction.[16] And for someone like Lyotard in *Libidinal Economy*, the notion of critique is worthy only of laughter, "since it is to maintain oneself in the field of the criticised thing, and in the dogmatic, and indeed paranoiac, relation of knowledge".[17]

---

[10] Louis Althusser, *Pour Marx,* La découverte, 2005 [1965], p. 19-20

[11] Cf. Max Horkheimer, *Traditionelle und kritische Theorie*, Fischer, 2005. p. 223.

[12] Ibid, p. 215.

[13] Theodor Adorno, "Zu Subjekt und Objekt" in *Schriften*, 10.2, p. 748.

[14] Michel Foucault, "La torture, c'est la raison", Interview with K. Boesers, December 1977, *Dits et écrits III,* Gallimard 1994, pp. 397-8.

[15] Cf. also his "What is critique?", transl. Lysa Hochroth in *The Politics of Truth*, eds. Sylvère Lotringer and Lysa Hochroth, Semiotexte, 1997, where the role of critique is described thus: "a means for a future or a truth that it will not know nor happen to be, it oversees a domain it would not want to police and is unable to regulate.", p. 25.

[16] "Letter to a Japanese Friend", *Derrida and Difference*, ed. Robert Bernasconi and David Wood, Northwestern University Press, 1988, p. 3.

[17] Jean-François Lyotard, *Libidinal Economy*, Continuum, 1993, p. 95. Lyotard targets both Marxist and variants of Kantian critique, proposing a philosophy of humour instead of critical justification.

The notion of the human has thus in the history of philosophy been seen both as an expression of ideology (antihumanism) and as the possibility of its radical questioning (humanism). It is this categorial undecidability, which the idea of the human convokes with respect to the possibility of critique that I seek to explore through the philosophy of Emmanuel Levinas.

The Contemporary Discursive Situation

What I would like to show is how Levinas intervened upon the scene of philosophy's treatment of the human, actively reshaping the idea, and showing how such a notion of the human carries with it the very condition of possibility for critique. Already in the title of this study, it is claimed that we must understand him as "resaying" the human. For a start, the notion of resaying is ambiguous. Is this to be understood as a conservative insistence on the notion of the human, or does it mean a radical transformation of the notion as we know it? And how is one to differentiate between these two options? Certainly, a radical transformation can spring from deeply conservative motives, just as the insistence on the validity of an ancient concept can be the source of a radical critique. In fact, Levinas's philosophy is both an attempt at safeguarding the notion of the human by reforming how we understand it in philosophy, and at retrieving in the notion of the human the condition of possibility for philosophical critique, that is, the very possibility to think beyond any seemingly safeguarded consensus. Even if this investigation aims to show how Levinas's thought can be used for radical rather than conservative thought, the philosophical question of the human transcends the opposition between the radical and the conservative, preserving this difference within itself. Levinas's aim is best understood if we are to understand his philosophy as operating metapolitically, rather than as a specific mode of politics, tied to a concrete programme, aligned to a particular ideology.[18]

In this book (as indeed it is for Levinas), the central notion is "the human", rather than "man", "mankind", "humanity" or "human being". The purpose of this, admittedly, in English somewhat strained and awkward adjectival noun is to place the emphasis on the discursive quality of *l'humain* or *das Menschliche*, rather than making it appear as if we were speaking about metaphysical man, humanity in the sense of mankind or human being as a species. It is not a category (ontological or biological) under which we human beings are counted as individuals. Rather, the notion of the human interrupts this relation between the particular and the universal. It serves to draw attention to the singular, irreducible to the relation between universality and particularity, opening up thereby another way of thinking the universal. It will be shown, how Levinas can con-

[18] For the coining of this term in relation to Levinas's philosophy, cf. Miguel Abensour, "Anarchy between Meta-Politics and Politics", *Parallax*, Volume 8, Issue 3 June 2002, pp. 5-18.

ceive of universalism as a process, rather than as a reference to a pre-given universal essence.

The centrality of the notion of the human in Levinas's work ties him to the debates of the 1960s and 70s about the future of humanism, in terms of both its philosophical and political utility. Where is he to be placed in this debate? Since, for a certain period of time, Levinas chose to associate his philosophy with humanism, calling it a "humanism of the other man", the case may seem closed. In later texts, however, from the mid 1970s, one can detect a change in tack; thereafter, humanists are addressed by him only in the third person, and, more intriguingly still, antihumanism is, to a certain extent, championed by the French-Jewish thinker as revitalising the notion of the human.

In spite of this, for many interpreters Levinas fits squarely into the humanist camp. For example, Leonard Rosmarin talks of a "renewed humanism" in his work.[19] In a similar fashion, Catherine Chalier reads Levinas as inviting us "to leave the dwelling of being and advance without prudence towards the 'light (*clarté*) of utopia' (NP 64; PN 44), where the human shows itself".[20] In contrast, I place emphasis on the growing prudence that Levinas shows in the descriptions he issues about this "advance". Furthermore, I have certain misgivings about her claim that the human "shows itself". The notions of showing and light seem to allude to an association of truth with light, as if the human were a phenomenon showing itself with clarity.

On the contrary, the notion of the human plays a very complex role in Levinas's work. To map out this overdetermined category is a central aim of this investigation. Levinas's insight about the precarity of the notion of the human also means that one cannot simply classify him as a humanist. The force of his contribution derives from a certain confrontation with antihumanism and humanism. Of course, one may wonder why Levinas's relation to the battle between humanism and antihumanism would be relevant for us today. The project may seem dated—humanism has after all, in much of what is referred to as continental philosophy, come to function as a pejorative description of a "pre-poststructuralist" position, typically personified by Jean-Paul Sartre.

However, even if in contemporary philosophy humanism has become a non-word, an archaism, humanist slogans are never too far from the political scene, albeit uttered in a somewhat subdued voice. "Humanism" is seen as a notion

---

[19] Leonard Rosmarin, *Emmanuel Lévinas, humaniste de l'autre homme*, Éditions du Gref, Collections L'un pour l'autre, no 1, 1991, p. 117.

[20] "Lévinas convie donc à deserter la demeure de l'être et à s'avancer, sans prudence, vers 'la clarté d'une utopie' là où se montre l'homme" (Catherine Chalier, *Lévinas. L'utopie de l'humain*, Albin Michel, 1993, p. 11. It should be noted that when Levinas here talks about a clarity of utopia, he is interpreting and quoting Paul Celan. Even if he quotes Celan favorably, it is not the same thing as if he had formed this conceptuality on his own. In fact, as we will see, Levinas argues against Husserl's notion of clarity as a telos for a philosophy on the human.

with immense pretensions; to describe oneself as a humanist means to claim to be working for the best of mankind, thereby implying that one's opponent is not doing so. Humanism and hypocrisy are words that seem to call for each other. Nevertheless, were one to conduct an experiment and ask the average educated citizen of the Western world what motivates their views on political practice, I would venture the hypothesis that he or she would eventually refer to some form of humanism. Even if most decisions and opinions will, when prompted, be justified on a much smaller scale, these justifications will in their turn be motivated by—and in the end point to something like—"what is good for human beings" as the final, unquestionable, horizon.[21] Concern for the rest of the living species is most of the time, if not always, conceived as a concern for the *environment*, a concept lacking any sense without the central focus on the human being dwelling therein. This is by no means the same as saying that these verbal motivations are the actual or fundamental causes for actions. I am saying, more modestly, that it is precisely in its resourcefulness in providing verbal justifications that humanism plays a dominant role.

On the scale of world politics, it seems that the political convulsions of the late eighties and early nineties have, depending on one's viewpoint, led to either an inflation or a deflation in humanist rhetoric. It might seem to have been strengthened: one could write the story of the struggles of Charta 77 in Czechoslovakia, of Andrei Sakharov and the Moscow Human Rights group in the Soviet Union and other similar movements in Eastern Europe; how, having defeated totalitarianism, such political mobilisations opened up the possibilities for democratic reform. "A victory for humanism!" some will exhort.

Perhaps, however, it pays to be a little less sanguine. If there were before, at least on the level of political rhetoric, two conflicting Western projects, battling for world dominion, now the situation is more of the West against the Rest. The individualist universalism of Western market liberalism is no longer challenged by a socialist universalism; now the power struggles are less clearly translatable into a battle over the definition of humanism. More often, the battles are rhetorically portrayed as standing between Western liberalist universalism and conservative or "fundamentalist" particularisms. However, since the market liberalism of the West so clearly has the upper hand in this conflict, the emancipatory language of humanism rings rather hollow. And in this scenario, humanism appears all the more as a euphemism, as hiding a system of power, a newspeak for military interventions and imperial domination. We need only to be reminded of the so-called "humanitarian interventions" by NATO bombers in the former Yugoslavia in 1999. Possibly this overexploitation of the humanist jargon is sufficient justification why humanism is

[21] One could object that this is only valid for a post-monotheist, secularised attitude, held only by a minority of the world population. And yet is this not the moral attitude most interculturally translatable and therefore most feasible as a "world ideology"?

best viewed with some scepticism, and politically, why the notion of the human in the economy of political discourse has undergone a deflation in its value.

This deflation can perhaps account for an upsurge in political realism and neoconservatism at the turn of the millennium; there was a tendency towards a more direct way of expressing power interests: whereas G.H.W. Bush senior had named military interventions "humanitarian", the US administration under Bush junior more often spoke of strategic alliances, speaking somewhat less about the protection of democratic rights and the championing of humanitarian causes.

Nevertheless, the humanitarian discourse remains a source from which the hegemonic power of the West, in relation to its most proximate others (now the Muslim and Arab world) is justified, and with the help of which one can make out the emerging power of China as a threat. The humanitarian foreign aid programmes, from the US and Europe, are in this context akin to pouring oil on troubled waters of dissent. The intellectual leftist opposition has become, as a result, even more typically antiuniversalist and rhetorically antihumanist. On the other hand, the humanist discourse is also present in the critique of the dominant power, ranging from specific criticisms, for example the criticism of the treatment of prisoners in the camps of Guantánamo Bay, to the more general critique of capitalism as the enslavement of human beings under the forces of capital.

The way in which Human Rights have come to command much attention internationally gives a good example of the duplicity of humanist discourse, of which Human Rights is seen as the legal formalisation. In this way, they have an important role in legitimising (or questioning the legitimacy of) political actions. Recent examples showing the political importance of Human Rights include: the US government invoking Human Rights for their campaigns in the Middle East; indictment of war criminals in the aftermath of the Yugoslavian civil war; the criticism directed towards multinational companies for violating Human Rights by exploiting workers in poor countries.

However, Human Rights may be a favoured rhetoric, and indeed a concern for many individuals. Does it carry a force in politics, though? Is it not just a rhetoric one instrumentalises in order to get other things done? For now, I wish to hold aside the question of hypocrisy or weakness of will, leaving open the extent to which an actual concern for Human Rights motivates the rhetoric of Human Rights. My interest here is with the fact that Human Rights are invoked to such a large extent, the fact that they have such a high rhetorical value. The question is: What is the notion of the human intended in humanism as formalised in Human Rights?

Antihumanism—defined as the definite break with the view of an autonomous and universal human subject as an ontological foundation for politics and ethics—can, at least in the humanities departments, be said to have won the battle of the 1960s. The universalism promised by classical humanism is surely no longer what the human sciences aspire to. The general paradigm for human and social sciences today can be said to be what Paul Ricoeur referred to as the "hermeneutics of suspicion".[22] There is a general understanding that the world is open to interpretation, and that different stories about the world have different ways of justifying their validity-claims. Between different stories and perspectives, between different ways of interpreting the world, a struggle invariably takes hold. The corollorary here being that once humanism submits itself to this *Kampfplatz* between interpretations, the humanist narrative becomes just one among many discourses, its universal pretentions subject to a power analysis. But outside the humanities departments, the scene might look different. Even if the humanist rhetoric has lost some of its valour, it remains the idiom of justification for what we could call (for lack of any better terms) modern Western states. Certainly, there are also reactions towards this "hegemony" of the anti-humanists within the humanities departments—and it is not uncommon in these cases to refer to Levinas for support.

In his preface to the English edition of his work *Ethics*,[23] Alain Badiou protests against this recent return to humanist ideology. He claims that this ideology employs the notion of ethics as a convenient way of warding off any emancipatory politics as unleashing an exorbitant amount of violence, and potentially sowing the seeds for totalitarianism. This "ethics", says Badiou, with its call to "human rights" is nothing but an ideology conserving the "principles of the established 'Western' order".[24]

His verdict against this tendency is harsh; therein he sees an

> intellectual counter-revolution, in the form of moral terrorism, imposing the infamies of Western capitalism as the new universal model. The presumed 'rights of man' [serve] at every point to annihilate any attempt to invent forms of free thought. (p. li).

Badiou identifies two central abstractions around which this ideology of ethics coheres: "Man", and "The Other". The abstraction of the notion of man enables the doctrine of Human Rights to be deployed as a form of "moral terrorism". Badiou associates the "ethics of the other" with Levinas, noting in fairness however that in its widespread form it has little to do with him. Whereas the Levinasian notion of an "ethics of the other" for Badiou is utterly dependent on religion, the contemporary politicised usage of Levinas (Badiou mentions no names) is secular. A secularised ethics of alterity, an ethics of respecting differ-

[22] Cf. Paul Ricoeur, *Freud and Philosophy: An Essay on Interpretation*, Yale University Press, 1970, pp. 32-35.
[23] *Ethics*, Verso, 2001 [1998].
[24] Badiou mentions "ethics" and "human rights" only within scare quotes, since his aim is to establish another understanding of ethics, and of the human.

ences, is according to Badiou utterly vacuous, directionless. Being is difference, everything is difference, says Badiou, and therefore, a non-theological ethics of alterity is a banality, if not plain nonsense. In practice, Badiou contends that the political application of the rhetoric of difference (he seems to be thinking of multiculturalist rhetoric) does precisely the opposite from what it claims. The others are accepted only insofar as they are similar enough to me.

Opposed to this ethics, Badiou evokes the legacy of antihumanism. He summarises antihumanism in the following way:

> What was contested in this way was the idea of a natural or spiritual identity of Man, and with it, as a consequence, the very foundation of an 'ethical' doctrine in today's sense of the word: a consensual law-making concerning human beings in general, their needs, their lives, and their deaths, and by extension, the self-evident, universal demarcation of evil, of what is incompatible with the human essence.
>
> Is it to say, then, that Foucault, Althusser and Lacan extol an acceptance of the status quo, a kind of cynicism, an indifference to what people suffer? [...] [T]he truth is exactly the opposite (p. 6).

Badiou continues by describing the ethico-political *engagement* of the antihumanists, vociferously arguing that

> [i]n reality, there is no lack of proof for the fact that the thematics of the 'death of man' are compatible with a rebellion, a dissatisfaction with the established order, and a fully committed engagement in the real of situations [*dans le réel des situations*], while by contrast, the theme of ethics and of human rights is compatible with the self-satisfied egoism of the affluent West, with advertising, and with service rendered to the powers that be. Such are the facts (p. 7).

Badiou seeks to revive or prolong the debate on humanism, describing his book as a defence of the antihumanism of the 1960s (p. lvi), as an "ideological polemic" against the "democratic' totalitarianism" which is supported by the rhetoric of human rights." Ethics must, according to Badiou, be dissociated from the abstract categories of "Man or Human, Right or Law, the Other", and refer to particular situations".

More specific for our purposes, Badiou makes clear that anyone who wants to map out a secularised philosophy of the human in Levinas, will stand accused not only of ideology, but of an intellectual mess on the level of "cat food" (*de la bouillie pour les chats*; p. 23): "In truth Levinas has no philosophy—not even philosophy as the 'servant' of theology. Rather this is philosophy [...] *annulled* by theology, itself no longer a theology, [...] but precisely an ethics." (pp. 22-23).

Let us first grant Badiou the description of "the facts". A humanitarian rhetoric is indeed the perfect shield for an undisturbed consensus over unjust politics. However, Badiou himself wants to find a new philosophical meaning for the word "human", and for the word "ethics". Without intending to delve deeper into the philosophy of Badiou, it is of particular interest that ethics for him can in a positive sense only be an 'ethics of truth'. By "truth", Badiou means the singular events that break with a consensus—he protests against an ethics of happiness, of living well (which is nothing but nihilism (pp. 30-39)). The notion of the human is no longer to be connected to the mortality of a finite animal, but to what Badiou calls "the Immortal", which is the condition of possibility for the break with consensus (p. 35).

Structurally, this is strikingly similar to the alleged cat food that the work at hand is about to serve. As regards Badiou's claim that Levinas is a "religious" as opposed to a "philosophical" thinker, this simply seems to be an unfair way to delimit a thinker from the scene of his or her discourse. Even if he found inspiration in the discourse of the prophets, Levinas was unequivocal that his task was to philosophise. Moreover, his understanding of Judaism is that of an already secularised attitude towards the world. The Bible does not lead towards, as he puts it, "the mysteries of God, but towards the human tasks of human beings" (DL 409; DF 275, translation altered). The challenge we receive from Badiou's pamphlet is to show in what way Levinas's philosophy of the human is, contrary to Badiou's belief, philosophy, and how it provides us with a notion of the human which is precisely the condition of possibility for critique; i.e., for a break with consensus. The intention of the present work is to show how Levinas does not provide the "ethics of difference" for which Badiou rebukes him, but rather opens the space for thinking an ethics of dissensus (or as Robert Bernasconi says, an "ethics of suspicion" (ES)), which is the height that Badiou claims this discourse is incapable of attaining. This is something we will hold on to, not only against the critics of Levinas, but also against some of his followers. The distinction between an ethical alterity or proximity (that the other is my neighbour) and the cultural difference of the other to me is often blurred in the secondary literature. This distinction will receive clarification during the development of this investigation.

If one wishes to criticise humanism—and criticise the notion of the human entailed therein—one must be attentive to what it is one is criticising. In Blanchot's understanding (referring to Kant), "Humanity is communicability".[25] I find this phrase to capture something very relevant for this debate. In order to perform a critique of the human, we must communicate. What, may we say, are the conditions for this communication—how do we take care that this critique can be heard? If humanity is communicability, the idea of humanism—a nurturing of

[25] Maurice Blanchot, *The Infinite Conversation*, University of Minnesota Press, 1992, p. 457.

what is human—is actualised in our every relation to the other. This goes equally for my relation to the other researcher, whose view I want to criticise, as well as to the people who are subjected to the power structures I seek to criticise. As will be shown in this investigation, for Levinas, the human is the very condition of possibility for critique, in that it implies the ethical sensibility necessary for critical self-reflection.

Argument and Structure of the Investigation

That is, in compact form, the thesis I shall develop and make clear, providing all the while the necessary historical context against which a novel contribution on the philosophy of the human comes to be articulated by Levinas. In both a more systematic and economic fashion, I shall now develop the main points somewhat further. In this investigation, it will be shown how the notion of the human was central for Levinas from his very first texts onwards. At first it stands for a vague notion of ethico-political transcendence. By the middle period of the 1950s and 1960s this takes on the famous meaning of the ethical experience of the other. The subject's relation to the other is marked by an asymmetrical structure: I am infinitely responsible for the other before I can ask the same responsibility from him or her. This is an asymmetry that precedes and yet still calls for a universalism according to which all human beings are equal. In his later texts, after the encounter with antihumanism and after Derrida had presented his path-breaking reading, in "Violence and Metaphysics",[26] this structure loses its dependence on experience, but retains its ethical structure as the condition of possibility for critique. During this middle period, he announced his philosophy as a "humanism of the other". When later he no longer chooses to describe the relation to the other in the language of experience, he develops a more complex relationship towards the term humanism, refraining from its use as an unambiguous description of his own philosophy. Further, it will be shown that Levinas does not propose an "ethics of difference" in the sense in which it is often portrayed. The alterity of the other does not relate to a difference in (cultural) identity, but to the very asymmetrical ethical relation to the other. In this way, alterity must be read as the opposite to ipseity, rather than to identity. For this reason, in later texts, Levinas often prefers to employ the concept of proximity so as not to evoke this categorial confusion. To my mind, this is an aspect of Levinas's work that has not been sufficiently stressed. His insistence that the notion of the human is to be understood from the notion of the other is therefore not an appeal to a respect for difference. It is an attempt to formulate a universalism that does not take the autonomy of the individual, but the responsibility for the other as its starting point.

---

[26] Cf. *Writing and Difference*, Routledge, 1978.

The investigation is thus divided into two main parts:

- a first part, which follows the development of the notion of the human throughout Levinas's work until the 1960's. This exegetical treatment will, at certain points, be punctuated by sections that situate his thought in a wider field of philosophical and political debates. This includes presentations of the debates surrounding humanism and antihumanism by other influential thinkers of this time, as well as Derrida's important reading of Levinas in "Violence and Metaphysics".

- a second part, treating the notion of the human as it appears from the seventies onwards, with special focus on *Humanism of the Other and Otherwise than Being.* The notion of the human is here shown to be strongly linked to the idea of the possibility of critique. In this part, special considerations are also given to how the political in general, and Human Rights in particular can be understood from this perspective. In a final section, the historicity of the notion of the human is critically scrutinised.

Taken as a whole, this investigation has both a historico-exegetical and a systematic agenda. It asks both how Levinas's discourse on the human unfolded—and what his positions were—and how one can systematise these positions in order to understand the possibility of critique and the concept of Human Rights. Even if the first part lays more emphasis on exegesis and the second operates more speculatively, both ambitions are present in both parts.

The reason for the extensive space dedicated to the historico-exegetical discussion is at least twofold. Firstly, in the flood of discussion of the other around the turn of this millennium there has appeared a common, straw man version of Levinas, used both by those who are fascinated by what they believe to be his philosophy, and by his critics. According to this reading, he is the thinker of an ethics of difference, respecting the other so different from me that I can never understand him or her. This interpretation bears most resemblance to the position developed in *Totality and Infinity,* but, even there, it does not reach the core of his thinking. With the historical narrative I develop here, it becomes easier to show how this picture has appeared, and in what sense it is not fitting to his own texts—especially not the writings from the seventies onwards. The second reason concerns the internal development of Levinas's philosophy: his later thought is to a large extent self-reflective, and easier to understand against the background of the earlier thought. Since the notion of the human is far from a strictly defined concept, it is necessary to trace it through a number of works in order to conceive of the specific signification that it gains in the thought of Levinas.

Finally, a historical description is always a game of emphasis and omission. With respect to the description of thinkers who were important for Levinas's development of the notion of the human, one could enumerate many, such as for example Franz Rosenzweig, Gabriel Marcel or Martin Buber. Of course, these philosophers inspired Levinas to think the human from the vantage point of the relationship to the other, and as such the formative contribution that each had on the development of his thought is not to be underestimated. However, Levinasian scholarship on his connections to Rosenzweig and Martin Buber is already extensive (whereas there has not been so much done on the significance of Gabriel Marcel[27]). One could question the focus that is given in this investigation to a writer such as Michel Foucault, whom Levinas hardly ever mentions. The main reason for blending out certain influences while making others more apparent is the stress this investigation places on the debate surrounding humanism in France during the 1960s and 1970s. Even if he seldom directly treats the interlocutors of this debate, such as Foucault, it becomes a very important trope in his later texts.

The purpose of this investigation is however not merely to show how Levinas's thought developed and what his influences were. With the help of Levinas, the aim is to rethink the notion of the human, showing that it is a concept indispensable for philosophy and for political thought.

[27] Samuel Moyn, however, gives a good description of the relations between Levinas and Marcel in his *Origins of the Other. Emmanuel Lévinas between Revelation and Ethics*, Cornell University Press, 2005, pp. 221ff.

Part I

Origins of the Human

The purpose of this first part is to show the genesis and development of the notion of the human in the early to middle work of Levinas. This stretches over a long period of time: from his first reception and introduction of phenomenology in France, until his reception by Jacques Derrida in "Violence and metaphysics" (ED 117-228; WD 97-192) in 1964.

Levinas is known as a philosopher of ethics. But he never developed an ethics in the sense of a certain set of rules or even a worldview on human beings that could be harnessed as a guide for how to live one's life. Rather it is a philosophy that tries to highlight what the ethical as such could be, or as Derrida has called it, an "ethics of ethics" (ED 164; WD 138). In fact, in his earliest works, there is rarely any mention of ethics, and it is certainly not at the centre of Levinas's concern. And even later, when summing up his work, Levinas more often preferred to describe himself as a thinker of transcendence or of the holy. In "No exit: Levinas's aporetic account of transcendence",[28] Robert Bernasconi argues that Levinas's thinking is always a quest for the meaning of transcendence, which at one point finds ethics to be this meaning (p. 101). Thus with Bernasconi, one can make a "distinction between transcendence as a formal structure and ethics as its concretization" (p. 102). Transcendence was thus from the start at the heart of his philosophy, only at a later stage would he associate transcendence with ethics. Bernasconi's thesis is controversial in that it claims Levinas's philosophy is essentially a philosophy of transcendence and only accidentally—or at least less importantly—a philosophy of ethics. In the following, agreeing with the gist of Bernasconi's interpretation, I would like to dig deeper into this account of transcendence in Levinas's early work, showing how for him it is always related to the notion of the human, which was from the start a politically and ethically charged concept. Altering Bernasconi's account somewhat, I claim that the ethico-political back-drop is always present in his work; what is more accidental to Levinas's philosophy than is generally understood is the particular jargon of ethical *experience* (this is indeed often taken for the core of his thinking)—which though characteristic of his middle period (with its climax in *Totality and Infinity*), nonetheless ceases to be, in his later thought, the portmanteau through which transcendence is accessed. The ethico-political signification of the notion of the human, however, is present from his very first truly independent philosophical text, "Reflections on

---

[28] *Research in Phenomenology*, 35, 2005, 101-117.

the Philosophy of Hitlerism", from 1934 (QRPH; RPH), and remains present throughout his work.

Already in his earliest texts, the notion of the human becomes connected to transcendence, to the concept of the beyond. The "beyond" is in Levinas's descriptions always connected with a certain performativity of a movement, an escape. What exactly the object, or sphere, that one moves beyond is, is less determined; Levinas talks about an escape beyond oneself, beyond the egosphere, or (most abstractly) beyond being. He means that this possibility of the human—the possibility of a movement beyond—is fundamental for Western philosophy and civilisation, but that Western philosophy has failed to provide an understanding of this escape in its concreteness. In clinging to a description of the beyond, Western philosophy has betrayed the insight of the need to escape beyond. This escape, so he says, is inscribed in being as such or in facticity itself. I will show how the notion of the escape, even if it is often clothed in religious terms, is mainly presented as an ethico-political necessity.

A problem with the texts from these early years is that the ideal of concreteness, which Levinas sets for himself, is never met. The discourse of escape seems to end in a phenomenological *via negativa*. This evokes a dilemma: how can this movement beyond be described by a thinker who, as we shall come to appreciate, is so mistrustful of mysticism? Levinas searched for a non-mystical concretion for this movement beyond. In the beginning this would be described as a promise that philosophy had yet to fulfil. Later, in his post-war writings, he was to find points of anchorage to think the move beyond in its concretion, found in the relation to the other. But this relation would be subject to redescription: first, the relation to the other was couched in terms of the erotic relation, to be later replaced with the ethical experience, and finally to be understood in terms of the vulnerable responsibility of the subject itself. Once the discourse on the ethical entered into the work of Levinas in the late 1940s, it was never far away from his concern.

The ethical is, according to Levinas, never to be reduced to the political, but must, on the other hand, find political expression. In order to be conceived beyond a cynical understanding, the political must be understood from the never-ending project of reconciling irreconcilable ethical concerns. In this sense the ethical is metapolitical[29]—the ethical is for Levinas the very possibility of justice in society. Already his first independent texts, written in the mid-thirties, were consonant with this metapolitical agenda. In these writings, he expresses the need for civilisation to retrieve a possibility of defending itself against forces of barbarism—an expression later made impossible, in an intellectual climate associating the glorification of civilisation with the naïveté of humanism, hiding the

[29] This term is used by Abensour to describe Levinas's relation to the political in "Anarchy between Metapolitics and Politics", *Parallax*, 2002, vol. 8, no.3, 5-18.

cynical cruelties of colonialism. Placing this theme in relation to the concern for a just politics, developed in the later texts, can shed some light on both periods of his thinking. On the one hand, it can help us extract some meaning and direction from the seemingly empty and ideologically charged juxtaposition of civilisation and barbarism in his early works, and on the other, it might give us reason to raise a question to his later texts about the remnants of Western chauvinism that his thought sometimes harbours.

One way in which to link the ethical and the political in philosophical discourse has traditionally been with the notion of the human. And one understanding of the word "humanism" is precisely the belief that politics is to be subordinated to ethics—this might also be the reason why Levinas during a certain period of time would consider the label "humanism" as adequate in distilling the essence fof his own thinking. Throughout his life, however, he was a thinker of the notion of the human, which was always attached to a moment of transcendence. This was the case already in the earliest texts, which we will now discuss. However, Bernasconi's claim that Levinas's philosophy always was oriented towards transcendence is not sufficient as a characterisation; this transcendence had from the very start an ethico-political meaning, which will be shown to be already operative in this first part. Levinas's later insistence on the notion of the ethical is thus not as contingent as Bernasconi would describe it. Levinas's later texts to a certain extent work out what was already residing in the notion of the human from the very beginning.

1.1
Phenomenology as the Path to the "Concrete Human" (1930–1934)

Levinas began his academic career as an expert on phenomenology, introducing the new thought of Edmund Husserl and Martin Heidegger to the French speaking public. Apart from his thesis on Husserl, (TIPH; TIHP) completed in 1930, he co-translated Husserl's *Cartesian Meditations* into French and wrote many essays on Husserl and Heidegger, later assembled in *En découvrant l'existence avec Husserl et Heidegger* (EDE). Phenomenology was to strongly influence the fate of an entire generation of French philosophers, and it was the philosophical tradition Levinas considered his own thought to be indebted to throughout his life.[30] On the one hand, phenomenology can be seen as a reaction towards idealism; a philosophy that was too much caught up in systems no longer justified in a contact with the phenomena of the world. On the other hand, phenomenology was a reaction against the efforts to naturalise philosophy, to reduce the perceived world to psychological, sociological or scientific data, wrongly presumed to be the ultimate strata of reality or of scientific explanation. These scientific perspectives are nevertheless valid in their own right—seen as developments of the natural attitude according to which we impute a real and objective existence to that which we perceive. And yet for phenomenology the future of philosophy lay elsewhere. What philosophy should do is instead to perform a phenomenological reduction, in which one brackets these assumptions of the existence of the perceived phenomena as independent objects. The phenomena should be described as they are given, in their concrete givenness for the intentionality of the subject. In *Totality and Infinity,* Levinas would give the following explanation of this intentional analysis:

> Intentional analysis is the search for the concrete. Notions held under the direct gaze of the thought that defines them are nevertheless, unbeknown to this naïve thought, revealed to be implanted in horizons unsuspected by this thought; these horizons endow them with a meaning—such is the essential teaching of Husserl (TI 14; TaI 28).

[30] Even in his latest major work, *Otherwise than Being,* Levinas would write: "our analysis claims to be in the spirit of Husserlian philosophy" (AE 280; OB 183).

The task of phenomenology is to show what these horizons are that make possible the notion to be analysed, that is, its condition of possibility. This is a reflection that turns towards the phenomena as they appear for the subject, revealing the givenness of the phenomena at the same time as they reveal the perceiving subject. Even if phenomenology is a method, rather than a philosophical system of theses, it has, undeniably, one central thesis: the irreducibility of the first person perspective. This, we will see, would later on receive a particular alteration in Levinas's description of the subject's relation to the other.

The main achievement of Husserl's methodological revolution was, according to Levinas, that acts of consciousness were to be studied from the viewpoint not of an underlying substance, but from the act itself. This, Levinas saw as a new possibility of understanding the human subject in its *concreteness*.[31] In his dissertation, Levinas writes: "The phenomenological reduction is precisely the method by the means of which we return to the truly concrete Man" (TIPH 209; TIHP 146, translation altered).[32] It is this, an investigation into concrete human subjectivity (and not the thematisation of intersubjectivity) which during these years will hold Levinas's interest in phenomenology.

On closer inspection, Levinas found that Husserl betrayed this ideal of concreteness. According to Levinas, Husserl tends to mistakenly interpret the horizons revealed by intentional analysis as analogous to thoughts aimed at objects; the primary attitude is that of contemplating things as things (TIPH 184; TIHP 128)[33]. Even if Husserl provided the tools for a parting of the ways from the image of the human subject as a substance of consciousness opposed to a world of things, he did not draw all the necessary consequences. Levinas often summarised this problem such that the doxic act is the act with which all other acts are seen as analogous. [34] This comes from Husserl's insistence on starting

---

[31] Cf also Jean Wahl's book: *Vers le concret: Études de histoire de la philosophie contemporaine*, Vrin, 1932.

[32] Husserl did not read Levinas's book. However, when someone in the early 1930s had suggested to translate the young Frenchman's dissertation into English and use it as an introduction to phenomenology, Dorion Cairns wrote a critique of Levinas's thesis and sent it to Husserl. The critique was translated in 2007 and published together with Husserl's comments to the critique on www.dorioncairns.net/levinasreview.htm [accessed on March 6, 2010]. Reading the above quote, cited also in Cairns's critique, Husserl added: "That shows that Levinas has entirely misunderstood the phenomenological reduction (misled by Heidegger)" (Ibid).

[33] Husserl goes so far as to say that in the subject's constitution of the world, the material sphere is the foundation of all other spheres. In *Ideen*, §152, Husserl writes: "Als unterste Stufe liegt schließlich die materielle Realität allen anderen Realitäten zugrunde" (*Gesammelte Schriften. Band 5. Ideen zu einer reinen Phänomenologie*, Felix Meiner, p. 354.). This might seem to stand in stark contrast to Husserl's transcendental idealism, but it is for Levinas, from his then Heideggerian point of view, to be understood as a direct consequence of Husserl's intellectualism, privileging the objectifying relation to the world.

[34] On the topic of the doxic, Husserl noted in his letter to Cairns that "...in general, [Levinas] cannot distinguish between doxa as an ontic belief taken universally and the specific, theoretically interested doxa whereby we do not only universally undergo ontic certainty but also live in theoretical interest, i.e., striving, willing, actualizing true being oriented to the continuation of harmonious experience and predicative determination in experience. Theoretical interest is

from the ego in its act of self-reflection. By privileging the theoretical attitude, Husserl is, in Levinas's eyes, prolonging the modern philosophical tradition of understanding the revelation of being as a free act of knowledge. [35] As Levinas saw it, the definite break with this tradition was to come only with Heidegger. On Heidegger's view, which thus far Levinas embraces, the intellectual relationship to being is only one relation among others, and not the privileged relation to being. Heidegger also further emphasises the passivity of understanding, such that my discovery of being must be primarily understood as being revealing itself to me. Truth, the very event of being revealing itself is what constitutes my "being there" (*Dasein*) in the world.

Who or what is *Dasein*? Against the letter of Heidegger's own texts from this time, Levinas insists on the identification between *Dasein* and the human subject:

> that my *Da* is the very event of the revelation of being, that my humanity is truth—this is the chief contribution of Heideggerian thought. The essence of Man lies in this work of truth; man is thus not a noun, but initially a verb: he is in the economy of Being, the "revealing itself" of Being; he is not *Daseiendes*, but *Dasein* (EDE 85-86, my translation).

Here the term "economy of Being" is not further explained. We can however understand it as the goings on, the transformations of Being, in all its historical contextualisations.[36] These transformations are according to this expression not the cause of the human subject as a perceiving agent, nor are they totally inde-

---

a special form of praxis—its practical telos is true being or correct and ultimately valid predication." (www.dorinoncairns.net/levinasreview.htm). In support of Levinas, we could say that Husserl's claim of the difference between the "theoretically interested doxa" and "doxa as an ontic belief" contains the crux of the whole Husserlian phenomenology, which can never be entirely founded. On the one hand, theory is a particular form of praxis, says Husserl, on the other, it is "specific" and must be distinguished. What Levinas poses as a problem is the confidence which Husserl shows in assuming an analogy between the doxic and the other practices. This is the reason for the "imperialist" tendency of Husserlianism, which we shall discuss below. Cf. below section 2.5.

[35] Much of Husserlian research of the last decades has been focused on rehabilitating Husserl in this regard, showing how the criticism of Husserl by Levinas and others is due to misreadings, and simplifications, and, furthermore, how the positions of his later critics are anticipated by Husserl himself, especially in his unpublished writings. There seems to be a large consensus among contemporary Husserl scholars that Levinas's interpretation did not do justice to Husserl (Cf. Rudolph Bernet, "Levinas's Critique of Husserl" in Critchley and Bernasconi (eds), *The Cambridge Companion to Levinas*, Cambridge University Press, 2002; Søren Overgaard, "On Levinas's Critique of Husserl" in Dan Zahavi et al (eds), *Metaphysics, Facticity and Interpretation*, Kluwer, 2003; Daniel Birnbaum, "Den andre och tiden—om alteritet och närvaro i Husserls filosofi" in Alexander Orlowski and Hans Ruin (eds), *Fenomenologiska perspektiv. Studier i Husserls och Heideggers filosofi*; Dan Zahavi, *Self-Awareness and Alterity*, Northwestern University Press, 1999). This is however of minor importance for the following discussion on Levinas, which is not so much focused on whether he correctly understood or criticised Husserl and Heidegger, or whether or not he was faithful to the tenets of phenomenology, but on how Levinas developed an understanding of the notion of the human.

[36] We will discuss the concept of economy in section 1.7.

pendent of this. This appearance of the human subject or Dasein is the moment of Being revealing itself to itself, and is as such a part of the economy of Being.

Levinas finds that Heidegger perfects the phenomenological approach—the core of which for Levinas consisted in discovering the concreteness of Man. This was achieved to its full only with Heidegger's placing of Man in the moods (*Stimmungen*) of his everyday life, and his concrete historical situation (his facticity). For Heidegger, every specific understanding of the world is founded in a mood that allows for the disclosure of the world in this particular way. "Understanding" is not only a theoretical understanding; it is an existential category, expressing the self- and world-revelation of Dasein. Dasein is therefore the understanding of Being, the event of Being being understood. But this understanding is not only, and not even primarily a theoretical understanding; it is first and foremost care. "Understanding Being is existing in the manner of caring for one's own existence" (EDE 88, my translation). The subject understood as consciousness is secondary: "It is because there is a finite existence—*Dasein*—that consciousness can be possible" (EDE 89, my translation).

Levinas finds Husserl lacking also because he understands the human subject as an ahistorical entity (It must be noted that he is writing this before the publication of *Krisis*). Levinas remarks, inspired by Heidegger:

> [T]his historicity is not a secondary property of man as if man existed first and then became temporal and historical. Historicity and temporality form the very substantiality of man's substance (TIPH 221; TIHP 156).

This understanding of human being as a historical entity would never be entirely abandoned by Levinas, but in the years to come, he would be forced to question the Heideggerian understanding of historicity.

During these early years, it could not be claimed that Levinas was an original thinker. Rather his main task was to contribute to the reception of Husserl and Heidegger in France. But this was by no means a neutral process; in his idiosyncratic reading one can discern the beginning of an independent agenda. He tended to transform their transcendental philosophies into anthropologies, into philosophies of the human, an interpretation which neither Husserl nor Heidegger would have approved of. Indeed Husserl is ambiguous in his usage of the notion of the human; sometimes he uses the concept to represent the transcendental subject, and even describes his philosophy as a transcendental anthropology. Most of the time the term is associated to the modus of the natural attitude, before the epoche and the phenomenological reduction. Heidegger, for his part, did not want to identify the notion of the Dasein with that of the human, nor with that of the subject, because of the entanglement of such notions with the history of Western metaphysics.[37]

[37] Cf. *Sein und Zeit,* Niemeyer, 1993 [1927], §10, pp. 45-50.

When Levinas insists on the notion of the human—both when referring to the transcendental subject of Husserl and to the Dasein of Heidegger—it is not merely out of an insensitivity to their respective standpoints. By introducing Husserl and Heidegger as philosophers of the human, Levinas brings them back into dialogue with one another and with the philosophical tradition as a whole. He views the contribution of phenomenology as lying in its search for a concrete understanding of human being. Thereby, Levinas is preparing the ground for what is to become his own philosophy of the human.

Until 1933, it seems adequate to describe Levinas as a Heideggerian phenomenologist, understanding Man as the event of Dasein, the self-revelation of the "economy of Being" (EDE 86). However, when on May 1st, 1933, Heidegger joined the National Socialist Party and publicly associated his philosophy to the politics of the Führer, it was a shock for the young Jew, a shock that would have an irrevocable impact on his own philosophy. Heidegger's activities in National Socialism seem to have been decisive, leading Levinas onto the philosophical route for which he was to become famous. But even if the break with Heidegger was the birth of Levinas as an independent philosopher, his own philosophy would be in constant dialogue with the German thinker.

1.2
Riveted but Restless (1934–1939)

To summarize Heidegger's adventure in the National Socialist Party is a difficult task, which has been attempted in a large number of articles and books.[38] And to claim the final word regarding the relation between Heidegger's philosophy and his political commitments seems not only difficult, but misguided. The claims that establish a certain causal relation seem just as shadily argued as those that disclaim any relation between these two domains of his life. However, since Heidegger's political involvement was to mark such a distinctive turning point in Levinas's philosophical itinerary, it is necessary to at least touch on the subject. The purpose is here not to add to the stigmatisation already affecting Heidegger's thought because of his political involvements, nor to dismiss the relevance of Heidegger's thought today. Indeed, Levinas himself always acknowledges how deeply he is in debt to the German thinker. However, it is necessary to emphasise that the relation between Heidegger's thought and his political activities cannot be dismissed offhand.

A key text for locating this relation in Heidegger would be his *Rektoratsrede*, his inaugural address as a Rektor for Freiburg University.[39] Its particular importance lies in the explicit way in which philosophy and politics come to be conjoined. In it Heidegger describes his view on the role of education for the German nation. The whole rhetoric of the text attempts to articulate the Western philosophical tradition with the movement of the German spirit during the thirties. It takes up a classic academic theme, that of the independence of science, mutating it until it becomes a self-affirmation of the German nation through science. Science must be "for and through us", says Heidegger, which he later lays out as the preservation of the spiritual world of the nation. The "spiritual world of a nation [*Volk*]", writes Heidegger, "is the power which most deeply preserves the forces stemming from the blood and soil [*Blut und Boden*] of this

---

[38] The list is already very long; to mention a representative few, cf. Hugo Ott, *Martin Heidegger, Unterwegs zu seiner Biographie*, Campus, 1988; Victor Farías, *Heidegger et le nazisme*, Verdier, 1987, Rüdiger Safranski, *Heidegger, Between Good and Evil*, Harvard University Press, 1998; Silvio Vietta, *Heideggers Kritik am Nationalsozialismus und der Technik*, Niemeyer, 1989.

[39] *Die Selbstbehauptung der deutschen Universität*, Korn, 1933.

nation, as the power which most deeply moves and profoundly shakes our being" (Ibid, p. 9). Education is thus dissociated from any universalist ideal and put into the service of the destiny of the German people. Here we can see, that the moment of historico-cultural concretion, which Levinas had especially admired in Heidegger's reformation of the phenomenological movement, now receives, to say the least, a problematic air. At that time Heidegger understood his philosophy to be in line with the National Socialist doctrine. In retrospect, however, Heidegger came to see his philosophy of this time as an opposition to National Socialism. It might pay to be circumspect about drawing any quick conclusions in this regard. Over and against both attempts by Heidegger to politically assess his own philosophical thought, we must allow ourselves not to take for granted that the connection between his philosophy and his politics is in any way crystal clear.

In 1934, a year after Heidegger's Rector's address, Levinas published what was arguably his first independent philosophical work: "Reflections on the philosophy of Hitlerism"(QRPH; RPH). This text sets as its goal an analytic of the fracture line dividing "Hitlerist philosophy" from the philosophy of European civilisation—Judaism, Christianity, Liberalism, Marxism. As a description of Hitler's own rather simplistic thought, "philosophy" is of course a much too generous term. This choice of syntagm is however far from unimportant. Levinas's reason for using this term is, that Hitlerism is an expression of

> a soul's principal attitude towards the whole of reality and its destiny. [...] The philosophy of Hitlerism therefore goes beyond the philosophy of Hitlerians. It questions the very principles of a civilisation. (QRPH 7-8; RPH 64)

With the term Hitlerism, Levinas does not mean to propose a commentary of Hitler's own texts or speeches, nor that of the more refined Nazi ideologists. What Levinas labels "Hitlerism" is what he sees as a more general movement, a break with our philosophical tradition, the tradition in which the free subject is cherished and venerated as an ideal above history. Hitlerism denies this transcendence of the human subject. The revolution that Hitlerism promulgates springs from a particular "sentiment" that the age of Hitlerism bears within itself, one different from the sentiment of the philosophy of the European tradition. It would not be imoprudent to take "sentiment" as a translation or a transformation of Heidegger's concept *Stimmung*, or even *Grundstimmung*, the mood fundamental for a certain culture to disclose the world in its particular way. Levinas employs Heidegger's phenomenology in order to analyse a worldview, in which the German philosopher was himself implicated.[40]

---

[40] However present the German philosopher might appear in this text, he is never mentioned by name. Yet, it is almost impossible—given Levinas's background as a keen reader of Heidegger, as well as the theme and title of the text, and the time of publication—to read it without thinking of Heidegger's political involvement. Let us note that to associate Heidegger

The sentiment Hitlerism grounds in Levinas will call *enchaînement*: the condition of being bound to one's historical situation, to one's biological body, to one's race, to one's people.[41] But not only does Hitlerism differ from the European tradition in that it senses itself as enchained rather than free—inasmuch, for example, as the soul was always thought of as imprisoned in the body. The sentiment of *enchaînement* is particular in that the subject identifies itself with the very contingencies to which it understands itself as enchained. In this sense, the condition of enchainment is self-generating. It is a subjective world-view that is transformed into reality. Contingent identifications are internalised as essential to one's being, so that one understands oneself as *being* one's body, as *being* one's own national heritage, et cetera. The identification with these contingencies is not merely ontological—it is an existential affirmation; the ideal of this philosophy is to affirm the rootedness in one's proper situation and promote the force that emanates from these contingencies. While it is from the first sentence onwards taken for granted that the reader will join him in rejecting Hitlerism,[42] the critique of the phenomenon is not meant to function as a mere repudiation of a particular ideology, by which, from a position outside it, one's own conscience remains unscathed. Hitlerism is understood as an irreversible event, shaking the foundations of Western civilisation and forcing it to change the way we understand our collective identity. Even, then, if it is never explicitly stated, some of

---

with Hitler was by no means an act of heresy in 1934. There was nothing in the least bit controversial about such an equation. At the time, even if Heidegger did not hold the so-called thinkers of National Socialism in high regard, he probably would not have had much to object to the association to Hitler, and to the widespread nationalist movement in Germany between the world wars.

[41] This view of National Socialism as a radical antitranscendentalism was repeated in a more elaborate version by Hannah Arendt in *Origins of Totalitarianism*. She argued that the goal of totalitarianism was the transformation of the very human nature, a change that makes it irreceivable for transcendence (*Origins of Totalitarianism*, Harcourt, 1976, p. 458). Her view was found self-contradicting by Eric Voegelin, who meant that a "change of nature" is a contradiction in terms. He sees it as a clear-cut concession to the immanentism with which he also characterised the totalitarian ideology. Voegelin defines "nature" as "that which identifies a thing as a thing of this kind and not of another one" (Voegelin, "The Origins of Totalitarianism", *Published Essays*, Volume 11, University of Missouri, 2000, p. 21)—the transcendent must therefore be unchangeable. However, things change, and so do kinds. As we saw in the preface, the notion of the human has always been changing. In *The Human Condition* Arendt wrote: "The human condition comprehends more than the conditions under which life has been given to man. Men are conditioned beings because everything they come in contact with turns immediately into a condition of their existence." (*The Human Condition*, p. 9). This is to say, in any relevant understanding of human nature, it changes constantly, because new elements always come into play to change the conditions for our existence. This interpretation of National Socialism and Fascism as immanentism was shared by the historian Ernst Nolte, *Three Faces of Fascism: Action Française, Italian Fascism, National Socialism*, trans. Leila Vennewitz, Holt Rinehart, 1966), part. 5, "Fascism as a Metapolitical Phenomenon", esp. 429-34 and 450-54.

[42] In "L'inspiration religieuse de l'alliance", published the following year, Levinas would write that racism is a "test that has to be overcome, rather than a problem to be solved. It is *unworthy of refutation*" (He 145, Levinas's emphasis).

the traits ascribed to Hitlerism are bound up with his own philosophical heritage. Hitlerism is a reaction against the empty abstractions of Western thought, and as we saw in the previous section (1.1), Levinas saw phenomenology as the path to a *concrete* understanding of the human. This does not lead him to reject the phenomenological method along with Hitlerism. In his very analysis of this movement, the primacy of the concrete guides him still. As such, the opposition between Hitlerism and traditional Western thought must not be treated as a logical contradiction between particularism and universalism, but as a concrete event. As he writes:[43]

> A logical contradiction cannot judge a concrete event. The meaning of a logical contradiction that opposes two forms of ideas only shows up fully if we go back to their source, to intuition, to the original decision that makes them possible. It is in this spirit that we are going to set forth the following reflections (QRPH 8; RPH 64).

In order to trace the source of the event of Hitlerism, Levinas sketches a short history of Western civilisation, proceeding through Judaism and Christianity to Liberalism and Marxism. The purpose is to show that the defining element of Western thought has always been the view of the human being as essentially free; civilisation is then assigned the role of assisting the human being's claim to freedom. For Levinas, the trouble is that, along the unfolding of this historical trajectory, the liberation of the human being was coupled with an increasingly abstract conception of humanity. In the era of liberalism, the human being lacks a certain sense of embodiment in flesh, history and culture:

> In the world of liberalism, [...] the possibilities open to [human being] [...] are only logical possibilities that present themselves to a dispassionate reason that makes choices while forever keeping its distance (QRPH 13; RPH 66).

This dispassionate relation to the ideas can result in scepticism, and so the arbitrariness of the idea of freedom that liberalism nourishes can turn against itself. "The gap that separates man from the world of ideas" (QRPH 20; RPH 69), reduces thought to being but a game, where the power to doubt is often a symptom of a "lack of conviction". Civilisation becomes too weak to defend its ideals of human dignity and freedom; the venerated ideals are marked by insincerity. In this rarefied atmosphere, "the Germanic ideal of Man seems to promise sincerity and authenticity" (QRPH 21; RPH 70). Since the free choice (cherished by liberalism) between values and between ideals is marked by an arbitrariness, the

---

[43] According to Levinas, this was claimed by certain journalists at the time (QRPH 8, RPH 64). Levinas does not give any references as to whom he his referring, but it is a position that has often since been repeated. Cf. Ten Hoor (http://www.kenyonreview.org/issues/archives/tenhoorS1941.php [Accessed January 15, 2007].

restitution of the communitarian bond (linked to the soil, to birth and blood) seems to become the only resource for the grounding of values. The temptation is to think of oneself as linked by birth and blood to some people rather than others, to some ideas and values rather than others. Whence the category "enchainment".

In Hitlerism, the attachment to one's *proper* body, to one's *own* situation and to the force that is connected with this sense of 'propriety' sets itself up against the traditional Western universalist image of the human soul. Where one often would see Hitlerism as a particularism reacting against universalism, Levinas instead finds in Hitlerism a modification of the idea of universalism. For Hitlerism universality is understood from the idea of expansion. (QRPH 22; RPH 70). Even if it is first described as an idea, it is in fact not an idea, but a force, which develops in a totally different manner from how an idea is propagated. Whereas the propagation of ideas depends on the discursive conditions under which peers can communicate freely and equally, force, on the other hand,

> is attached to the personality or society exerting it, enlarging that person or society while subordinating the rest. Here the universal order is not established as a *consequence* of ideological expansion; it is that very expansion that constitutes the unity of a world of masters and slaves (QRPH 22–23; RPH 70–71).

This becomes a conflict between "civilisation and barbarism", a conflict that concerns—as the last line of the article suggests—"the very humanity of Man".[44] The way I read Levinas, the notion of humanity is the key concept in this article. His purpose is neither sociological nor psychological, but thematic. Clearly he does not purport to capture the essence of National Socialism, nor is he interested merely in drawing up a character profile of some of his contemporaries lost to Nazism. Rather if one wishes to locate the key characteristic of "Hitlerism"—and an aspect that therefore joins Nazi ideologists with certain contemporary philosophers—it lies in the thematic of man's enchainment or rootedness (in culture, in the present, in history—in "Being"). This rootedness is not only seen as a necessary starting point for an analysis of the human, but also as a condition which is ethico-politically affirmed by these ideologists.

Since this article on Hitlerism appears so soon after Heidegger's open allegiance to National Socialism, it is tempting to read the essay merely as a covert criticism of Heidegger. This is only a part of the truth. There are too many elements of his description of Hitlerism that do not fit with Heidegger—such as the

---

[44] The full last three sentences read: "Peut-être avons-nous réussi à montrer que le racisme ne s'oppose pas seulement à tel ou tel point particulier de la culture chrétienne et liberale. Ce n'est pas tel ou tel dogme de démocratie, de parlemantarisme, de régime dictatorial ou de politique religieuse qui est en cause. C'est l'humanité meme de l'homme" (QRPH 23-24; RPH 71).

importance placed on the role of the body as well as the emphasis on race, neither of which playing any prominent role in Heidegger's philosophical thought.[45] Levinas's object of analysis, Hitlerism, must be read as a conglomerate of thoughts, an attempt to capture a certain discursive atmosphere. Methodologically, he proceeds by constructing philosophical alloys, composites made from thought-figures that partially—though never fully—mirror actual philosophers. Philosophers are themselves recast, as Levinas distils and amplifies certain features, which are then integrated into his own philosophical orientation. This is a method he will adopt consistently during his philosophical career.

What is then the thought-figure that can be distilled from his juxtaposition of Hitlerism and Western Liberalism? Even if Levinas does not here reach this conclusion explicitly, from the way the neither/nor alternative between these two ideologies is presented, it stands clear that what Levinas was looking for was a way, on the one hand, not to belie the concrete phenomenon of human facticity as a starting point for philosophy, and, on the other, to insist on what he saw as philosophy's intrinsic connection of the human to the beyond. Thirty years later, the starting sentence of the first chapter of *Totality and Infinity* would still express this key element of his philosophy in the following way:

> 'The true life is absent'. But we are in the world. Metaphysics arises and is maintained in this alibi (TI 21; TaI 33).

Philosophy is a movement beyond; it is an affirmation of the beyond. Of course, we might ask, what is there to prefer in the idea of transcendence over an affirmation of immanence (which, in our present time, is *de rigueur* in thinking a transformative philosophy)? In this text Levinas emphatically claims that the opposition between the movement towards transcendence and the affirmation of immanence boils down to a question of choosing between a civilised vis-à-vis a barbaric understanding of the human. Still, this gives rise to a question, namely what specifically hangs on this difference between immanence and transcendence? Put otherwise, what rides on this commitment to a philosophy of transcendence? Even if it is not put so explicitly, the thought Levinas is entertaining here is that "Hitlerism" violently departs from civilisation because it leaves unacknowledged "the equal dignity of each and every soul" (QRPH 15; RPH 66). In his short history of Western civilisation, Levinas writes, developing the position of Christianity:

> The soul's detachment is not an abstract state; it is the concrete and positive power to become detached and abstract. The equal dignity of each and every

[45] As has been shown by Robert Bernasconi in "Heidegger's Alleged Challenge to the Nazi Concepts of Race", in James Faulconer, *Appropriating Heidegger*, Cambridge University Press, 2000, Heidegger shared common racist views, displaying them in his lectures. However, he did not see race as a biological, but as a "spiritual" category.

> soul, which is independent of the material or social conditions of people, does not flow from a theory that affirms, beneath individual differences, an analogy based on a 'psychological constitution'. It is due to the power given to the soul to free itself from what has been, from everything that linked it to something or engaged it with something, so it can regain its first virginity (QRPH 15; RPH 66).

The notion of the equal value of everyone is for Christianity not a historical construction; it is based on the freedom of the soul over and against history. This ideal is retained in Liberalism, and in a sense also in Marxism. Even if Marxism entailed a critique of the notion that there would be a human soul or spirit that was not determined by material history, freedom is still an unquestioned ideal: "to become conscious of one's social situation is, even for Marx, to free oneself of the fatalism entailed by that situation" (QRPH 15; RPH 67).[46] From Christianity to Marxism therefore the freedom cherished is a concrete possibility of not being determined by history. As was described earlier, Liberalism is treated less favourably by Levinas, diagnosed as a stagnant period where freedom becomes increasingly a negative abstraction.

Even so, there seems to be something self-contradictory in his appeal to the concrete. He stops far short of questioning the Christian idea that the dignity of each soul depends on the "concrete and positive power" to detach oneself from one's situation. It is clear from his description that this power of liberation is even more "concrete and positive" in Marxism. But can such a power, which seems to be the power of free reflection, in its concretion really be equal to all? If this power is not equal to all, however, how can the equal dignity of all human beings rely on a power that is not equally distributed? If Levinas would still insist on this claim, has he not landed in the position he accused Liberalism of, reducing the human to an abstraction? Moreover, does not this discussion reveal the self-contradiction in the notion of civilisation that Levinas relies on—are "the civilised" not after all more free, and therefore more dignified? To put it bluntly, who is to say who counts as civilised and who does not? This was a question that he did not think to ask himself in this text. Later, however, when he thinks the human from the viewpoint of the transcendence beyond power, he will no longer have the luxury of positing that civilisation emanates from a certain capacity of the subject.

What is consistent in Levinas's view, however, is the way in which Hitlerism was a possibility that the Western tradition carried within itself, showing a devastating blind spot in that very tradition. In his prefatory note to the Hitlerism

[46] Samuel Moyn (*Origins of the Other. Emmanuel Levinas between Revelation and Ethics*, Cornell, 2005) thus clearly goes too far when he says that Levinas depicts Marxism as an "important precursor to Nazism" (99n), or as a "liminal" position between Liberalism and Hitlerism. Even if Marxism criticises the view of the subject as pure freedom, this is only to better find a concrete freedom. "To become conscious of one's social situation is for Marx to free onself of the fatalism entailed by that situation" (QRPH 15).

text, added more than fifty years later,[47] he would make the point more plain: Nazism was not an anomaly of reason, but instead derives from an

> essential possibility of elemental Evil, into which we can be led by good logic and against which Western philosophy had not sufficiently assured itself. This possibility is inscribed within the ontology of a being concerned with being—a being, to use the Heideggerian expression, "dem es in seinem Sein um dieses Sein selbst geht". Such a possibility still threatens the subject correlative with being as gathering together and as dominating, that famous subject of transcendental idealism that before else wishes to be free and thinks itself free. We must ask ourselves if liberalism is sufficient for an authentic dignity of the human subject. Does the subject arrive at the human condition prior to assuming responsibility for the other man in the act of election that raises him to this height? (QRPH 25-26; RPH 63, translation altered).

Here it bears repeating that this summation comes at the very end of his philosophical career (five years before his death in 1995), as a comment to his earliest independent work, thus opening a span of thought from 1934 to 1990. It is a very compact statement, from which two preliminary remarks can be distilled:

Firstly, even if the text from 1934 never mentions the German philosopher, no reader of Levinas would need this prefatory note to suspect that Heidegger is present in this text. Yet, and as has been said already, one must not conflate Heidegger with Hitlerism, thinking that the essence of each amounts to the same. At least from the later comment, we receive a very complex picture of his relation to Heidegger. In fact, Heideggerian thought-figures appear on both sides of the opposition that Levinas paints between Hitlerism and Liberalism. To add to the complexity, they appear also in the language that Levinas himself deploys in his analysis. He uses a Heideggerian formula to provide, if not the solution, then a statement of the problem. Idealism and Liberalism are here brought together as two sides of the same coin, as representatives of the Western tradition "insufficient for the authentic dignity of the human subject" (QRPH 26; RPH 63). This is a clear allusion to Heidegger's statement from "Letter on 'humanism'" (cf. infra section1.5), where Heidegger says that "the highest humanist definitions of the essence of Man [exemplified by Heidegger in the preceding sentence as "animal rationale, as 'Person', as a being of spirit, soul and body"] do not realise the authentic dignity of Man" (WM 330; PM 251, translation altered)[48]. A few lines further down in the same text, Heidegger

[47] More precisely, it is added as a "prefatory note" in the publication of "Reflections on the Philosophy of Hitlerism" in *Critical Inquiry* from 1990. In the French republication (Rivages, 1997), it is the "post scriptum". Thus, very fittingly, it is the prefatory note as well as the post-script.

[48] "daß die höchsten humanistischen Bestimmungen des Wesens des Menschen [als animal rationale, als 'Person', als geistig-seelisch-leibliches Wesen] die eigentliche Würde des Menschen noch nicht erfahren."

adds that humanism does not "estimate the Humanitas of the human high enough" (Ibid). Levinas thus uses a Heideggerian formula against the very tradition that he sees crowned by Heidegger, a tradition that, even at its peak, proved to be insufficient for "assuring" itself against Hitlerism.

It is clearly wrong then to read the article on Hitlerism simply as a commentary on Heidegger's philosophy, as a text providing nothing more than a long accusation against Heidegger.[49] Rather, Levinas's claim is different. He considers that Heidegger's philosophy—a philosophy he judges to be the apogee of the Western tradition—is nonetheless not sufficiently "insured" against the evil of Hitlerism. But how can an ontology or a philosophy insure itself against evil? For Levinas, it seems that the answer is: through transcendence. Certainly, Heidegger's philosophy claims to be a philosophy of transcendence too. In its care for its own being, Dasein is at the same time always beyond itself, in front of itself in the world. This formulation of transcendence, however, did not stop him from assuming the jargon of blood and soil. As such, Levinas deemed the idea of transcendence that can be located in Heidegger inadequate.[50] As we saw in his addendum, attached more than fifty years later, Levinas's philosophy of transcendence would find its assurance in an ethical sensibility towards others.

This search for a transcendence, which here is understood by Levinas in terms of both a restlessness and wakefulness, and which he pursues as an assurance against evil, will however only introduce a contradiction at the centre of his early thought. Is not the assurance, the guarantee that Levinas is looking to secure at variance with the very attribution of restlessness that will at this stage come to be attached to transcendence? Can an essential restlessness at the heart of the human really at the same time be described as in terms of an assurance? This is a problem which is central to my reading of Levinas, and shall be discussed in more detail later on.[51]

Secondly, by the final rhetorical question of the preface ("Does the subject arrive at the human condition prior to assuming responsibility for the other man in the act of election that raises him to this height?"), Levinas's point is to locate a deficiency in the tradition's account of the human. Both Heidegger and the Idealist tradition have elided something central in the very notion of humanity. In this preface, Levinas proposes that humanity can be understood only from the viewpoint of the responsibility for the other man, not in the terms of freedom

[49] As Agamben writes, "The text is not so much an accusation as a topographic revelation, which concerns us in every way" ("Introduzione" In Emmanuel Levinas, *Alcune riflessioni sulla filosofia dell'hitlerismo*, translated by Andrea Cavalletti and Stefano Chiodi, Quodlibet, 1996, 10).

[50] This does not mean that the Heideggerian understanding of Dasein as transcendence cannot be put to other political uses, notably that of Jean-Luc Nancy in *Being Singular Plural*, Stanford University Press, 2000.

[51] section 1.7, section 2.5.

emphasised by the tradition, and still in a sense, by Heidegger. In the Hitlerism article, this outline of a positive answer to the tradition, to Heidegger, and to Hitlerism, is never presented. The other does not appear as a term in his philosophy until *Existence and Existents,* (DEE; EE) in 1947, and is not given the ethical meaning for which his philosophy is renowned until "Is Ontology Fundamental?" (EN 12-22; ENO 1-12) from 1951. So if indeed this is the viewpoint from which to understand the notion of the human, we must conclude that, in the text from 1934, Levinas was still searching for it.

But even before the elaboration of Levinas's own philosophy, we can nonetheless find some scaffolding for his philosophy to come. His early writings, from this point on, are all directed toward a philosophical formulation of the possibility of breaking what he here had named an enchainment to being, a logic into which, not only "Hitlerians", but the modern human being as such is drawn. In this way, the struggle transcends the field of philosophical theory. Hitlerism consists not only in proposing a certain view of man, but in erasing the possibility of promoting an idea of the human; the force of the enchainment serves only to promote itself as enchainment. But if Levinas and "civilisation" would wish an encounter on the level of ideas, while Hitlerism would shape the encounter as collisions of forces, will not force always win? Will not the ideas be unmasked as weak forces in the field where everything is force? Can we not say Levinas is engaging in a battle that he cannot be expected to win? Does this not condemn Levinas to work within the crisis of Western thought, never moving beyond it?

More than sixty years later, Giorgio Agamben described the Hitlerism text as even today constituting "the most valuable contribution to an understanding of National Socialism".[52] In *Homo Sacer,*[53] as well as in his introduction to the Hitlerism text in its Italian translation,[54] Giorgio Agamben notes that Levinas is not only talking about Hitlerism as such, but already about something that is fundamental for contemporary Western thought. He sees the allusions to Heidegger, but does not take such coded references as grounds on which to dismiss him as a Nazi thinker. On the contrary,

> [w]hat makes Levinas's diagnosis incomparable is the courage by which he recognises the same categories to be operative as those which during these years would be central for his own philosophical project (and implicitly also for his master from Freiburg).[55]

---

[52] *Homo Sacer,* Stanford University Press, 1998, p. 153.
[53] *Homo Sacer,* p. 151.
[54] Giorgio Agamben, "Introduzione", in: Emmanuel Levinas's, *Alcune riflessioni sulla filosofia dell'hitlerismo,* transl. Andrea Cavalletti and Stefano Chiodi, Quodlibet, 1996, pp. 7-17.
[55] Ibid, p.7.

As Levinas, Agamben finds the characteristic of Heidegger's analytic of Dasein overlapping with the ideology of National Socialism to be the readiness to transform a historical facticity into a political mission. For both Levinas and Agamben, every ontology harbours a politics, and their critique of a philosophy understanding itself as ontology is associated with a critique of a certain view of politics. Agamben opens the potential for a philosophical self-criticism in this text.

Instead of following this trail, however, Agamben uses the interpretation of Levinas's early text as a springboard for bringing forth his own agenda. Here their thoughts deviate in an interesting way. The challenge for "the coming politics", as Agamben messianically puts it, lies in doing nothing but showing how all ontologies are intrinsically political: all previous political ontologies are results of man, essentially without a mission, constantly seeking to define himself (through biology, history or religion) in order to receive a political destiny. These politics would, according to Agamben, derive from an insight into the essence of Man as without any defining function to fulfil, his *inoperositá*.

Levinas also saw a necessity of escaping an identification of human beings with their historical or biological particularity. He would have been in agreement with Agamben concerning the danger that arises from subordinating the political to ontology. Unlike Agamben, however, he did not see the human as a concept that needed to be emptied of content. For Levinas, negative definitions of the human are insufficient. With the last sentence of the article he inscribes himself in a struggle concerning the "humanity of man". The notion of the human would for him be crucial, tied to the very possibility of escape, the break with being. The idea of not being able to escape one's destiny, of being enchained, riveted (*rivé*)—to being, to one's proper situation, and perhaps most significantly, to oneself—is arguably the central theme in his early philosophy, finding its most poignant expression in *On escape*, first published in 1935.

On escape shares the point of departure with the Hitlerism text, namely that for traditional philosophy man is essentially separate from the world. It commences with the claim that "The revolt of traditional philosophy against the idea of being originates in a discord between human freedom and the brutal fact of being that assaults this freedom" (DE 91; OE 49). Philosophy—and Levinas is thinking of idealism specifically—is moved by an attempt to escape being, whereby being is typically understood as that which is non-human, i.e., not belonging to the human ego. But on Levinas's account, traditional philosophy deceives itself; it announces a break with being, only to land in a higher form of being (e.g. God as the Supreme Being or the Platonic "world of ideas" as the true being) with which humanity will find harmony.

> And Western philosophy, in effect, has never gone beyond this. In combating the tendency to ontologize [ontologisme], when it did combat it, Western philosophy struggled for a better being, for a harmony between us and the world, or for the perfection of our own being. Its ideal of peace and equilibri-

> um presupposed the sufficiency of being. The insufficiency of the human condition has never been understood otherwise than as a limitation of being, without our ever having envisaged the meaning of "finite being." The transcendence of these limits, communion with the infinite being, remained philosophy's sole preoccupation (DE 93; OE 51)

This means that the "rebellion of traditional philosophy against the idea of being" is not radical enough: it sets the I up against the non-I, "but it does not break "the unity of the 'I,' which—when purified of all that is not authentically human—is given to peace with itself, completes itself, closes on and rests upon itself." (DE 91; OE 49). As a description of German Idealism as a whole, this would be far too sketchy. For example, it would be a far from adequate rendering of Schelling's *Freiheitsschrift*, where the whole orientation of the system lies in a rupture of unity, the system itself being rupture and movement—a movement that is not realised in an equilibrium or in a Hegelian *Aufhebung*. All the same, Levinas's analysis has relevance for an understanding of the way in which society has assimilated certain suppositions and intuitions of idealism.

It has become possible, claims Levinas, for philosophy to strike an unholy alliance with a bourgeois self-satisfied life form. This life form is essentially conservative: the restlessness of capitalism is accepted only insofar as it helps to conserve an (imaginary) interior peace, a peace with oneself. For this, one needs a certain materialism: an instinct of possession. The capitalism of the bourgeois appears as an "imperialism" which is "a search for security" (DE 92; OE 50). When a prolonged peace is valued as the highest goal, being is also emphasised over becoming, owning over enjoying. In Levinas's description of the bourgeois life form, we find a parallel with the critique of Liberalism advanced in the Hitlerism text, a philosophy and a life form that flags its humanist ideals as an ideology, and by its lived hypocrisy leaves itself open for the "Hitlerist" critique.

Understanding being as becoming—as was the vogue in a France strongly under the influence of Bergson—will allow us to break from the imprisoning view of the subject as enclosed in the present. Ultimately, though, it will not allow for the exit from being that Levinas is looking for. Even if the notion of the human is thought from the viewpoint of activity, this will still not account for the escape that he envisages; human beings viewed as agents are still attached to themselves in their activity. Levinas explains thisin the following way:

> While it breaks with the rigidity of classical being, the philosophy of the vital urge does not free itself from the mystique of being, for beyond the real it glimpses only the activity that creates it. It is as though the true means of surpassing the real were to consist in approximating an activity that ended up precisely with the real. For fundamentally, becoming is not the opposite of being (DE 97; OE 54).

In the most radical understanding of escape, Man must escape himself. This does not mean suicide or loss of identity, but an attempt to think a duality between me and myself. "*The most radical enchainment*", writes Levinas—thus reintroducing the word associated with Hitlerism in the previous text—is "*the fact that the I* [*le moi*] *is oneself* [*soi-même*]" (DE 98, OB 55; Levinas's emphasis). Philosophy as an escape from being is thus compromised by a conservative insistence on being. "Ontologism", states Levinas, the reduction of all thought to ontology, remains "the fundamental dogma of all thought" (DE 124; OE 71). This can be seen as a description of the decadence of the philosophical ideals that made it possible for movements affirming the human rootedness in being to appear as more sincere than traditional philosophy (QRPH 21; RPH 70). Here, Levinas ties his project to a neologism: excendence (DE 98; OE 54). By this term, he affirms the intention of idealism to move beyond being but is suspicious of what he sees as the ontologising tendencies of transcendental idealism. While the prefix "trans-" suggests a movement from one sphere of being to another, and thus a detainment in ontologist thought, "ex-" suggests a departure from being per se. In the 1947 preface to *Existence to Existents*, Levinas lets the term 'excendence' reappear as a "departure from being and the categories which describe it" (DEE 9; EE xxvii).

To avoid any confusion at this stage it must be understood that Levinas does not want to find a higher level of being, but an escape from being, or better still, an escape that retains a foothold in being. The question is: how are we to understand such an escape? Levinas does not want to rely on religious mysticism, but on phenomenology. By way of phenomenological analyses of pleasure, pain, nausea, shame and malaise, Levinas tries to show that needs are inscribed in human existence not as a lack in mundane being—which idealism has traditionally argued—but as an abundance, allowing the human being to exceed itself. Gripped by the state of nausea, for example, one wants nothing but to leave—but it is an effort of utter despair in which one cannot think or act, be a subject.

> In nausea—which amounts to an impossibility of being what one is— we are at the same time riveted to ourselves, enclosed in a tight circle that smothers. We are there, and there is nothing more to be done, or anything to add to this fact that we have been entirely delivered up, that everything is consumed: this is the very experience of pure being (DE 116; OE 66-67, Levinas's emphasis).

In the same sense, shame is analysed as a shame of nothing but oneself, one's "being there". Thus, the necessity of escape is described in terms of being as such. Pleasure, on the contrary, is an ecstasy, a momentary departure from being, and a temporary and therefore ultimately insufficient loss of oneself (DE 108-109; OE 61-62).

But we are never told how or if escape is at all possible. All we are told is that it is a human necessity to take flight, and that the described modalities of existence are not sufficient for a true escape, but lead back to being, and back to oneself. Nor for that matter are we given an answer to the question that Levinas poses to his concept of excendence at the beginning of the text: "What is the ideal of happiness and human dignity that it [excendence] promises?" (DE 99; OE 56).

Even if no successful philosophical attempt to "leave" being has been made, in this path lies the value of European civilisation, Levinas writes. "Every civilization that accepts being—with the tragic despair it contains and the crimes it justifies—merits the name 'barbarian'." (DE 127; OE 73). Here we encounter anew the polarity between civilisation and barbarism, encountered first in the Hitlerism text. As was the case on that occasion too, the question as regards how this escape, this taking "leave" of being—which separates any civilisation from the sacrilege of barbarity—comes to pass is left in abeyance. If, in these texts from 1934-35, Levinas provides an analysis of a problem, he would not at this stage come to something resembling a solution. How is this transcendence which he seeks to be conceived? Since Levinas is often in his reception set apart from philosophy as a "religious thinker", and since he writes with such an insistence on the need to escape being—all the while not providing a philosophical answer to the question—one might suspect that it is not philosophy but religion that holds the key to a real escape.

Indeed, in the years leading up to the war and the Holocaust, one can find Levinas looking to Judaism to solve this philosophical problem, all the while trying to inspire hope in fellow Jews in facing the terrifying situation that befell them. In my reading, this did not mean a turning away from philosophy to religion, but rather a statement of the same philosophical problems in a Judaic context.

Levinas developed some reflections on Judaism in a series of articles in the Jewish journal *Paix et droit* in the years between 1935 and 1939.[56] If "Reflections of the philosophy of Hitlerism" tried to hold a sober distance from the phenomenon under scrutiny, in these texts he makes clear that it is impossible for a Jew to think antisemitism from a detached point of view: before the upsurge of antisemitism, Levinas writes, "[t]he Jew is ineluctably riveted to his Judaism." (He 144) The situation is analysed in a Heideggerian manner, distilling a mood that allows a certain disclosure of the world: "the great pains are not always blind. Their burns are also a light.". "Before the reality of Hitlerism one discovers all the gravity of the fact of being Jewish" (He 150).

This is never meant as a plea for a Jewish politics. In "L'inspiration religieuse de l'alliance", (He 144-146) Levinas claims that the Jewish identity is strictly religious; he refuses the idea of a Jewish national identity, the formation of an

[56] This was the journal of *Alliance israélite universelle*. The articles were later republished in *Cahiers de L'Herne*, 1991 (He), with an introduction by Catherine Chalier.

Israeli state. But as is the case also in his later texts on Judaism,[57] he never claims to write from the viewpoint of Judaism in the sense of claiming the privilege of a pious or mystically experienced perspective. In a text from 1935 on "L'actualité de Maïmonide" Levinas treats the 12th century Jewish Aristotelian as exemplary in this respect. "Maimonides brings more prudence than ecstasy, more logic than enthusiasm, more grammar than mysticism to the sacred texts". For Maimonides, "the rabbinic science *allowed no spontaneous faith*" (He 143, Levinas's emphasis).

> But still, Judaism is here understood as bearing a mission, the mission of bringing the opportunity of a thought that extends beyond the world. Levinas contrasts this task with paganism, defined as an incapacity to think beyond the world (He 144). What Maimonides shows in his "Guide for the perplexed" is that Aristotle's concept of the *primus motor* could never account for the creation of the world. As a pure act, it cannot find its motivation outside itself. It can thus never be more than the perfection of created things. In contrast, the *creatio ex nihilo* of biblical creation announces a God who cannot be thought along the lines of perfection. Levinas sees this as the discovery "of what six centuries later one would call the critique of pure reason", it arrests the logic of the world in its dominion over the beyond (Ibid).

This is regarded by Levinas as bringing a "definitive victory of Judaism over paganism" (Ibid). The victory lies not in the strength of faith per se, but in its very pointing beyond the world: the strength of the Jewish tradition therefore lies in its resistance to the ontologisation of transcendence in Western philosophy. Still, he never really makes clear what this indication of a beyond amounts to; why is this statement itself not ontological, not drawn back into ontology, in the way he described the general workings of idealism? Considering Levinas's admiration of Maimonides, this much alone is clear: the escape from a riveted existence cannot lie in any mystical communion with the beyond, or in an actual afterlife in another world.

Rather, his concern is always with our lives in the only world we know; for him there is no other world. In this text, he gives a sketch of two rival moralities: the pagan morality is "self-sufficient", satisfied with and settled in the world (another take on the conservative ontologism that Levinas criticised above), whereas Judaism views the world as "provisional", and therefore cannot use it as a measure (Ibid). But as Levinas would remark in his continued reflections on Judaism in 1938, in "L'essence spirituelle de la antisémitisme" (He 150-151): "The attachment to the world that [the attitude of Judaism and Christianism] refuses is not necessarily the joyful sensualism denounced by all doctrines of

---

[57] Later, he would write in *Humanism of the other*: "Biblical verses do not function here as a proof, but as testimony of a tradition and an experience. Don't they have as much right as Hölderlin and Trakl to be cited? The scope of the question is broader: do the Holy Scriptures read and commented in the West incline the Greek writing of philosophers, or are they only united teratologically?" (HAH 98, HO 66).

virtue, Jewish, Christian or Greek." (He 150). It is thus not sensualism *per se* which is problematic; what Jewish morality opposes, according to Levinas, is the simple satisfaction with the state of nature, with the order of things. However, he does not want to reduce Judaism to a certain morality—the distinguishing factor is rather "an immediate sentiment of the contingency and insecurity of the world, a *restlessness* of not being at home and the force to leave it" (Ibid, my emphasis). Here we find Levinas claiming that the restlessness, the non-identification with one's own situation, one's being in the world, is the fundamental situation and *Grundstimmung* of Judaism. Even the revelation of the one God is not as central to Judaism as this antipagan practice of not being at home (cf. He 152). Levinas is concerned with descriptions of the ethical rather than the otherworldly, though the ethical attitudes will gain their meaning by indicating a beyond. Paganism meanwhile serves as a counterpoint, and is given the following vivid description:

> the cult of the power and grandeur of the earth, the legitimacy of force to affirm itself as force, loving and hating spontaneously, riding horses, going hunting, waging war happily, the gift of being well at ease in the world (Ibid).

In the eyes of this "*Herrenmoral*", Judaism is but a folly, persisting in an election which means nothing but suffering. It is accused of the foolishness "of separating human dignity from force and success" (Ibid). Thus, in a sense he has answered his question posed four years earlier in *On Escape* (about the "ideal of human happiness and dignity" of the philosophy of excendence) by partly rejecting its premises. The philosophy of excendence dissociates human dignity from happiness. Here the Jew becomes the enemy of the Nazi precisely because he stands for a form of life which affirms the human as going beyond being, as an opponent to a doctrine which affirms immanence.

Interestingly, Levinas repeatedly uses the word "force" to describe the main element of the anthropology of what he earlier named Hitlerism. The aim of his own investigation is to find a description of the human that "separates human dignity from force and success". And this attitude is itself described as a folly, i.e., a weakness. Yet, on the very same page, the human is described as a 'force', inspired by restlessness and homelessness, to leave the world. It is also interpreted as the sentiment of not identifying with one's sentiment—in many senses Judaism is formulated in the terms of the world it wants to leave behind. This seems to raise the general question of the possibility of formulating a transcendence from within immanence. Can there be a force that leaves the world of forces, i.e. itself as force, and does not "affirm itself as force"?

The way in which, at least in these texts, Levinas tends to interpret National Socialism not only as a danger for Jews but as a historical ordeal—a trial for Jews and Judaism—can be difficult to accept, knowing the full horror of the atrocities enacted against the Jews. It is as if he comes close to saying the unavowable, namely ascribing to the senseless suffering of the Jews a certain meaning of historical necessity. One does not have to read him in this way—as trying to give a historical meaning to the Shoah—but rather, following Catherine Chalier's suggestions, in her introductory remarks to the republications of these texts in *L'Herne*, as trying "to choose life" (He 140), i.e., to construe the philosophical thought from the standpoint of the imminent and concrete events affecting him, making something out of them (even in the most desperate circumstances), rather than contemplating the notion of the human *sub specie aeternitatis*.

Levinas is writing about the particular situation into which he and his fellow Jews are thrown; he describes the struggle between the conflicting views as a struggle over life and death. This must be seen, as he said in the "Reflections on Hitlerism", not as a logical contradiction but as a concrete event. In this he shows acute historical awareness. Even if the concept of the human denotes the perhaps utopian dream of escaping the given, it seems that the necessity by which this "force" (He 150) of the Judaic notion of the human is summoned is produced by the urgency of the historical situation at hand. The notion of the human that Levinas introduces is perhaps, as I ventured above, a name for the force to leave a situation where only force matters.

A force that allows us to leave the play of forces might seem a contradiction in terms—and it must be clear that the expression is not his own, but is my way of creating a model, juxtaposing two seemingly conflicting thoughts in the early work of Levinas. He is trying to open up a new philosophical field of reference for thinking the human in a new way. On the one hand, he does not want to reduce the human to an immanent play of forces. On the other, in his attempt to think the human as transcendence, he wishes to resist the subordination of the human to the otherworldly. Framed in this way, Levinas is developing a problematic relation to the notion of the transcendent. He affirms, on the one hand, the philosophical and Judaic traditions of connecting the human to the beyond, and concomitantly associates the human with the immanent as a dangerous threat to Western civilisation. On the other hand, he sees in the notion of transcendence an equally potent threat of leaving the figure of the human both empty and abstract, and thereby exposing itself as an easy target for the forces of immanence. The term excendence stands for this movement out of being within being, that cannot allow itself the illusion of a standpoint outside. It is a transcendence in immanence—insisting that one starts in the concrete yet demanding a direction beyond, rather than in an ethics affirming the forces of immanence.

Levinas is searching for an understanding of the human as a facticity departing from a state of pure self-affirmation—the affirmation of one's own force, a force affirming itself. He performs a critique of this view, of this culture—criticizing a culture that denies the possibility of any such critique and that claims there is no point outside the condition of enchainment.

1.3
Incipit Alter
(1940s)

If so far as the notion of the human beyond being had been little more than an expression, unable to fulfil the concretion to which it aspires, in his work from the 1940s Levinas started to establish a proper description of what this would entail. From now on, the human "excendence" from being would find its focus in the relation to the other.

Even if Levinas is known as the philosopher of "the other", he did in no way single-handedly pull the figure of the other into philosophical discourse. One important source of inspiration came from within the phenomenological movement. Levinas co-translated the original publication of Husserl's *Cartesian Meditations*,[58] where Husserl sets the goal for philosophy as absolute science to find its own foundation in subjectivity. Husserl discovers, however, that the step towards objectivity must go via intersubjectivity. In the fifth Meditation Husserl therefore poses the problem of the other. How can the other, whose consciousness is closed to me, provide the basis for objective knowledge? At first, the gap may seem unbridgeable. Since it is an integral characteristic of my conscious acts that they are mine, how can I even perceive of the other as another consciousness, an alter ego? Husserl's solution is that first I perceive the other as a body, then I notice that it is a body such as mine, and finally, based on this categorial perception I come to perceive the other as a sentient creature such as myself. This is a phenomenon that Husserl calls "pairing", a general phenomenon of passive synthesis according to which separate entities which share characteristics are associated with each other and are identified as belonging to the same kind. But what is it that makes the other's body other and not my own? (Hu I, 142-143) In the perception of normal objects, the term apperception stands for the givenness of that which is not directly perceived, typically the backside of an object. The correlative term for the constitution of the other is *appresentation*, which is an utterly different case of indirect givenness. Whereas the backside of an object can always potentially become directly given by perceiving the object

[58] Published first in French, translated by Levinas together with Gabrielle Pfeiffer as *Méditations cartésiennes*: Introduction à la phénoménologie, Vrin, 1966 [1929].

from the other side, the appresentation of the other is more radically and irrevocably foreign to me.

When later in *Totality and Infinity* (TI 63-65: TaI 68-69) Levinas reviews the field of thinkers writing about the other in the years preceding that book, he fails to mention Husserl in particular, choosing rather to emphasise Gabriel Marcel and especially Martin Buber. Buber is commended for stressing the difference of the relation between subjects from that of the subject-object relation, but Levinas also shows that his approach differs from Buber's. Where Buber focuses on the I-you relation as reciprocal and symmetric, Levinas brings forward the originality of an asymmetric non-reciprocal relation to the other.

Even if this was to be done more elaborately in his lectures from 1946/1947, later published as *Time and the Other* (TA; TO), Levinas introduced the relation to the other for the first time in his writing in *Existence and Existents* (DEE; EE), written during Levinas's years of captivity in a Nazi work camp 1940-45. These two studies have essentially the same general outlook and ontological framework and will, for the present purposes, be treated together. The focus of each text is different, however. *Existence and existents* is not primarily a book about the other, but about the subject's relation to its own existence. It deals with the subject as a break with the *il y a* (there is)—Levinas's name for anonymous existence without an existent. This notion, which is not to be associated with the generosity implied by Heidegger's *Es gibt*, is rather filled with allusions to horror. In the description of the *il y a*, Levinas imagines "the plenitude of the void or the murmur of silence" (TA 26; TO 46). It is not attached to an existing subject or object, but is to be read as the same kind of verbality as found in other subjectless phrases such as the French *il pleut* (it is raining). He uses insomnia as an example: the force that keeps me awake is not my own; it has no goal. The moment to which one is attached in failing to fall asleep has no beginning and no real ending (DEE 109-113, TA 27; EE 61-64, TO 48). Being impersonal, it is also immortal. For Levinas, this is the only possible conception of immortality, since subjectivity always implies commencement and finitude. It is the immortality before which even suicide stands helpless—its absurdity will go on without me. Even if it is only described in detail in these two works, the notion of *il y a* retains a systematic function in his two major texts, *Totality and Infinity* and *Otherwise than Being*. For our purposes, the concept is of a certain interest, serving as a contrasting backdrop against which to view the human subject. Whereas Heidegger's critique of humanism focuses on the blindness or forgetfulness it causes towards the generous movement of Being, in contrast, Levinas sees the need to safeguard the human from the inexorable advance of the *il y a*. But what is the phenomenal validity, the experiential basis of this kind of limit concept? Why must anonymity be threatening? Is it not a matter of making a personal and contingent attitude into a fundamental ontological pre-structure of the subject? Even if Levinas wishes to put distance between himself and Heidegger's *Es gibt*, is it not precisely in opposition to Heidegger's notion that *il y a* appears as such? With the descriptions of the *il y a*, Levinas attempts to make it phenomenologically evident that the human subject appears threatened by the ominous forces of Being. The subject is the break with this anonymous existence, or more precisely the subject is "the transmutation, within the pure event of being, of an event into a substantive—a hypostasis" (DEE 125; EE 71). Levinas adopts the concept of hypostasis in contrast to Heidegger's *Ekstasis*. Whereas the latter concept is used to describe *Dasein* as the opening of and toward the world, "hypostasis" focuses instead on the subject as the sinking down, the becoming substance, as being a thing in the world. This is consonant with an attack on Heidegger's idea that it is the essence of the subject to care for its own existence, that everything in the world points to the existence of the subject. For Levinas, this means reducing the things of the world to their utility; he claims against Heidegger that "[w]e breathe for the sake of breathing, eat and drink for the sake of eating and drinking." (DEE 67; EE 36).[59] Levinas substitutes a work-oriented philosophy for a philosophy of life and enjoyment. Of course, for Heidegger, this utility meaning is always threatened by anxiety as the rupture of all meaning. But at the same time as anxiety has the role of laying bare the contingency of all meaning, it shows also how Dasein's projects are indeed the source of all meaning.

Inspired by Marxism, Levinas describes Heidegger's view of Dasein's care for its non-thingly and authentic existence as bourgeois ideology thinly veiled by quasi-religious jargon. Accusing Heidegger in this way, Levinas writes: "Under the pretext of saving the dignity of man, compromised by things, it is to close one's eyes to the lies of capitalist idealism and to the evasions in eloquence and the opiate it offers." (DEE 69; EE 37). In *Time and the Other*, he counters existentialism with support for a humanism of the working class, a "humanism springing from the economic problem" (TA 42; TO 60).

The subject is (as subject) alone. The possibility of a radical solitude of the subject is in these works structurally necessary in order to describe the other as radically other. Levinas here brings in "the alterity of the other who does not simply have another quality than me, but as it were bears alterity as his quality" (DEE 161; EE 97). This is a reaction against the Durkheimian idea of sociality as a commonality belonging to an entity that is "more than the sum of individuals", and "higher than the individual" (Ibid). Although not mentioning him by name, Levinas argues also against Husserl's understanding of sociality as "the imitation

[59] As an attack on Heidegger, this seems misguided. As we saw in the previous section, Levinas had himself commended phenomenology, and Heidegger in particular, for understanding the human subject concretely, i.e. not from an underlying substance, but from the act itself. Thus, when Heidegger writes that *Dasein* cares for its own existence in all its doings, it can very well be its existence *as* the act of eating and drinking, not necessarily in the sense of its survival.

of the similar", such that the other is immediately understood as an "alter ego" (DEE 162; EE 98), another such as me. These two approaches, which might initially appear miles apart, coalesce for Levinas around the same problem: the assimilation of the other to the same, sociality as fusion. In the first case, the other is assimilated to the anonymous commonality, in the second, to the ego. From a Levinasian perspective, we can infer that the Heideggerian notion of *Mitsein* (*Dasein* as always already being with other "*Daseins*") is the proof that these two mistaken understandings of sociality have something in common. *Mitsein* manages to combine the worst of both worlds: the anonymity of the *Durkheimian* notion, with the idea of a multiplication of the ego.[60]

Levinas is not arguing against the second perspective that imitation is not a central element of the psychological enfolding of an individuality, nor is he arguing against the first perspective that all social phenomena can be reduced to the relations of individuals. The potency of this description lies instead in what we might—with some caution—call the 'ontological' level of the subject's relation to the other. The key idea is that the alterity of the other is more than just the specific physical, mental, social and cultural differences that make us two unique and therefore differing individuals. This kind of difference always refers back to something common that we share in different respects or to a different degree. Levinas starts out from the relation to the other as other than me, the fact that the other is not me, and I not the other. Central to his approach is the difference in positions between me and the other, which make out what I as an I and the other as other are: the ipseity of the I and the alterity of the other.

> Intersubjective space is initially asymmetrical. [...] The other is the neighbour (*prochain*)—but proximity is not a degradation of, or a stage on the way to, fusion. In the reciprocity of relationships characteristic to civilisation, the asymmetry of the intersubjective relationship is forgotten. The reciprocity of civilisation—the kingdom of ends where each one is both end and means,[61] person and personnel, is a levelling of the idea of fraternity, which is an outcome and not a point of departure [...] (DEE 163-164; EE 98-99).

---

[60] This is my inference, not Levinas's. Most often he simply aligns the Heideggerian idea with the privileging of the collective. According to Levinas, the ethical singularity of the other eludes Heidegger, who instead envisages the social as gathering around the common. The other is not encountered face-to-face, but as part of this collective understanding of being, *around* being (cf TA 19, 88-89; TO 40-41; 93). As a consequence, claims Levinas, the relation to the other in *Mitsein* "rests on the ontological relation" (EN 17; ENO 9).

[61] This is a merging of two of the many formulations of Kant's categorical imperative: the humanity formula (*Menschheitsformel*) and the Kingdom of ends formula. The humanity formula is "Handle so, daß du die Menschheit sowohl in deiner Person, als auch in der Person eines jeden anderen jederzeit zugleich als Zweck, niemals bloß als Mittel brauchest." (*Grundlegung zur Metaphysik der Sitten*, BA 67) The Kingdom of ends formula is "Handle so, als ob du durch deine Maxime jederzeit ein gesetzgebendes Glied im allgemeinen Reich der Zwecke wärest". *Grundlegung zur Metaphysik der Sitten*, BA 87).

These are key ideas that will follow Levinas throughout his career. The political ideal of equality is watered down unless one appreciates that the point of departure must lie in the positing of an original asymmetry: the other is never to start with an equal or an alter ego; "the other is what I am not: he is the weak one whereas I am the strong one; he is the poor one, he is 'the widow and the orphan' […] Or else he's the stranger, the enemy and the powerful one" (DEE 162; EE 98). These notions of the stranger, the weak and the enemy function as qualifications of the very alterity of the other—"the essential thing is that he has these qualities through his very alterity" (Ibid). Here we see that the notion of equality is no longer, as in *Reflections on the Philosophy of Hitlerism*, derived from the notion of freedom,[62] but from the asymmetry of the intersubjective relation and from alterity as a quality—even if this argument is still not fully elaborated at this stage. These loaded qualifications of the other ought not to be interpreted from a philanthropic point of view; the other does not refer exclusively to the disenfranchised, the stranger, the poor in the third world, the less fortunate, and so on. Rather, it is a way of saying that what he here names alterity receives its meaning from the ethical (even though Levinas does not yet explicitly state it as such).

Arguably, this alterity as a quality is a first step towards giving content to his notion of humanity beyond being, a new specification added to his understanding of humanity. For Levinas we do not relate to the human other as a specimen in the category of Mankind. The human relates to the other *qua* other. Even the most abstract notion of *humanity* presupposes this understanding of the human. This is not yet spelled out as such by Levinas; what he says instead is this:

> The cosmos that is Plato's world is opposed by the world of spirit, where the implications of eros are not reducible to the logics of genera, where the same is substituted by the ego, and *l'autre* by *autrui* (DEE164; my translation (cf EE 99)).

This declaration can be taken as emblematic for all of Levinas's thought from now onwards, and its programmatic status is affirmed by its exact reappearance as the last phrase of the *Time and the Other* (TA 89; cf TO 94). "Plato's cosmos" here stands for the neutral perspective which Levinas perceives as permeating the contemporary philosophical world-view in general. In Plato's *Sophist* "the other" was found to be equal to non-being, otherness being nothing else but "other than", i.e. negation[63]. Levinas wants to conceive of eros from the interhu-

---

[62] Infra, section 1.2.

[63] In "Plato and Levinas: The Same and the Other," *Journal of the British Society for Phenomenology*, 1999, 30(2), pp. 131-150, Stella Sandford reads Levinas as if he thought that Plato had the same understanding of alterity as him. She shows that Plato's identification of non-being and the Other is not Levinasian, that non-being is only a non-being in a predicative sense, "other" always means "other than x", i.e., "not x". Thus, the other for Plato remains a difference within being and is never otherwise than being. But, although Levinas borrows the terms Same and the Other from the *Sophist* and put them in play as an integral part of his own philosophy, he is knowingly transforming their usage for his own ends. Stella Sandford's article is

man and intersexual encounter. The words that I left untranslated in the quote above, *autre* and *autrui*, are key concepts from this period on. *Autrui* denotes nothing but the other person, and is in everyday and literary French mostly used in moralist proverbs. *L'autre*, on the other hand, can be used as the English equivalent, "other", to denote all kinds of otherness, be it the human other or any other other. This versatility affords Levinas the possibility of approaching the traditional concept of otherness in order then to let it slide so as to denote a human other, allowing him to claim that "l'autre, c'est autrui".[64] The reason why this is far from a tautology is that the human element is smuggled into the concept. Alterity, claims Levinas, is first and foremost human. But why so and in what sense? In *Time and the other*, he poses the following question:

> Does a situation exist where the alterity of the other (*l'autre*) appears in its purity? Does a situation exist where the other would not have alterity only as the reverse side of its identity, would not comply only with the Platonic law of participation where every term contains a sameness and through the sameness contains the other? Is there not a situation where alterity would be borne by a being in a positive sense, as essence? (TA 77; TO 85; translation altered)

As we saw from the previous quote (about the Platonic cosmos), Levinas wants the conception of eros to be transformed. At this point, he is experimenting with the idea that the duality of the sexes would provide a model for the relation of alterity. This is a model for which he would be heavily criticised. In *The Second Sex*, Simone de Beauvoir exposed and attacked the notion of the woman as the Other, which she claimed to be the hidden presupposition in next to all descriptions of the masculine and the feminine. Interestingly, she would use Levinas as the first and primary example.[65] Unlike the rest of the tradition, however, the othering of woman is not stored away in the vault of unquestioned presuppositions. Levinas writes openly and explicitly thematises relations of sexuation, and in this way de Beauvoir's attack could be said to break an already open door. Levinas claims plainly in *Time and the other* that "alterity is accomplished in the

---

therefore misleading, even if correct in detail. The problem lies in the way she reads Plato through Levinas, asking Plato's *to heteron* to perform what Levinas claims that *autrui* does, claiming then, that *to heteron* fails to meet these standards. This is correct, but to claim, as Sandford does, that the Other is betrayed by Plato, is missing the point. Levinas and Plato are talking about different things. Levinas cannot deny the existence of *to heteron*, a difference within being; an otherness within the same exists even for Levinas, only this is not the otherness of the neighbour, which only can be the human Other. The differentiation of concepts is not a function performed by Levinas's Other. *To heteron* does not play the role of *autrui*! The inspiration for the Platonism that Levinas would later espouse lies rather in the notion of the Good beyond Being.

[64] Some writers on Levinas consistently translate '*autrui*' by 'Other' and '*autre*' as 'other'. In order not to join the tendency of mystification of Levinas's notion of "the Other", I choose not to adopt this translation, allowing myself other linguistic possibilities of expression through capitalisation.

[65] *The Second Sex*, Penguin, 1986, p. 13.

feminine" (TA 81; TO 88). Whereas the effort of Beauvoir's work lies in exposing a supposedly neutral philosophy as androcentric, Levinas's philosophy is here indeed openly androcentric. Even if they are miles apart when it comes to the advancement of gender consciousness, Levinas would agree with his feminist interlocutor that the putative sexless subject is an illusion. He makes explicit the point of view of a certain masculine subject, for whom the feminine is the other. His aim is not in this early work to show the feminine as the other and therefore a limitation, negation or a lack, but the other way round, to show an alterity that is not mere limitation, negation or lack: to show an alterity with a certain content.[66] This of course makes his position no less androcentrically essentialist in its cementation of gender stereotypes. Moreover, even if the sexless subjects are an illusion, it might appear equally limiting to view them as already sexed: I as masculine, the other as feminine.

However, Levinas would not persist in his claim that the idea of femininity was the answer to his quest for alterity and transcendence. When with some embarrassment he later discusses this thesis on the feminine as the other, what he finds salvageable therein is the notion of alterity with a content. But in what sense is this a content of alterity? In *Totality and Infinity* the feminine would be reduced to a more intimate alterity, less other than the stranger, the ethical and absolute other. Subsequent to that work, the feminine would no longer play any systematic role. Since the femininity on which *Time and the Other* in particular rests did not provide this alterity as quality, what content will this alterity then have? Jean-Luc Marion would later suggest that Levinas relied on an ontology that merely inverted Heidegger's ontological difference; claiming that (human) beings had been neglected by the philosophy of Being, the consequence being that Levinas instead privileges the existents (*étant*) over existence (*être*), beings over Being. Marion thinks that the notion of *Autrui* is too empty, too insufficiently determined to introduce anything new to overthrow the reign of ontology. He sees Levinas's criticism of ontology as coming from outside of philosophy, from the words of the prophets and the wise.[67] This is not how Levinas ever understood his own position—even if he was inspired by "religious thinkers", he always referred to his own intellectual practice as philosophy.

As an answer to Marion's criticism, Levinas would, in his untranslated preface to the second edition of *Existence and existents* from 1978, stress the accomplishment of the book as the "de-neutralisation of being, finally giving a glimpse of the ethical signification of the word good" (DEE 12, my translation). This refers to the original preface to the book, where Levinas announced that this "preparatory" work was concerned with the "relation to the Other (*autrui*) as a movement toward the Good" and guided by "the Platonic formula that situates the Good beyond Being" (DEE 9; EE xxvii). And it refers of course to the interhuman

[66] We shall return to the discussion of a content of alterity in section 2.5.
[67] Jean-Luc Marion, *L'Idole et la distance*, B. Grasset, 1977, p. 278.

framework that was meant to replace the Platonic cosmos as the sense-giving background of philosophical discourse. But still, it seems that this works as a reply to Marion only in hindsight; of the ethical signification of *autrui* there is in this earlier work indeed only a "glimpse". There is certainly an ethico-political undercurrent in all his early texts, but this was never developed as a theme in its own right. All the same it is clear that these early works open up a thought of transcendence, connected as it is in *Time and the Other* and *Existence and Existents*, to the human subject's relation to the other.

1.4
Existentialist Humanism

It is from the 1950s onwards, that both the terms "ethics" and "humanism" appear all the more frequent in Levinas's corpus. In order to understand why, we need to come to terms with how these concepts were circulating in the historical context out of which his thought would develop. In this regard, Levinas's texts often place a demand on the readers that they have a certain command over the specific intellectual and political conditions under which Levinas's philosophical vocabulary came to be established. For this reason, we will now sketch out the positions of the debate on humanism, partly viewed from the perspective of the questions which Levinas would later pose to the thinkers actively engaged in this debate.

After World War II and the Holocaust, many voices were raised in announcing the need to combat nihilism by regaining or reappropriating the tradition of humanism. Most of the time, however, this was not seen as an entirely unproblematic tradition. Even its advocates conceded it was in need of a new articulation.

Kojève's lectures on Hegel, held at the École pratique des Hautes Études from 1933 to 1939, had been formative in this regard. There, Kojève defined his/Hegel's position as an atheist humanism, as the antithesis of Christian theology. According to his understanding of Hegel,

> everything that Christian theology says is absolutely true, on condition that it is not applied to an imaginary transcendent God, but to the real human being living in the world.[68]

This secular humanism had as its aim a combative struggle against alienation; the absolute otherness that Christian Man had attributed to God turns out to belong to himself. Like Feuerbach, Kojève interprets all the divine attributes as human in the stage of absolute self-consciousness.

This understanding of humanism as the transformation of Christianity was to be the starting point also for Sartre, who like many of his generation was greatly influenced by Kojève's lectures. For Sartre, the foundation of humanism is a converted and assimilated Cartesian theology. The genius of Descartes consists

---

[68] *Introduction à la lecture de Hegel*, p. 572-3, Gallimard, 1968 [1947].

in teaching us to see the eternal truths as *created.* Descartes, of course, held God to be this creator, but in the modern era, which allows for no absolute transcendent foundation, cartesianism would instead provide a place for an atheist humanism. The important point is that Descartes's divine freedom, the model for human freedom, was not grounded in the framework of the eternal order of truths, but was on the contrary the foundation for Being, Truth, and the Good. Humanism in Sartre's understanding transposes the origin of these entities from the divine onto human freedom.

> Two centuries of crisis would be necessary—crisis of Faith, crisis of Science in order for Man to regain the creative freedom that Descartes had placed in God and for one to be able to have an inkling of this truth, which is the essential basis for humanism: Man is the being whose appearance makes a world exist.[69]

How are we to understand Man and the subject? Let us take a moment to recapitulate a brief history of the relation between Reason, Man and the Subject, as it came to be traced in the "history of philosophy". Plato associated Man with Reason, *nous*, as the perception of truth. With Kant, the perception of truth is connected to an idea of the subject, albeit on a universal plane. The subject constitutes the world. With Hegel, this constitution is shown to be a historical movement, or *the* movement of history. With phenomenology and existentialism, the subject and its constitution of the world is individualised and, with Heidegger—and to a certain extent also with Husserl's *Krisis*—historicised. Sartre, building on Kierkegaard, Nietzsche and Heidegger, is part of a movement that takes heed of these insights, but takes this process one step further; now, the individuality of the subject is impossible to understand as an instantiation of the categories of universal reason, or as a process of reason returning to itself.

When Sartre says that man makes the world, it is a question of the origin of meaning. The meaning that is to be found in the world does not transcend the sphere of human subjectivity; it is in this sense man-made. In his famous lecture *Existentialism is a humanism* his humanist position is expressed thus: "There is no universe apart from the human universe, the universe of human subjectivity".[70]

There is, however, something altogether ambiguous about Sartre's relation to the humanist tradition, something almost schizophrenic. Throughout his career he appears both as the scornful ridiculer and the fiery spokesman of humanism. This ambivalence appears already in his first ambitious philosophical work, "La légende de la verité",[71] of which only the first part was published by Sartre. This is a Nietzschean genealogy of the universal: not only of universal truth but also of the ideal of equality for all. In the published part, Sartre describes the birth of

[69] Jean-Paul Sartre, "La liberté cartesienne", *Situations 1*, Gallimard, 1947, s. 334.
[70] *L'existentialisme est un humanisme*, Gallimard, 1996 [1945], p. 76.
[71] *Écrits posthumes de Sartre, II* (ed. Juliette Simont), Vrin, 2001, pp. 27-59.

"The City of equals"—it is a democratic and just, but sterile and dull place, devoid of any real life, with high walls protecting it from the nature outside.

In this first part of the legend, the dissident heroes, freedom-seeking prophets ("thaumaturgs") leave the City to live in the dangerous but lively woods outside the city. The City's rule relies on the power of *savants*, learned men who teach that there is nothing beyond the democratic point of view. They go so far as to launch expeditions against the dissidents in the woods, with the purpose, and the successful achievement of their extermination.

In the second (unpublished) part, State philosophers are given the role of imitating the thaumaturgs in order to appease the nostalgia of the people. They go out into the woods and hurry back. But there is an unexpected turn of events. The *savants* suddenly come to appreciate that equality is not merely an ideological abstraction, and join with the people in revolution. If one were to compare this ending with the tenor of the story as a whole, then such a turn of comes across as unexpectedly sanguine in its treatment of the ambiguous position that the *savants* occupy—portraying as they do both the emancipatory potential of the universal character of a humanist ethics and the mechanisms of exclusion and domination that such a discourse equally entails. This originally unpublished addition sets to light an ambiguity of the entire Sartrean philosophy: Is humanism an ideology that must be surpassed or is it the name for the critical movement as such?

The problems generated here have a certain resonance with those we have already enumerated in Levinas's early production. We can recognise the critique of a stagnant liberalism—a critique typical for its time—from Levinas's analysis of the kingdom of ends in *Existence and Existents*, which is "the outcome and not the departure" of civilization (cf. above, section 1.3). Both Sartre and Levinas view modern democratic society as in need of being reminded what it is supposed to stand for. For both thinkers, it is the concern for the singular that is the only justification for universalism, but which in the self-reflection of the modern State tends to be forgotten, or even repressed. In this shared concern for the singular, however, the crucial difference between the two thinkers becomes apparent. Whereas for Sartre it is individual freedom that is forgotten in the City of equals, Levinas, understands this forgotten origin to be the asymmetrical relation to the other. From *Existence and Existents* onwards, Levinas's work is oriented towards a concretion of transcendence in this asymmetrical relation to the other. The central structure for Sartre, on the other hand, is arguably the authentic self-relation. To be authentic is to realise oneself as a for-itself preceding the in-itself, as an existence preceding its essence. A philosophy thus attuned Sartre calls existentialism, a philosophical position finding its clearest expression in *Being and Nothingness*, published in 1943.

Fundamental for Sartre's entire philosophy is the categorial distinction between the for-itself and the in-itself. Only the subject is for-itself, and as such is the point of view from which all things in the world (as in themselves) are perceived and reflected. But on the other hand, in reflecting upon itself, the subject also objectifies itself, perceiving itself as an in-itself. This means that I (as for-myself) am not identical with myself, for my reflection always leads me one step beyond myself as reflected. The subject, seen as for-itself, is without any specific content other than its freedom; an honest and truthful self-reflection will therefore discover the subject as empty and meaningless. This is a tragic position—and here Sartre strongly identifies with Ivan Karamazov: "if God is dead than everything is allowed". There are no values that I can accept in good faith but the ones that I create, and even these are mine to change: "I am the foundationless foundation of values," Sartre writes. This is, and should be, a cause of anxiety—but this anxiety contains in itself the way out of this bleak view of existence; Sartre interprets the tradition from Kierkegaard and Heidegger as describing anxiety as the motor for authentic self-liberation. The anxiety over the meaninglessness of life is at the same time a certain ontological insight: there is no intrinsic meaning to life. This realisation, however, need not be paralysing and depressing, it can instead serve the role of indicating that meaning is there to be created. For Sartre, this self-liberation is the subject's realisation of its own freedom, the possibility of an authentic life.

But since this anxiety weighs heavy upon us, we also seek to flee from it. In this act of taking flight, which Sartre calls "bad faith", the for-itself understands and treats itself as a certain in-itself, as if it were not always different from itself; it is an act of self-reification.

I cannot perceive the other as a for-itself; my glance objectifies. The extent to which the other extends the in-itself can be perceived merely as a lack. And vice versa, the glance of the other objectifies me. Therefore, even if I desire the recognition and the love of the other, the Sartrean conceptual toolbox is such that the relation between me and the other becomes one of conflict. The impossibility of the for-itself sharing the view of the other for-itself is sometimes expressed by Sartre rather cynically, holding a pessimistic view of interhuman relations, expressed on a global level as scepticism towards the project of humanism.

In *Nausea*,[72] Sartre's protagonist Roquentin mockingly pokes fun at a number of representatives of humanism in Parisian society: the catholic humanist; the communist humanist; the leftist humanist; the laughing humanist; the philosopher humanist and the weeping humanist. All these figures function in the novel as political expressions of bad faith. In each of these cases the characters fail to see the difference between themselves and their projects.

It comes as somewhat of a surprise therefore that in his lecture, "Existentialism is a humanism", Sartre endeavours to appropriate the notion of humanism. In so doing, Sartre takes great care in separating out the existential humanism he

[72] *La Nausée*, Gallimard, 1938.

is pursuing from what he labels classical and Comtean humanisms. Both these positions rely on something outside the individual human subject for their understanding of humanity—whether this be intrinsic human values (classical humanism) or a common human project, the project of modernism (Comtean humanism). There is, as we have seen, for Sartre nothing that unites different individual subjects. There is no subjective "we" of humanity; in the plural, there can only be objectivations. The original intersubjective situation is that of a conflict between absolutely free subjects.

Sartre's existentialism was often derided by his critics, who described it as an apolitical philosophy, or worse, nothing more than a popularistic nihilism. Sartre's "Existentialism is a humanism", must therefore be understood as a rebuttal addressed to his less charitable critics. His purpose is to show that a life led according to the existentialist ideals will be a life in some sense for the good of humanity. The notion of the human takes its lead from the concept of freedom. The radical freedom and emptiness of the existentialist subject makes "objective values" impossible. At the same time, however, one can say that Sartre reintroduces freedom as the value replacing all other values. Freedom is the value to struggle for; a realised freedom becomes the difference that separates the authentic from the inauthentic life, not only for me but for others. But moreover, my freedom is dependent upon the freedom of others, so that the more I struggle for my freedom, the more I realise that my freedom is dependent on the emancipation of others. When discussing this, Sartre takes over a topic introduced by Kojève's Hegel lectures,[73] the "Life-and-Death Struggle": the encounter of two subjects, each searching to be recognised as a subject by the other. In order to confirm myself as subject (in order to truly become subject) I need the recognition of the other. The problem is that this recognition must be given by the other seen as a subject with free will. This leads to a struggle of life and death, according to which only another subject willing to put its life at stake in order to be recognised suffices for the recognition of me as a subject.

But for Hegel, this struggle is only a transient stage. I can force the other to recognise me, but to do so would annul the freedom that makes possible authentic recognition. Hegel's solution is well-known: the *Aufhebung* of the Life-and-Death struggle in the State, where the aggressive mutual quest for recognition is constitutive of the State yet is cancelled by that State. Only in the State will both be able to see that it is rational and good to recognise the other as a subject. Through the achievement of such recognition, the conflict can be reconciled.

However, in the French reception of Hegel—and such is the case for Sartre—the reconciliation in the (Prussian) State is bracketed, as is the notion of *Aufhebung*. In the French reception, the struggle between free wills is never sublat-

[73] Shortly before Sartre, Simone de Beauvoir treated the topic in *Pyrrhus et Cinéas*, 1944, further developing her argument in *Ethics of Ambiguity* (PMA; EA) discussed below. Cf. Ulrika Björk, *Poetics of Subjectivity*, Filosofisia tutkimuksia Helsingin yliopistosta 21, 2008, p. 140.

ed. Here, Beauvoir expresses it succinctly: "each is interested in the liberation of all, but as a separate existence engaged in his own projects. So much so that the terms 'useful to Man,' 'useful to this man,' do not overlap. Universal, absolute man exists nowhere" (PMA 140; EA 112).

But, if there is no overlap or articulation between particularity and universality, then a key question emerges: why must my struggle for freedom result in a struggle for the freedom of others? How is this move to be understood from an intersubjective situation of conflict that is never reconciled since it is never to be transcended in the form of a Hegelian *Aufhebung*? How can someone like Sartre, who, after all, puts so much emphasis on conflict and the ultimate impossibility of reconciliation, claim that the struggle for one's own freedom will necessarily benefit the freedom of others? Does Sartre really succeed in distinguishing his own from the Comtean project, which is based on a "belief in humanity" and which Sartre otherwise claims to be impossible?

One line of argument in support for his existentialist humanism is the categorical imperative: I should always act so that the maxim for my action can become a law for all human beings. In Kantian vernacular, Sartre writes:

> [If] I decide to marry and to have children, even though this decision proceeds simply from my situation, from my passion or my desire, I am thereby committing not only myself, but humanity as a whole, to the practice of monogamy. I am thus responsible for myself and for all men, and I am creating a certain image of man as I would have him to be. In fashioning myself I fashion man.[74]

This would be a good description of a Kantian humanism. But why would this maxim apply to a subject who is never understood as an instantiation of universal reason, but rather one who is first and foremost a nothingness always situated?

Turning to the thoughts of Simone de Beauvoir will help us appreciate the problem better and will supply an answer—lacking in Sartre's account—from within the bounds of existentialism. In *Ethics of ambiguity*, she steps in to defend the existentialist position, with the aim to close the loophole between the essential conflict between subjects and the need to fight for the freedom of the other:

> [F]or existentialism, it is not impersonal universal man who is the source of all values, but the plurality of the concrete, particular men projecting themselves toward their ends on the basis of situations whose particularity is as radical and as irreducible as subjectivity itself. How could men, originally separated, get together? (PMA 24; EA 17-18)

[74] *L'Existentialisme est un humanisme*, pp. 32-33

Beauvoir's main line of argument relies on the subject's dependency on the other in order for the world to be meaningful: the others take part in the creation of meaning in my world. Without the others' freedom, my world would be meaningless and empty (PMA 90; EA 71). To "will that there be being", i.e. to will existence, "is to will that there be men by and for whom the world is endowed with human significations" (Ibid). Still, would not this description relegate the others' to the production of meaning *for me*? Beauvoir assumes this objection and her response starts in Hegelian fashion:

> Man can find a justification for his existence only in the existence of others. Now, he needs such a justification, there is no escaping it. Moral anxiety does not come to man from without; he finds within himself the anxious question, "What's the use?" Or to put it better, he himself is this urgent interrogation. He flees it only by fleeing himself, and as soon as he exists he answers. It may perhaps be said that it is *for himself* that he is moral, and that such an attitude is egotistical. But there is no ethics against which this charge, which immediately destroys itself, can not be levelled; for how can I worry about what does not concern me? I concern others and they concern me. There we have an irreducible truth. The me-others relationship is as indissoluble as the subject-object relation (PMA 91-92; EA 72).

When she claims that my concern for the other is an irreducible truth beyond egoism and altruism one might think that, for a moment, Beauvoir sounds like Levinas *avant la lettre* (Beauvoir's *Ethics* preceded Levinas's "Is ontology fundamental", the first text in which his own ethics of the other takes shape). But Beauvoir is not concerned, as Levinas will be, with how the other can appear as the one before whom my self-affirmation comes to a halt, before whom I "can no longer be able" (*je ne peux plus pouvoir*). Rather, her idea is in fact consonant with Henri Bergson: the struggle for freedom for me and for others is a constant struggle for the extension of my capability to act. The subjects, the other and I, are always understood as capabilities in becoming, as "élan vital".[75] This is Bergson's term for "an internal push that has carried life, by more and more complex forms, to higher and higher destinies."[76] For Bergson this process is not restricted to a subject; it is in its core life affirming, furthering itself over individuals and generations. Beauvoir more than Bergson ties the notion to an individual subject and its continuous life project[77]: "The tendency of man is not to reduce himself, but to increase his power" (PMA 115; EA 92).[78] Power contains an inherent posi-

[75] Beauvoir uses the notion of *élan* mostly in *Pyrrhus et Cinéas* and in her philosophical diaries. The importance of Bergson's notion of *élan vital* for Beauvoir's understanding of the formation of the subject has been shown by Ulrika Björk, *Poetics of Subjectivity*, Filosofisia tutkimuksia Helsingin yliopistosta 21, 2008, pp. 46-50.
[76] Henri Bergson, *Creative Evolution*, translated by Arthur Mitchell, University Press of America. 1983, p. 87 (*L'évolution créatrice*, P.U.F., 1959 [1907], p. 95).
[77] Cf. Björk, ibid, p. 49.
[78] It is noteworthy that Beauvoir in this quotation more or less equates Man with his power.

tivity, a belief in the affirmation of the force of life, which may explain why Beauvoir finds the movement from the affirmation of my freedom to the affirmation of the freedom of the other self-evident.

Beauvoir's departure from Hegel is clear: there is no Hegelian belief in a higher state securing my recognition; rather the hope is invested in the élan of life itself. However, she also preserves a Heideggerian gesture: any concern or anxiety seemingly caused by others in reality reflects my concern for myself, for my own finitude. Levinas would, in contrast, here make a sharp distinction between concern and interest. I have an interest for myself, my own happiness, *élan vital*, which can be confronted by my concern for others, the latter being provoked in spite of myself.

Beauvoir continues her argument, by extending her concern towards the political, stridently arguing for an interdependence between me and the others. Not working for the other's indirect realisation of his or her freedom is, by way of consent, tyranny (PMA 108; EA 86). Why tyranny of necessity would be in bad faith is not explicitly stated in her argument—can I not be a tyrant, by consent or directly, without believing this to be my essence? Later, when speaking about the oppressor, she intimates that the oppressor will always have to defend his position with reference to some impersonal higher entity (values, civilisation, institutions); it cannot merely be justified by his own freedom (PMA 114; EA 91). She shows that only by primarily relating one's freedom to that of others, rather than to impersonal entities, does one set freedom at stake, thus saving it. In this sense the tyrant cannot be authentic. For Beauvoir, as well as Sartre, then, the ideal of authenticity remains the key concern. Projected as the unchanging universal ideal, above all values, it is "through his own struggle, [that man] must seek to serve the universal cause of freedom" (PMA 112; EA 90).

Authentic freedom is understood as the realisation of the non-identity between the subject and itself, the non-identity between the subject and its projects. This is, so to speak, the minimal form of universal freedom, for Existentialism. Leaning on Husserl, Beauvoir claims that Existentialism is merely a method (cf. PMA 14, 19; EA 145, 180) not an ontology of Man. In keeping with this, Beauvoir writes: "We repudiate all the idealisms, mysticisms, etcetera which prefer a Form to man himself" (PMA 180; EA 145). The question, though, is whether an inconsistency here shows itself between method and the ethical value that guides this method. To what extent has authentic freedom not become the "form" for humanity by which the struggle for justice is measured? Beauvoir's reflections on Don Passos's *The Adventures of a Young Man* are helpful in this regard. The protagonist in this novel is put before the choice of either saving the lives of a few miners, or forsaking these lives for the good of the communist party. She commends Don Passos's hero for choosing to save the miners. "Of course", she begins, "if one had to choose between the revolution as a whole and the lives of two or three men, no revolutionary could hesitate", but here it is just the matter of strengthening the communist party in the USA, which is only "hypothetically" linked to the revolution (PMA 187; EA 151). What is the revolution and how might it be linked to authenticity? What would constitute for Beauvoir a non-hypothetical connection to the revolution, justifying thereby the sacrifice of individual lives? And, how does this relate to the "absolute value" which her existentialism ascribes to the individual? (PMA 193; EA 156) In what way are these reflections not privileging a certain Form of Man (free, revolutionary, authentic) over individual humans, only then to deploy this Form as the basis on which to value their lives?

Both Sartre and Beauvoir have been heavily criticised for their political naïveté. Here, the aim is not to repeat or refine this criticism from yet another ethical or political standpoint. The intention is rather to establish the problem with which the two thinkers were attempting to grapple, namely, of establishing an ethics, or even a humanism, that would no longer be dependent on a certain abstract image or Form of "Man".[79] This is, after all, the problematic with which Levinas is struggling, and Existentialism is a philosophical tradition through which this problem takes its contemporary form for Levinas.

Already in *Time and the Other*, Levinas reacts against the existentialist glorification of authentic freedom, writing: "[t]here is something other than naivety in the flat denial the masses oppose the elite when they are worried more about bread than about anxiety" (TA 42; TO 60). Diametrically opposed to Sartre, Levinas sees the "greatness" of a "humanism starting from the economic problem" (Ibid). He does not want to grant existentialism the sole privilege of defining what is empty prattle; for a socialist humanism, he says, existentialism can be seen as ostrich behaviour. Levinas finds that, despite his atheism, Sartre shows a non-secular tendency when glorifying the loneliness of the choice. "The revolutionary struggle is divested of its true signification and its real intention when it serves simply as a base for a spiritual life" (TA 43-44; TO 61).

None of the critical questions posed in this section are meant moralistically. They have as their aim to reveal the problems that appear when one claims to found a certain ethics in a certain ontology, or a certain ethical behaviour (the engagement for the freedom of the other) in a certain ontological "insight"

[79] Sartre is, from the viewpoint of a more classical humanism, often described as falling back into a weaker version of dogmatic anthropocentrism. It is seen as a weaker position because, in its attempt to formulate a new humanism, it tries to do without a description of a human essence. Cf. Alain Finkielkraut's *In the name of humanity*, Columbia University Press, 2000 where he regards Sartre (and even Foucault!) as merely repeating the position of Pico de la Mirandola's classical humanism. But Finkielkraut paints with so wide brushstrokes that it is indeed difficult to see how philosophers at all can distinguish themselves from each other; Cf. also Dominic Janicaud's "L'humanisme: des malentendus aux enjeux", *Revue philosophique de Louvain*, Vol. 99, no 2, May 2001, pp. 183-200, where he describes Sartre's and Heidegger's positions as "outbiddings" of classical humanism ("postures de surenchères". p. 185, 199). Without an anthropology, reasons Janicaud, the freedom of Sartrean humanism becomes empty.

(there are no fundamental values, but we are free to create our own). The question is whether that which is said to be founded is not already presupposed. Sartre seems to presuppose a concern for the other, a concern that is universalised through political struggle. But this concern is never just a concern for the freedom of the other, which is all that Sartre—from his minimalist perspective—can ascribe to the human subject as a for-itself. Juliette Simont catches the existentialist dilemma rather well, when she writes:

> This freedom is the moral inspiration running through all of the work, and at the same time (paradoxically) that which stops the work from being taken for a treatise on morality: it is precisely due to the fact that freedom is free that it is impervious to the prescriptive register of morality.[80]

On the one hand, an ethical pathos resonates throughout all French existentialism, a pathos of liberation. On the other hand, this ideal of freedom is never meant as an ethical prescription.

Sartre never published a treatise on ethics, though he was intensely working on such a project in 1947-48, after both the humanism lecture and *Being and Nothingness*. There, he experimented with a notion of "ontological generosity", which would consist in offering the other his own being in-itself, i.e. those parts of him that are not in the strict sense subjectivity, for-itself. This is also called love: a reconciliation of the in-itself and the for-itself of the other. I love, this is Sartre's example, not only the dancer in her relation to her own dancing, but also in her pure physicality, her sweat and her trembling breasts.[81]

The "ontological generosity" of love in these unpublished writings of Sartre serves as a way of shoring up the strength of an existential humanism against the vociferous criticisms otherwise waged against existentialism as a nihilism. Even so, the implications of this supplementary role for love remain uncertain. Does love appear in the garb of a regulative ideal in Sartre's work? Even if the perfectibility of a conciliation between two lovers is an impossibility for Sartre (given that even in the amorous encounter between two subjects each objectifies the other), nonetheless the perfect fusion could be claimed to be present in its absence, even in the earlier texts. Indeed, in order to understand the subject as lack (as Sartre does) one must already have hypostasised an idea of fullness. The anxious loneliness of the subject in these published texts in this sense starts a trajectory, ending in the "ontological generosity" of love in these posthumously published writings.

Levinas, who saw the relation to the other as the key to understanding the subject, did not orient his project towards this possible or impossible amorous

---

[80] Juliette Simont, "La morale de Sartre, entre humanisme et anti-humanisme", *Daimon, Revista de Filosofia*, no 35, 2004, p. 23-24.

[81] Posthumously published as *Cahiers pour une morale*, Gallimard, 1983.

reconciliation. He saw the asymmetry of my relation to the other not as a problem of objectivation needing to be solved, but as the founding element of democracy. For Sartre, objectivation would mean understanding the other as a certain essence: e.g. "the foreigner" or "the worker". Levinas is also concerned with this reduction, but the hope of its resolution lies not in love. He has already mapped out the notion of alterity as a quality, deriving as it does from the asymmetrical intersubjective situation: there is a certain quality to being me, and a certain quality to being the other. In his later work, this formulation will receive an ethical signification, according to which these positions find their meanings in my responsibility for the other. For Levinas, this relation is the very prerequisite for universalism and for philosophy, and cannot be founded by philosophy—which, one could claim, is what Sartre was attempting in "Existentialism is a humanism".

1.5
Heidegger's Letter

In the "Letter on 'Humanism'", written in the autumn of 1946, Heidegger made it clear that he did not see himself as part of the existential humanism with which Sartre had associated him in his lecture, "Existentialism is a humanism".

Originally, the text was conceived as a response to a letter from the young French philosopher Jean Beaufret, who had asked how sense could be returned to the word "humanism". The question has an air of desperation; the world events preceding the missive would account for this. Penned a year after Sartre's "Existentialism is a humanism", the letter offers Heidegger the opportunity for a rebuttal. Here Heidegger reacts to Sartre's conscripting him into the philosophical programme of existentialism.

Heidegger's response to Beaufret's question is at first puzzling. He writes:

> If Man is to find his way once again into the nearness of being, he must first learn to exist in the nameless. [...] Before he speaks, Man must first let himself be claimed by being, taking the risk that under this claim he will seldom have much to say. (WM 319; PM 243, translation altered).

Let us rephrase this as: one should be wary of subscribing to a doctrine before having investigated what it is, even though at first glance it might seem obvious that what it promotes is good. So what is humanism? Heidegger aims for the core of the movement: should we understand this as an effort to care for Man, to make the human being more human? How should one otherwise understand the direction of the humanistic concern, if not as bringing the human being into his essence as human? But what is the essence of Man? Heidegger gives some examples to show how such a question undergoes contextual variation. Marx, for example, sees the true nature of human being as living in the society which provides for his needs; Christianity sees the human being as the image of God, as that which belongs to the divine, but is not God. Heidegger points to how, already among the Romans and Greeks, *humanitas* gained its intelligibility only by what it opposed, i.e. the in-human in the form of what was deemed barbaric and base. For the Renaissance humanists, who reactivated humanism from within their Roman heritage, the in-human was now incarnated in the form of the Medieval Gothic scholastics. Heidegger then speaks about the connection between humanism and the humanist studies, later translated by 18th

Century German humanists as *Bildung*. Through this move he intimates that the focus on education served only to strengthen this exclusivist ideal of humanism—though he does not say who the in-human others are meant to be for Winckelmann, Goethe and Schiller. (WM 320; PM 244). Heidegger continues his argument: even if one restricts Humanism to mean simply that Man should be free for his humanity, to find his value there, this will still depend on the way freedom and values are understood, which is something that differs between different historical understandings of humanism, and their multiple interpretations of those human values. Values, claims Heidegger, are products of metaphysics, a statement that can be taken as a reproach to Nietzsche—but also to Sartre, who conceived human freedom to be the progenitor of value, and therefore, as the highest value. Heidegger says: "Every humanism is either grounded in a metaphysics or is itself made to be the ground of one." (WM 321; PM 245). This, for Heidegger, is connected with the fact that every humanism *defines* Man. All humanisms take a definition of Man for granted, a definition conditioned by its metaphysics. In "Plato's Doctrine on Truth" from 1940, which at first was published conjointly with "Letter on 'Humanism'". Heidegger spells this out more clearly, defining humanism as the occurrence

> where Man in different respects, but always knowingly [*wissentlich*], moves to the centre of being [*Seiendes*][82], without being the highest being [...] What is always at stake is this: to take "Man", *animal rationale*, defined by a region of a fixed metaphysical ground structure of being, to the liberation of his possibilities and to the certitude of his definition and to the securing of his "life" within this region (WM 236; PM 181; translation altered).

In the various moments of the history of occidental thought, which Heidegger gathers together, this liberation had been viewed differently. However, "[w]hat takes place in each instance, is a metaphysically determined revolving around Man, whether in narrower or wider orbits" (Ibid; translation altered).

What Heidegger views as problematic in metaphysical humanism is that the question of Being is never made apparent; the relationship between the essence of Man and Being is obscured, the proximity of Man to Being threatened. Both the animality and the rationality of the rational animal are defined according to what is rational and animal in a given epoch. Man's resistance to these categories—the fact that he never can be reduced to any such substance—is captured by Heidegger with the term ek-sistenz: man stands out outside them, being spoken to by Being. Distancing himself from traditional humanism, Heidegger is nonetheless proximal to Sartre's humanism in at least one respect: even if they criticise traditional humanism for binding humanity to an essence, both contin-

[82] When referring to the Heideggerian concepts, I translate "(das) Sein" as "Being" (with a capital 'B'), and "Seiendes"/ "das Seiende" as "being" (with a lower-case 'b').

ue to speak of the human being as an entity incomparable to other entities, in that its essence is indefinable, or is defined only by its projects.

For our present purposes, there is one notable difference—conspicuous in the texts of the later Heidegger. Rather than putting the emphasis on the fact that Man himself is responsible for his *engagement*, Heidegger emphasises that Man is "thrown" by Being; Being discloses itself historically by the projection of Man. His projects are never his but always the projects of Being. It is Man's role to be the attentive Guardian of Being. The ek-sistence of Man stands and falls with this play of Being. In taking its starting point in a principle, the metaphysics of traditional humanism blocks the question of Being, and thereby obstructs the passage towards a more primordial questioning concerning the essence of Man. By defining Man as Ek-sistence Heidegger is not aiming to discard the humanist definitions of man (as *animal rationale* or as "person" or as a spiritual-psychic-bodily essence). What he says instead is "that they still do not realise the authentic (*eigentliche*) dignity of man" (WM 330; PM 251; translation altered).

This sounds as if Heidegger were about to construct a new humanism, one that cares for the *authentic* dignity of Man. He almost admits to this being a kind of humanism, but if this were the case it would be a humanism of Man as the historically contingent openness for being, rather than Man as a creation of metaphysics. In a footnote added in 1949, he explicates the "eigentliche Würde" from the quote above: "The dignity proper (*eigen*) to him, i.e., that has come to be appropriate, appropriated in the event: propriation and event of appropriation". (WM 330n; PM 251n).[83] The footnote explains that by authentic ("eigentlich") we should not understand a timeless essence of man, but on the contrary understand the essence of man as temporal, as historically appropriated (*zugeeignet*) and at the same time as the event opening time (*Ereignis*). This is the dignity of Man. Heidegger thus toys with the thought of not rejecting altogether the title of humanism for his project: his humanism would thus have the essence of Man as essential for the truth of being, but only so that this truth would not be dependent on Man as such, but dependent on the way Being gives itself historically to Man. Ultimately, though, Heidegger rejects this idea, finding the label of humanism to be irrevocably associated with the forgetting of Being of Western metaphysics. Heidegger decides not to endorse the project of humanism therefore, arguing that its blindness to its own metaphysical origin would hinder us in concentrating on the openness to the play of Being (WM 321; PM 245).[84]

Humanism and metaphysics are part of the alienation of Man; they block the original relationship between Being and Man. Man becomes homeless, out of

---

[83] "Die ihm eigene, d.h. zu-geeignete, er-eignete Würde: Eignung und Ereignis".

[84] If one claims, as Tom Rockmore does, that Heidegger presents his philosophy as a "new form of humanism" (*Heidegger and French Humanism*, Routledge, 1995, 81), one misses the very thrust of Heidegger's endeavour.

touch with his relationship to Being. Heidegger analyses Nationalism (as well as Internationalism) as a symptom of this *Heimatslosigkeit* or alienation of Man; he even speaks of it as a result of Man being expelled from the Truth of Being (WM 341-2; PM 260). In this sense, Heidegger now attributes the upsurge of Nationalism (in which he himself was caught up only a decade earlier) to Humanism.

Ironically, Heidegger has been accused by some of his followers of slipping back into the very anthropocentric philosophy that the "Letter on 'Humanism'" takes as it object of critique. Miguel de Beistegui, for example, characterises the development of Heidegger as follows:

> While the problem of anthropocentrism was in a way "neutralised" [...] in Being in Time through the identification of man with the "there" of being, Heidegger's reopening of the question regarding the truth of being also means reopening the question of man [... In] *Being and Time*, [...] man was simply a solved issue, for it coincided absolutely with the advent of being. But now the question of man re-enters the scene [...] Man is not so much the site of *Wahrheit*, as he is the *Wahrer* of this *Wahrheit*.[85]

Thus, for de Beistegui, *Being and Time* offers a stronger criticism of humanism than the later works, since it tries to dissolve Man rather than fashion him a new role. In the case of the latter one takes an unavoidable step back into humanistic discourse.

Obviously, though, Heidegger did not merely wish to dismiss the philosophy of Man in order to write about something else. He wanted to work himself out of anthropocentrism, an anthropocentrism he now concludes that the *Daseinanalytik* from *Being and Time* was not free from.

Is there not though, in another sense, a slip back into metaphysics? Already Derrida found a tendency towards a new variant of humanism or metaphysics in Heidegger—the human is described along the parameters of a certain proximity and distance to oneself and to Being.[86] Moreover, Heidegger assumes a "we", a fellowship oriented around the question of the understanding of Being, and assumes that the being posing the question of Being, Dasein, is an exemplary being, a key to the meaning of Being. The reason for this is that Dasein is the Being that we (*jeweils*) are.

When Heidegger says that Nationalism and Internationalism, as well as Individualism and Collectivism, are just symptoms of the forgetting of Being, he seems to be very close to what he labelled ontotheological reasoning. The relationship between Man and Being becomes the only worthy or dignified principle with which to view society. But according to Heidegger, a metaphysical principle is such that it reduces all Being to a privileged being. Is it then not just a question

[85] Miguel de Beistegui, *Truth and Genesis. Philosophy as Differential Ontology*. Indiana University Press, 2004, p. 140.
[86] "The Ends of Man", *Margins of Philosophy*, University of Chicago Press, 1985, p. 124

of names? "Metaphysical" or "non-metaphysical": is not what is happening in this text nevertheless a reduction of diversities according to a principle? A valid response to this criticism would be to point to the difference between *Sein* and *Seiendes*, which Heidegger challenges us to think. Being (*Sein*) can never be anything like a principle of metaphysics; it is rather one of his ways of stating that there can be no such ultimate principle. Principles manifest themselves historically from the play of Being, and it is in being attentive to this play that we can see the *Ereignis*-character of principles. It is to enter into a freer relationship with principles, to think them in terms of a process of becoming, rather than as fixed and eternal points.

In an earlier text, "Die Zeit des Weltbildes"[87], Heidegger puts a slightly different inflection on the term humanism; there it is explicitly used only to describe the situation of modernity (*Neuzeit*). Once Nature and Man have become the object of scientific research, so that its beingness can only be understood as objectivity, Man starts to understand himself as a subject, as *hypokeimenon*; "Man becomes the being, which founds all other being in its way of being and in its truth. Man becomes the referential centre (*Bezugsmitte*) of being as such."[88] Being is now understood as Man's representation, as a picture. All understanding of Being proceeds via an understanding of the human subject as representing Being in this or that way. The more accurate the techno-science, the greater the role of the subject. Where the world becomes the subject's objective representation, any world picture (*Weltbild*) becomes an anthropology. This becomes the foundation for a new development of humanity—humanism. Man thinks of himself as having the power to change the course of the development of humanity, as "deliberately" (*wissentlich*) holding the central position in Being.

Where Heidegger chooses to draw the borders around the notion of humanism is here not of importance. Of greater significance is that the entire Western tradition is implicated in this veneration of Man. It is therefore a tendency in the history of Being that commences in Platonism and culminates in modernity. When Heidegger examines the development of modern views of society, he is not so much interested in the shifts and historical uniqueness of these -isms and ideologies; instead he tends to understand them somewhat reductively in the light of the constellation of Man and Being. Heidegger's notion of the history of Being is in a sense ingenious, in that it sees man as a historical being, while refusing all ideas of abstract laws governing the turns of history. Yet there seems to be no apparent way of responding to someone who would claim that Heidegger has introduced a law more abstract than all others and would further claim a

---

[87] "Die Zeit des Weltbildes", *Holzwege*, Vittorio Klostermann, 1994, pp. 75-114; in English as "Age of the world picture"; *Off the Beaten Track*, edited and transl. Julian Young and Kenneth Haynes, Cambridge University Press, 2002, pp. 57-85.

[88] Ibid, p. 81; pp. 66-67, translation altered.

dubiousness about Heidegger's efforts to provide a philosophical solution to an alienation, which itself is couched in political terms.

On the other hand, one could say that this criticism is demanding of Heidegger what he has no interest in providing. Heidegger is using political concepts as arbitrary examples; he has no political agenda in this text, but just wants to turn our eyes from the thoughtless involvement in the play of politics to the self-sufficient thinking of being. This seems to be in line with his own self-interpretation. In the concluding pages of the "Letter on 'Humanism'", Heidegger tries to respond to the hypothetical question of the use this thinking of Being might serve. He says that it should be seen as neither practical nor theoretical; rather he seems to conclude that it is a way of life, more fundamental than the active or the theoretical life. He says: "Such thinking has no result. It has no effect. It satisfies its essence by being." (WM 358; PM 272). A few pages later, close to the end of the letter, Heidegger continues: "[Thinking] surpasses all contemplation, because it cares for the light in which a seeing, as *theoria*, can first live and move [...] Thinking is a deed. But a deed that also surpasses all *praxis*." (WM 361; PM 274). Heidegger goes on to ask himself where such thinking can find its measure. He never answers directly, but writes only that thinking is related to that which is to come, and that Being *is* as the fate of thinking.

> Thinking gathers Language into simple saying. In this way language is the language of being, as clouds are the clouds of the sky. With its saying, thinking lays inapparent [*unscheinbar*] furrows in language. They are still more inapparent than the furrows that the farmer, slow of step, draws through the field (WM 364; PM 276, translation altered).

These are the last words of Heidegger's letter. We should be alert, I think, to all the Platonist and antiplatonist motifs in the description of a thinking that seeks to disabuse itself of metaphysics. Where Plato spoke of a contemplation that is not seeing but surpasses it, Heidegger speaks of thinking as surpassing contemplation, i.e. as surpassing that which could only be described with the formula of surpassing. He goes on to explain that it surpasses in that it cares for the light, that is, the medium of philosophy. But in what sense? No orientation is forthcoming as to how thought should provide this care. Only that it is directed towards that which is to come. The coming can of course not be described from the present era, trapped as it is in metaphysical language. Rather, it must be understood in its difference.

How are we to understand the statement of the "inapparent Furrows (*unscheinbare Furchen*)" that thinking produces? In order to be more attentive to his choice of wording, a brief return to "Plato's Doctrine of Truth"is necessary. Here, Heidegger directs our attention to how Plato describes the Good, the subject-matter as well as the *telos* of Plato's philosophy as *to fanotaton* (WM 228; PM 175)—and which Heidegger translated with the German neologisms *das*

Erscheinendste and *das Scheinsamste*, signifying both that which shines most and that which above all lets appear. In Heidegger's reading the Good that lets appear is understood too much along the lines of the idea, letting truth as disclosedness or *aletheia* become secondary to the ideas. This is not a minor event; Heidegger describes it as truth being put "under the yoke of the idea" (WM 230; PM 176), and under the good. This equates with the dawn of metaphysics, which at the same time is the dawn of "humanism" (WM 236; PM 181). The concept of values is understood by Heidegger as a degenerate modern offspring to the idea of the good, because they are thought of as objects present at hand (*vorhandene*), rather than as that which lets being be.[89]

Returning to the "Letter on 'humanism'", we can therefore conclude that Heidegger's comment about the unapparent furrows is a distancing from the value-oriented philosophy of humanism. Thinking should not go for that which shines and is apparent, such as "The Good", or even worse "values", but it should do the humble and unapparent groundwork for that which is to come. Heidegger delivers a powerful critique of the humanism of the Western tradition, to which Levinas will see the need to respond. This he will do by retaining the critique, all the while preserving the possibility of a philosophy of the human.

[89] For a succinct defence of Plato against Heidegger, cf. Paul Friedländer, *Platon. Band 1: Seinswahrheit und Lebenswirklichkeit*, de Gruyter 1964, pp. 239-242. According to Friedländer, Heidegger unjustly locates the forgetfulness of the original concept of truth as *aletheia*. Rather, it is Plato who first makes the view of truth as *aletheia* visible to philosophers. Truth as *orthotes*, correctness, however, was according to Friedländer a relevant concept even for the Presocratics.

1.6
Ethics of the Other (1950s)

For Levinas, the rejection of humanism and the repudiation of a philosophical ethics was symptomatic of a problem in Heidegger's philosophy, which he now increasingly was to label "ontologism", namely, the tendency to give a priority to ontology over ethics, a priority of a philosophy of Being over a philosophy of the other.[90] After World War II, when the full extent of the crimes committed by the political party supported by Heidegger was known, to draw a connection between Heidegger and an unethical philosophy was not unexpected. But this criticism had in fact been there from the beginning. His own disciples Karl Löwith and Hannah Arendt had (independently of each other) argued already in 1928 that Heidegger tended towards a solipsist account of human existence.[91]

Heidegger had responded to this criticism as early as 1929 in "On the Essence of Ground":

> The statement: *Dasein exists for the sake of itself*, does not contain the positing of an egoistic or ontic end for some blind narcissism on the part of the factical human being in each case. It cannot, therefore, be "refuted," for instance, by pointing out that many human beings sacrifice themselves *for others*, and that in general human beings do not merely exist alone on their own, but in community. The statement in question contains neither a solipsistic isolation of Dasein nor an egoistic intensification thereof. On the contrary, this is the

[90] Jean-François Courtine's interpretation ("Fundamentalontologin hos Levinas", translated by Jim Jakobsson, in Bornemark, Jonna (ed.) *Det främmande i det egna*, Södertörn Philosophical Studies, 2007), according to which the term ontologism aims to stigmatise a thought of Being in its purity and generality, is thus clearly misleading. Not the contemplation of the pure, but the ever-continuing assimilation of the other into the same is Levinas's characterisation of ontologism. In his "Philosophy and the Idea of the Infinite" where this association is given some extension, Levinas describes this ongoing assimilation of the other into the same in the following way: "The Ego, the Self, the ipseity ... does not remain invariable in the midst of change like a rock assailed by the waves (which is anything but invariable); the Ego remains the Same by making of disparate events of a history—its history. And this is the original event of the identification of the Same, prior to the identity of a rock, and a condition of that identity." (EDE 230). It is not Platonism but Hegelianism that is being caricatured here.

[91] Karl Löwith, *Das Individuum in der Rolle des Mitmenschen: Ein Beitrag zur anthropologischen Grundlegung der ethischen Probleme*, Drei Masken Verlag, 1928; Hannah Arendt, *Der Liebesbegriff bei Augustin: Versuch einer philosophischen Interpretation*, J. Springer, 1928.

> condition of possibility that human being can behave *either* "egoistically" or "altruistically" (WM 157; PM 122, Heidegger's emphasis, translation altered).

The scare quotes around the notions of both egoism and altruism indicate that Heidegger does not truly believe in these notions, presumably because they are too tied up with a modern philosophy of the subject. Heidegger adopts the strategy that attack is the best form of defence. According to him, this philosophical tendency—which Heidegger accuses of disfiguring the classical questions of philosophy, trying to force them through the aperture of subjectivity—is the cause of the misreading that would wish to convict Heidegger of solipsism. As we saw in section 1.4, however, Levinas's critique of the philosophy of sociality in Heidegger was not only a criticism of a solipsism, but a critical interrogation of the idea of the commonal bond of *Mitsein*, which both precedes and obscures the other's essentially asymmetric relation to me.

In the decades that followed, this asymmetrical relation to the other would come to be understood as ethical. "Is ontology fundamental?" from 1951, is the first of Levinas's texts which explicitly deals with ethics in a manner for which he was later to become famous. It is also the first text in which he finds a point of anchorage for his notion of the human. Here he presents a clear opposition between an ethical understanding of the human and an ontological understanding.

He describes the philosophy starting from the ontological view in the following way: "It is not because there is man that there is truth. It is because being in general is inseparable from its disclosedness; it is because there is truth, or, if you like, it is because being is intelligible, that there is humanity" (EN 13; ENO 2). This is how he understands Husserl and Heidegger, as the perfection of Western philosophy's propensity to "ontologise"; humanity is equated with truth and with understanding. From this point on, this view is the one against which Levinas will develop his own thinking of the human.

According to this view, all human existence is understanding; understanding a tool or a situation means handling this tool or this situation—and this is the primary mode of understanding. Levinas claims that Heidegger in this sense is a true heir to Aristotle, who opened his Metaphysics by stating: "All men by nature aspire to knowledge" (Met. 1.980a). Heidegger is misunderstood by many, who insist in thinking him as anti-intellectualist. On the contrary, for Heidegger "[o]ntology [...] is the essence of every relation with beings and even with every relation in Being... Every misunderstanding is simply a deficient mode of understanding" (EN 15; ENO 4).

The problem with Heidegger's position, for Levinas, is that the particular existent (*Seiendes, étant*) is understood from the horizon of its Being (*Sein, être*). In this sense he interprets Heidegger as belonging to the tradition of subsuming and subduing the particular under the universal. Levinas thinks that this is acceptable for understanding in general—understanding a being from Being also means letting it be. Its inadequacy is encountered when the other human being is at stake. Even though we want to understand the other, this relation goes beyond understanding. The other is by its own virtue an existent (*étant*) and not by virtue of its relation to a concept such as Being (*être*). The Heideggerian approach to the existent, letting it be (in the light of Being) is for Levinas an inadequate approach to the other. Understanding someone already means to talk to and be spoken to by her. Speech is thus a condition for understanding the other.

> Man is the only being that I can't meet without my expressing this meeting itself to him. That is precisely what distinguishes the meeting from knowledge. In every attitude toward the human being there is a greeting—even in the refusal to greet. (EN 18; ENO 7).[92]

Thus speech is not only to be understood as the articulation of an understanding (which is how it is described in *Being and Time*), but in instituting sociality—a sociality irreducible to understanding the other. Most important for Levinas is to describe a relation to the other that cannot be reduced to any exercise of power on the part of the subject.

> Perception does not project itself towards the horizon (the field of my freedom, my power, my property) in order to grasp the individual against this familiar background. It refers to the pure individual, the being [*étant*] as such (EN 18; ENO 7).

The relation to the other is in this sense a relation with a being (*étant*) as being (*étant*), or being in itself. This relation he also calls "religion", referring to the way Comte uses the word at the beginning of the *Politique positive*,[93] i.e. a secular agnostic humanism, always pronounced by Levinas in explicit contrast to any mystic understanding of religion. This relation is not to be understood as irrational, but rather as the relation constituting rationality. This claim was to be further developed in later articles; in this article the main accomplishment is that the other has a signification that is primarily ethical.

Earlier, Levinas would talk about the human as a force while still acknowledging the human as a weakness—this we expressed as "the force to leave a situation

---

[92] Levinas is thus advancing a claim of the following type: even the deficit of a certain trait is an example of this trait, since this trait is an anthropological constant. Arguably he thereby shows up the remnants of a Heideggerian heritage. This is exactly how Heidegger puts it in *Being and Time* when he shows that a characteristic of Dasein not only is *existentiell* but *existential*, i.e., that even the careless attitude is a mode of care (*Sein und Zeit*, Niemeyer, 1993 [1927], p. 192); even silence is a mode of speech (p. 164). For Heidegger this means that the phenomena of speech and care are "ontologically prior" (p. 194) to any particular modus of speech or care. Heidegger is in *Being and Time* explicitly in search for the "ontological foundations" of Dasein (pp. 196-197). Should not Levinas ask himself if he is partaking in an ontologisation of Man, the project he wants to be opposing? This will be discussed more extensively in sections 1.7 and 2.5.

[93] *Système de politique positive ou traité de sociologie instituant la religion de humanité*, Thunot, 1851-1854, especially preface and chapter VI.

where only force matters".[94] Here, this ambivalent relation toward the notion of force is given a more elaborated and systematic role: the ethical or human relation is described in terms of an end to power. On the one hand, the other is the only being that I *can* want to kill. On the other hand, truly being in relation to the other means already not being able to kill. Of course, murder is not an impossibility in the strict sense, but his point is that killing the other is precisely no longer relating to the other as other, but treating the other as the means to something else. It means perceiving the other as a part of my horizon rather than meeting the other face-to-face. The face-to-face relation means precisely the appearance of the other as other, as the one before whom I find myself no longer being able to exert power. Levinas says, and these are the final words in "Is Ontology Fundamental?": "The human gives itself to a relationship that is not a being able (*qui n'est pas un pouvoir*)" (EN 22; ENO 11). The face-to-face relation is thus the situation where I am, as a power, stopped by the one who is not a power. I, as a "force qui va", (Levinas here quoting Victor Hugo) can encounter three types of resistance: The passive resistance of matter; the active resistance of another force and the resistance of the other as a face. Only in the latter case is the subject no longer to be understood exclusively in terms of power. Of course, the encounter with the other can also be a conflict of powers, but Levinas takes interest in the specific otherness that lets me no longer be a power. Thus in contrast to the ontological understanding of man as understanding, and as truth, Levinas says that humanity is accessible as a face, that this specific relation *is* the human. This shows that the relation is not only given in the negative—the positive designation of this relation is speech as salutation.

"Is Ontology Fundamental" can be said to be the first sketch of what would subsequently be labelled a 'humanism of the other man'. Without mentioning either classical or existentialist humanism, or the Heideggerian criticism of them, this variant of humanism focuses on what is perceived to be a weakness of both Heidegger and existentialism, namely, the relation to the other. A challenge to any philosophy which pretensions to a humanism after Heidegger's criticism, is to show how the notion of the human does not need to be dependent on an ontologically fixed image of Man. For Levinas, this role was to be filled by the appearance of the other, preceding all ontological descriptions of Man.

If the term appears occasionally in earlier texts, then a text published in 1956, "For a Jewish Humanism" (DL 406-411; DF 273-276), will give humanism the first proper thematisation in his work. Here he proposed to connect this humanism to the Jewish tradition:

> A Jewish humanism: the phrase seems as suspect for its noun as for its adjective! Humanism, a much-used misused and ambiguous word, can none the less designate a system of principles and disciplines that free human life from

[94] Infra, section 1.2.

> the prestige of myths, from the prestige of myths, the discord they introduce into ideas, and the cruelty they perpetuate in social customs. But in that case, we have already defined not just humanism, but Jewish humanism. Its notion remains secular. (DL 407, DF 273).

Levinas is very consistent in reading the Jewish sources as bearing a message that does not only apply to the Jewish people; it is never to be understood as a belief in a deity privileging the Jews: "Monotheism is a humanism" (DL 409, DF 275). In order to make his case for this interpretation of Judaism, Levinas compares it to a humanism that has its roots in Greek sources:

> The rare privilege of the Jewish religion consists in promoting as one of the highest virtues the knowledge of its own sources. This knowledge can lead pious souls to forms of life that demand ulterior options. It does not impose these options just as the Hellenic humanism does not impose the sacrifice of a cockerel at Escalupe (DL 210, DF 276, Translation altered).

Even if he was a critic of its mainstream application in the era of liberalism, Levinas's allegiance to the notion of humanism will undergo yet further expansion, having thereby increasing centrality in his own thought. *Totality and Infinity* from 1961 would provide the ideology of humanism with a more systematic philosophical foundation.

1.7
The Other as Kath'auto (Totality and Infinity)

As we have seen in the preceding sections, the focus of Levinas's work, connected to the transformation of the notion of the human, has been to understand and defend philosophy's relation to the beyond. Having tied the notions of the human and the beyond to the ethical relation to the other, he can in *Totality and Infinity* now address this theme more systematically.

As the trajectory of this inquiry is guided by Levinas's critical recasting of a philosophy of the human, the reading I am to present of what is undoubtedly his richest investigation will have to be subordinated to this specific concern. In view of this, the aim of the present section is to tease out certain structural problems in *Totality and Infinity*, problems that in this study were not thoroughly resolved. These problems would be more clearly reflected as such by Levinas in both *Humanism and the Other* and *Otherwise than Being*, which from the perspective of this investigation are regarded as more consistent. It should be noted that even if the emphasis in this reading is on the problems surrounding *Totality and Infinity*, the seeds of their solution are nonetheless already planted therein.

Let us begin, however, at the beginning. As already cited, the opening sentences of the first chapter of Totality and Infinity proclaim: "'The true life is absent.' But we are in the world. Metaphysics arises and is maintained in this alibi" (TI 21; TaI 33). With these lines, Levinas pledges allegiance to the tradition of philosophy as a quest for the meaning of transcendence. This is now linked to a metaphysical desire, a desire "for the absolute other" (Ibid). This is a desire distinct from any lack in the subject that has to be filled or relieved. When announcing the possibility even to talk about such a desire, he sets himself up against a panoply of reductionist strategies—whether in the mode of a cynical materialist or historicist reductionism, or perhaps a psychologism, according to which such a desire is a "[d]emented pretension";

> the acute experience of the human in the twentieth century teaches that the thoughts of men are born by needs which explain society and history, that hunger and fear can prevail over every human resistance and every freedom. There is no question of doubting this human misery, this dominion that the

> things and the wicked exercise over man, this animality. But to be a man is to know that this is so. Freedom consists in knowing that freedom is in peril. But to know or to be conscious is to have time to avoid and forestall the instant of inhumanity. It is this perpetual postponing of the hour of treason—infinitesimal difference between man and non-man—that implies the disinterestedness of goodness, the desire of the absolutely other or nobility, the dimension of metaphysics (TI 23-24; TaI 35, translation slightly altered).

Here metaphysical desire for the other bears the promise of "humanity", of goodness, understood as the possibility of interrupting a totality of needs. The notion of the human implies the possibility of a consciousness of one's insertion in an inhuman totality. Therefore, it is not immedieate consciousness of oneself as a free subject but consciousness of a lack of freedom which distinguishes the human.

What is at stake for Levinas in this redefinition of the human is announced in the first sentence of the preface: "Everyone will readily agree that it is of the highest importance to know whether we are not duped by morality" (TI 5; TaI 21). This critical disposition against moral duplicitousness sets in motion the possibility of philosophy. The possibility of philosophy becomes the possibility of relating to something beyond a cynical politics, as "the art of foreseeing war and of winning it by every means" (Ibid).

Claiming the impossibility of transcending immanence is equal to claiming the impossibility of transcending a purely cynical outlook upon humanity, reducing all humanity to a play of forces. This is a theme that we recognise from his early work. On this occasion, however, the very possibility of philosophy has become implicated in this transcendence from the violence of immanence.

All the same, even if the possibility of both philosophy and the human is tethered to transcendence, this is not to deny but rather to underline the omnipresence of war, which the forces of immanence unleash:

> Of peace there can only be an eschatology [...] Peace does not take place in the objective history disclosed by war, as the end of that war or as the end of history. But does not the experience of war refute eschatology, as it refutes morality? [...] To tell the truth, ever since eschatology has opposed peace to war the evidence of war has been maintained in an essentially hypocritical civilisation, that is, attached both to the True and to the Good, henceforth antagonistic (TI 9; TaI 24).

One can ask about the value of such a notion of peace. Can it be anything but hypocritical? The philosopher intent on the suspending this hypocrisy is usually forced to choose either the emphasis on "eschatological truths" (Ibid)—proving a peaceful world untouched by the seemingly undeniable war of the present, belying that being "reveals itself as war" (TI 5; TaI 21)—or the affirmation of the omnipresence of war, in creative fashions performing the reduction of the hypocritical so-called eschatological truths, and showing them for what they really are—a philosophical strategy that Ricoeur would identify as a "hermeneutics of suspicion."[95]

Levinas does not seem to believe in either of these options; with an unconventional move, he insists that hypocrisy is a condition that cannot be permanently transcended: "It is perhaps time to see in hypocrisy not only a base contingent defect of man, but the underlying rending of a world attached both to the philosophers and the prophets" (TI 9; TaI 24). What Levinas here calls hypocrisy is the collision of two attitudes, one aspiring towards a Good beyond Being, and one seeking a totality of truths. For the "totalitarian" approach, any attempt to go beyond the totality can be exposed as hypocritical. But for Levinas, this approach is not enough for philosophy; philosophy draws its sustenance from the movement towards transcendence, a desire for a Good beyond Being. This applies, even though such a Desire carries the threat of being captured in a new totality, harbouring the risk of being exposed as hypocritical.

For Levinas, the possibility of philosophical discourse relies on a situation in which the totality is broken up. This rupture is performed by "the gleam of exteriority or of transcendence in the face of the other" (Ibid). This is an "experience" (Ibid) and a "situation" (Ibid) that not only breaks with totality, but also conditions totality itself. According to Levinas, a phenomenological description of the relation to the other has to start out from this relation, and not from a view outside of this relation. Seen from this point of view, my responsibility for the other is not dependent on the responsibility of the other for me. The latter, reciprocal relationship, is what he calls the commercial or contractual relationship, where I take responsibility for you, only as far as you take responsibility for me. In order to describe the ethical and asymmetrical relation to the other, Levinas often cites Dostoyevsky: "Everybody is responsible for everything and before everyone—and I more than the others".[96] In this phrase there is an unresolved conflict between the universality and extreme singularity of this responsibility. The phrase is valid for everyone, but still only "for me"; it is only when viewed from within the relation, that its meaning is truly received. As long as the relation to the other is seen from within the relation, the asymmetry is

[95] Paul Ricoeur, *Freud and Philosophy: An Essay on Interpretation.* transl. Denis Savage, Yale University Press, 1970, pp. 32-35.

[96] Cf. EI 95, and Jill Robbins (Ed.) *Is it Righteous to be? Interviews with Emmanuel Levinas*, Stanford University Press, 2001, p. 133. Levinas's slight alteration of the quote is not unimportant. Dostoyevsky's character actually says that everyone is *guilty* (in Russian. *vinovat*), whereas for Levinas it is important to emphasise that it is a case of a "responsibility without prior guilt", whether in a juridical, ethical or religious sense. The word "responsibility" (*otvetstvennost'*) was at the time of Dostoyevsky rarely used in Russia as well as in Western Europe.

irreducible. Only a view from outside can discover two subjects mutually and reciprocally responsible.

Once this central hypothesis is advanced, much of *Totality and Infinity* thereafter is concerned with describing the conditions for this asymmetric relation to the other. In order for this description to find its outlines, both the sphere of the ego and the sphere of the other have to be sufficiently circumscribed. These two spheres are drawn in constant opposition; the counterposing terms announced in the title are extensively varied: Totality and Infinity; Metaphysics and Ontology; the Same and the Other (*L'Autre*); the Ego and the Other (*Autrui*); the Interior and the Exterior, the Visible and the Invisible, et cetera.

But, in spite of his appeals to Descartes, Levinas does not wish to establish a new variation on the traditional dualisms of the ideal and the real, or mind and matter. These are already ontological distinctions, on the wrong side of the dividing line. Indeed, the experience Levinas is describing makes possible the break between metaphysics and ontology.

So what is at stake in his distinction between ontology and metaphysics? We have already encountered in his earlier texts how the desire for philosophy to go beyond has never been satisfied. Here, in *Totality and Infinity*, this is systematically described through the key terms ontology and metaphysics. Levinas uses these terms, which others use almost synonymously, to account for two distinct philosophical approaches.

> Western philosophy has most often been an ontology: a reduction of the other to the same by interposition of a middle and neutral term that ensures the comprehension of being (TI 33-34; TaI 43).

Favoured examples of this neutral term include the *concept* of classical Idealism, the *horizon* of Husserlian phenomenology, and the *Being* of Heidegger's ontology—the latter of which for Levinas crowns the Western philosophical propensity to "subordinate the relation of someone, who is existent, to a relation with the Being of existents" (TI 36; TaI 45). This reduction of the other to the same is an act of violence—it "neutralises" the other, it is a dogmatism.

This scepticism towards the philosophical concept is of course not Levinas's invention; it is probably as old as philosophy itself. In *Otherwise than Being*, he speaks of scepticism as philosophy's bastard son, a mostly unwanted, but also an undeniably inevitable offspring, which derives from the very movement of philosophy as critique. Nietzsche is possibly the modern philosopher most associated with the critique of the philosophical concept. Indeed, for Nietzsche, Idealism's relation to truth is akin to hiding something only in order to find it again:

> When someone hides something behind a bush and looks for it again in the same place and finds it there as well, there is not much to praise in such seeking and finding. Yet this is how matters stand regarding seeking and finding "truth" within the realm of reason.[97]

What one hides in order to search for and find again is of course nothing but concepts. "Every concept originates in our equating what is unequal".[98] Nietzsche views this as the inherent violence of language, of which philosophy must become aware in its own practice. There is no non-violent conceptual relation to the singular. By contrast, Levinas sees a discursive point of non-violence as necessary for philosophy to be possible at all. Philosophy must have access to a non-violent relation to the singular, to the other. The non-violent relation is the ethical; it is a metaphysical as opposed to an ontological relation. Levinas writes:

> Metaphysics, transcendence, the welcoming of the other (*autre*) by the same, of the Other (*autrui*) by me, is concretely produced as the calling into question of the same by the other, that is, as the ethics that accomplishes the critical essence of knowledge (TI 33; TaI 43).

Metaphysics is here the name for the movement towards alterity; it accomplishes *critique*—showing vigilance in the wake of the ego's spontaneous dogmatism. This critical operation is not something I can come to by myself; rather it is brought about by the encounter with the other. In this way, the possibility of metaphysics, of theory, of critique is entrusted to the experience of the other.

> The Other (*autrui*) alone eludes thematization. Thematization cannot serve to found thematization, for it supposes it to be already founded; it is the exercise of a freedom sure of itself in its naïve spontaneity—whereas the presence of the Other (*autrui*) is not equivalent to his thematization and consequently does not require this naïve and self-sure spontaneity (TI 85; TaI 86).

It is the appeal of the other that originally makes critique possible. The Other is the "Master" who helps me out of my egosphere.

This ethical movement out of the ontological has a political task as well. The ontological world-view serves as support for "the community of the State, where beneath anonymous power, [...] the I rediscovers war in the tyrannical oppression it undergoes from the totality." (TI 38; TaI 47). As we saw already in the Hitlerism essay, the very impulse from which Levinas's project came to promi-

---

[97] "Über Wahrheit und Lüge im aussermoralischen Sinne" in *KSA* I, De Gruyter, p. 883.

[98] "Jeder Begriff entspringt durch Gleichsetzen des Nicht-Gleichen.", Ibid, p. *880*

nence was political. By *Totality and Infinity* the meaning of the political undergoes a change in inflection. Here, the notion of the political is associated partly to the neutral and collective, threatening both me and the other (an abstraction leading away from the concrete appeal from the other), and partly to the struggle for recognition (brutally ignoring the appeal of the other). The political is locatable, as it were, on both sides of the ethical. It is at once beyond and before the ethical. Even if, in its essence, the ethical is irreducible to the political, nonetheless it always appears from within a political situation, and its significance always returns to the sphere of the political. This transience of the ethical is what makes nihilism possible: a political outlook towards life, or even a political philosophy, which so to speak, skips over the ethical, reducing it to its political conditions and outcomes. According to this view, social life is struggle—and in order to survive, one chooses to join with others, mutually recognising each other by law and contract. Ethics is viewed as secondary to politics; what we know as morality is a pattern of behaviours and attitudes nurtured by society for political ends. This view exists both as a rationalism, according to which this reduction of violence is for the benefit of all, and a non-rationalism, according to which morality is seen as one group oppressing others. One could attribute to the first a version of Kantianism, and to the second either a Nietzscheanism or certain tendencies of Marxism. The important thing here is not whether the thinkers from which the abovementioned labels originate are reducible to these standpoints, but that these are frequently encountered ways of reasoning, and therefore part of the philosophical heritage Levinas is examining.

The predominance of this view, where the ethical is viewed as a secondary instrument of politics, drives him most of the time at this point to reject the political construction of the human. When in *Totality and Infinity* Levinas speaks more affirmatively of the political, it is in terms of pluralism or multiplicity—namely, the possibility of not being reduced to the powers of history. The political in this second sense comes to signify the responsibility for more than one other. This concept of the political is organised around the idea of "the third": the one I am forced to neglect when responding to the other. The relation between ethics and politics is a question of a relation of relations—the relation to a singular other, and the relation to many others, according to which the others and my relation to them relate to each other. There can be no "purely" ethical relation, for there are always many others for whom I am responsible. Concomitantly, there can be no purely political relation either, for the political finds its justification only in the responsibility for the others as singular beings. "The epiphany of the face", says Levinas "attests the presence of the third party, the whole of humanity, in the eyes that look at me" (TI 235; TaI 213). The political, from the viewpoint of the responsible subject, appears as an irresolvable conflict between my obligations to different human beings. This does not reduce the urgency of an individual's obligations. What it does call for are calculations, compromises—the demand on responsibility is so to speak not only vertically, but horizontally infinite. As we shall examine in Part II, the question of the political will be given a more extensive treatment in his later works. In *Totality and Infinity*, however, the political sphere is most often approached through a criticism of the view according to which all other views must be reduced to the political. This reductive view also denies transcendence, denies metaphysics, by which one is to understand the movement that calls into question the same by the other. It is the establishment of a link between philosophy as metaphysics and an ethics of the other which constitutes the core of *Totality and Infinity*.

Metaphysics is the movement towards the absolute, as that which absolves itself from Being. Therefore, in order for Levinas to be able to found his metaphysics in the ethical experience of the other, he or she must be convincingly portrayed as *absolutely* other. Accordingly, a key term for the argumentational structure in *Totality and Infinity* is separation—the ego does not live in symbiosis with the other, but exists as separated, or "as separation" from the other and from God. Understanding this means the "dawn of a humanity without myths", a "metaphysical atheism" (TI 75; TaI 77). Man is naturally independent and atheist. Existing as separation makes it possible to start anew, to be a subject. But the separation as absolute also entails that *there actually is no experience of the ethical other.* In a sense, this experience of the other is a non-experience. The story Levinas tells is about a non-experience which relates that which is nonrelatable, "a relation without a relation" (TI 79; TaI 80). But even if he writes of experience only to say that what he describes transcends it, we shall note that Levinas still leans on the language of experience as a support for his notion of ethics—something which he later would find problematic. The language of experience leans on a vocabulary of presence, which would in his later work be questioned. This vocabulary is a first step in his establishment of a point of immediacy, a hierarchy where the other can appear as the *kath'auto.* The question I would like to ask is whether there is not the risk of complacency in his proclamation of a privileged discourse of ethical metaphysics. If his purpose is to emphasise the uniqueness of the ethical relation to the other, both as irreducible to ontology and as the condition of possibility for critique, does it then not run counter to his intentions to phrase it in an ontology of experience, tied to the notion of *kath'auto*, the most ontological of terms?

In order for the other to appear for the subject as absolutely other, the subject has first to be described as a sovereign ego, who puts the world at its feet, and understands the world according to its own interests and purposes. Only against this backdrop will the ethical encounter be described in its full radicality; so that the encounter takes the form of a solipsistic worldview suddenly interrupted by the other *qua* absolute other. Levinas introduces the absolute other as the purity that philosophy has always sought: the other is decided as the only *kath'auto*, with everything else mediated by the interests of the ego. Again, in order for the alterity to be described as radically as possible, the egosphere is reduced to a solipsistic or egoistic enjoyment. On the one hand, the subject enjoys, masters and devours the world, making it its own; on the other, the I is subjected to an absolute otherness that is its Master. Interestingly, both the ego's enjoyment of the elements (TI 142-149; TaI 135-140) and the face-to-face relationship (TI 44; TaI 52) to the other are related to as *immediate*. Moreover, when doing this, Levinas exclaims that this is "the human". Rather than jump to conclusions here, at this point it might be wise to leave room for self-critical reflection: he does not himself comment on this choice of syntagm; it is therefore unclear whether the choice of "the human" is in this context to be regarded as deliberate on Levinas's part. Perhaps, one could claim, these quotes are marginal to his philosophy, to be read as emphatic exclamations belonging to a certain style of writing, dismissing them as not having any ontological or otherwise central philosophical significance? Were one to interpret Levinas in the general spirit of his philosophical contribution, however, the exclamatory quality of these locutions would not justify their immediate dismissal. Would not the centre of a philosophy arguing for a metaphysical experience overflowing the concept lie not in its strictly conceptual argumentation alone, but in its exclamatory appeal also?

To recall the important passage from the beginning of *Totality and Infinity*, discussed above, Levinas holds that humanity is the possibility to break with totality. This totality gains a new determination, showing itself as now rooted in an economy of enjoyment. Here, the term "human" appears at a quite precise moment, namely where an experience in its originality irreducible to (transcending) these economies is described. We are presented with a three-step movement: first the positing of enjoyment, which then becomes the very currency of an "economy of enjoyment". Finally, the introduction of the face-to-face relation, which makes possible a rupture with that economy.

Let us start with enjoyment: according to Levinas, it is as enjoyment that the human subject arises as an ek-stasis in relation to the *there is*, to participation,[99] to mere Being (*être*). Clearly emerging from being it is the existent (*l'étant*) par excellence. Enjoyment is here described as the primordial relation to the world. This is not just an accidental or isolated fact about human existence. Enjoyment has an ontologically primary status; human beings do not primarily encounter objects in the world, but they enjoy the world in its elements. As such, Levinas will declare that enjoyment is the "universal category of the empirical" (TI 140; TaI 132-133). On this basis Husserl is criticised for conceiving the object too much from the viewpoint of mental representation.[100] Heidegger's conception of

---

[99] Cf. infra section 1.3.

[100] As a criticism of Husserl this is all too short-sighted. Husserl did not intend the mental representation of the object as an "original" or "elemental" representation, but as the starting point for the philosophical analysis, the goal of which is exactly to break down the illusion of such metaphysical propositions of reality. In this sense, Levinas's description of enjoyment as

the object as tool (*Zeug*) or ready-at-hand (*zuhanden*) is viewed as equally inadequate. Levinas attempts to show how taking pleasure in the elements of the world is more fundamental than encountering in it objects of representation or tools to use. According to him, the fresh air that we breathe and the loaf of bread that I eat can be seen as tools in no other world but one extremely marked by a Protestant work ethos in a technocratic, industrialist society.[101] Enjoyment is never a specimen of work; rather I work in order to be able to enjoy, and I can even take pleasure in working. Enjoyment, he claims, is our primary relation to life, our primary way of living—life is understood as enjoying in the sense of living from... (*vivre de...*). I live from that which I enjoy. By way of a sharp reversal of Plato (and much of the philosophical and psychoanalytical tradition afterwards), who understands needs as pain or as lack (cf. Phil. 46a), Levinas describes needs as the possibility of fulfilment, of accomplishment. So needs are not understood as privative, rather the human being is "happy for his needs" (TI 118; TaI 114).

Here, Levinas does not see the bodily needs as threats to the humanity of the subject, but as the necessary conditions for working the world: "my body is not only a way for the subject to be reduced to slavery, to depend on what is not itself", he writes, "but (it) is also a way of possessing and of working, of having time, of overcoming the very alterity of what I have to live from." (TI 120-121; TaI 116-117). Only as a bodily subject, can I experience myself as "I can", and thereby gain independence. Moreover, the personality of the ego is shaped in the search for happiness, in enjoying the world. Enjoyment is individuating; it confirms the subject in its self-identity—the subject is in a world seen as potential for enjoyment, and thus breaks with any view of an original neutral totality. In enjoyment, I am not reducible to "understanding Being" or to ontology: I am exalted above Being. This exaltation above Being makes Man "the existent (*étant*) par excellence". Levinas goes so far in this vitalist humanism as to assert that "human egoism leaves pure nature by virtue of the human body raised upwards" (TI 121; TaI 117). The ego is a hypostasis, a beginning, an arche, an origin. Even if normally Levinas connects value only to the relation to the other, he says that enjoyment is already *better* than mere existence, or ataraxia, or the

the basic relation to the world is a break with the phenomenological paradigm—from a Husserlian perspective this would be confusing method with ontology.

[101] The objection might seem close at hand (as uttered for example by Jean François Courtine in "Fundamentalontologin hos Levinas" in *Det främmande och det egna*, Södertörn philosophical studies, 2007, p. 140) that the background for the Zeuganalyse in *Being and Time* is more of a handicraft ethos than that of the age of industrialism. But this does not take into account that Levinas is reading Heidegger's analysis against the grain. Only in the age of industrialism could meaning be reduced to use in the pragmatism of the early Heidegger. And even if the romanticisation of the handicraft ethos might seem to strive beyond this, it is only thinkable in a time of industrialism. Heidegger would later abstain from terms like *Zeug* and *Zuhandenheit*: and with the term *Gestell* he performs a similar critique of the utility-view on the meaning of things.

virtue of rising above being (TI 154; TaI 145). There is no value in abstention if it is not for the sake of other, and life can only be for the other if first it is life in the sense of enjoyment. In this sense, the overfullness of need is a presupposition for the ethical. By implication the notion of the human is connected to fullness and overflow, a fullness that can never be contained in any economy.

What however does Levinas mean by economy? He never explicitly defines this concept, nor does he refer to any other sources for its signification. Let us, for a start, note that it obviously does not merely denote the circulation of money, services and goods. Already in *Existence and Existents,* he uses it with a certain systematicity, stating that "the economic world includes not only our so-called material life" (DEE 155; EE 92), but the subject in *all* its mundane existence. He goes so far as to speak of a "general economy of Being" (DEE 141; EE 83), from which the subject breaks. Since the notion of economy will be of continued importance to us in the following sections, and since to my mind there is no other work that contextualises Levinas's notion of economy, the ground will here be prepared by showing how the concept has been put to different uses by both Sigmund Freud and Georges Bataille.

In Freud's "The Unconscious", the economy principle is defined as one of the main principles by which the human psyche functions.[102] According to this principle, the human psyche is always compelled to search out pleasure. Many behaviours can of course not be immediately explained by this propensity. Nonetheless the economy principle advances the hypothesis that all that occurs in the human psyche can be reduced to an "avoidance of displeasure or production of pleasure"[103], in the sense that all events can be exchanged for pleasure. Pleasure-seeking is the axle around which the Freudian psychic economy turns.

In the same essay in which we find Freud proposing the economy hypothesis, Freud claims also that "consciousness only mediates knowledge of one's own state of mind, knowledge of other minds are only known per analogy" (p. 128). The notion of a non-transcendable economy of pleasure seems for Freud to be associated with an epistemological solipsism. For Levinas also, from the perspective of the economy of enjoyment, there is no contact with the Other; rather the encounter with the other as absolute other occurs only as a disturbance to this economy. In his description of the economy of enjoyment, he trades an epistemological for an ethical solipsism, so that this rupture is not a relation of knowledge of the other mind, but an ethical relation.

In "Beyond the pleasure principle", written in 1920, Freud found the idea of an all-explaining pleasure principle to be unsatisfactory. The notion of the death

[102] The other principles are the *topographical* principle according to which the psyche is divided into the conscious, the preconscious and the unconscious, and the *dynamic* principle, which explains the laws of repression. "Das Unbewusste". Freud, *Studienausgabe*, Bd. III, S. Fischer Verlag, 1915, pp. 119-154.
[103] *Jenseits des Lustprinzips*, Internationaler psychoanalytischer Verlag, 1921, p.1.

drive was introduced in order to fill in the lack that Freud had diagnosed in his earlier understanding of libidinal economies. The death drive served as the *explanans* to account for destructive and regressive human behaviour. In the same year, Freud would use this supplementary concept in order to explain "The economic problem of masochism", in an article thus titled.[104] In order to show how the masochist could transform displeasure to pleasure, the economy of pleasure has to be transcended, but only in order to preserve it as the general explanatory principle. The death drive operates as a back-up principle, explaining that which falls out of the system.

For our purposes, it is of particular interest that Freud explicitly formed his theory as a rejection of humanism, believing as he did in a distinctive "drive towards perfection"[105] of man. As Freud stated: "The development of Man thus far seems to require no further explanation than that of the animals" (Ibid). Already in Freud, then, the declaration of a libidinal economy from which there is no possibility of transcendence is associated with antihumanism.

It is against such a topos that Levinas can pronounce the transcendence of the economy of enjoyment to be the human distinction *par excellence*. But this is not out of a "drive towards perfection"; as we have laid out, the transcendence, as he envisages it, is effected by a desire which breaks with the needs and drives of the ego.

Another thinker who radicalised the category of economy was the French philosopher and novelist Georges Bataille. Bataille is especially interesting, since he was the first to give Levinas's work serious consideration. In 1947 he published a review of *Existence and Existents*, with the title "De l'existentialisme au primat de l'économie".[106] In this text, which has attracted little commentary, Bataille suggests that Levinas's work performs a necessary departure from existentialism, making possible thereby a thinking which gives ontological primacy to the concept of economy. Generally, the tone in Bataille's reading is sympathetic. He shows special interest in his descriptions of the *il y a*, but takes distance from the horror with which Levinas describes this pure subjectless existence. Rather, Bataille seems to see the "general economy of being" as a promise that Levinas himself does not deliver on. In *The Accursed Share,*[107] published two years subsequently, Bataille takes up the gauntlet, transforming Levinas's notion of the "general economy" into a cosmological thesis. The general economy for Bataille concerned "the play of living matter in general" (p. 23)). In this general economy the fundamental law is not balance but excess. The sun throws its rays

---

[104] "Das ökonomische Problem des Masochismus", *Studienausgabe*, Bd. III, S. Fischer Verlag, 1915 (Bd. III, 339-354).

[105] *Jenseits des Lustprinzips*, p. 38.

[106] "De l'existentialisme au primat de l'économie" in Critique, 19, 1947, pp. 127-141).

[107] Cf. Georges Bataille, *The Accursed Share, Volume 1: Consumption*, trans. Robert Hurley, Zone Books, 1991, pp. 19-26).

on the earth, constantly loading the system with surplus energy, a movement reproduced in animal and human life. Accordingly, Bataille takes a special interest in practices of excess, of luxurious expenditure, and sacrifice, practices in which wealth goes up in smoke. The idea that economy always strives towards balance is exposed as a bourgeois prejudice. Bataille, like Freud, wants to reduce the human distinction, and insert the human economy into a larger biological system. "Man is the only roundabout, subsidiary response to the problem of growth." (p. 37). Somewhat aporetically, however, Bataille retains the "sovereignty" of man in one sense:

> The general movement of exudation (of waste) of living matter impels him, and he cannot stop it; moreover, being at the summit, his sovereignty in the living world identifies him with this movement; it destines him, in a privileged way, to that glorious operation, to useless consumption (p. 27).

Here Bataille's reason for privileging the *il y a*, contra Levinas, becomes apparent. Whereas the human is defined through its break with the economy of Being, Bataille sees the specificity of man in his capacity to reside within the violent forces of Being. What fascinates Bataille about Man are those practices in which he lets himself be submerged in the pre-human: arts, rites, the mystical, and so on, practices which Levinas typically viewed with suspicion. In Bataille's own words, "Man is the most suited of all living beings to consume intensely, sumptuously, the excess energy offered up by the pressure of life to conflagrations befitting the solar origins of its movement".[108]

We can thus form a certain constellation: The early Freud uses the term economy to show how all acts of the subject, be they unconscious or conscious, can find their explanation in a striving for pleasure; pleasure becomes the currency in which all acts of the subject are exchanged. This economy is in principle not transcendable.[109] For Bataille, on the other hand, all life is excess. Economy in its Levinasian understanding is also constantly transcended, but this overflow of the economy does not reduce subjectivity to an effect of a cosmological law of a self-transcending economy. Instead, the subject's relation to the other is reserved as the place-holder for transcendence. Transcendence does not mean an overflow of the same currency (in the case of Bataille: energy; in the case of Levinas: enjoyment), but means that something resists currency conversion, thereby exceeding the limits of the economy.

---

[108] *The accursed share*, p. 37.

[109] When Freud later introduces the death drive, to account for that which the pleasure drive cannot, the economy becomes more complex. Nonetheless the description aims for an account of an economy that is never transcended. As a background for the notion of economy that Levinas aims for, the initial hypothesis of the pleasure principle is what is most relevant; it is also the most historically important and theoretically clear.

While this discussion on economy has afforded the possibility of understanding its conceptual morphology, it is now necessary to spell out the precise contribution that Levinas makes in *Totality and Infinity*. As we have already stated, he never explicitly defines economy. As an initial characterisation of how he uses the term in his texts, we can say that economy is the exteriorised organisation of life around enjoyment. This definition allows us to better think how Levinas's appropriation of the term is irreducible to both Freud and Bataille. Etymologically, economy returns us to its Greek origin, as the governance of a home. The building of an economy is the establishment of a home in order to preserve and optimize my enjoyment over time, and in order to survive—because being alive is the ultimate condition of possibility of enjoyment, as it is the ultimate condition of all possibilities. In economy, everything can be changed into the currency of enjoyment and is ultimately valued with respect to enjoyment. The economy is destined to work to the benefit of enjoyment, whereas enjoyment itself is not for the sake of any economy. Levinas explains: "To enjoy without utility, in pure loss, gratuitously, without referring to anything else, in pure expenditure—this is the human" (TI 141; TaI 133). It might be surprising that he uses the name 'human' for pure enjoyment, given that the name is given also to that which transcends the economy of enjoyment. So as to negotiate this putative inconsistency, we must understand that Levinas institutes a difference between enjoyment as such, and the *economy* of enjoyment, which is not necessarily enjoyment, but which subsists for the sake of life as enjoyment. There is nothing "wrong" with enjoyment *per se*. Enjoyment is "better" than ataraxia (TI 154; TaI 145). What he criticises is rather the unilateralisation of the economy of enjoyment which threatens to become an exhaustive description of human existence in a vitalist or libidinised philosophy of immanence.

Even if enjoyment is seen as egoist, it is not in itself violent with respect to the elements that it enjoys. Enjoyment does not encounter the other, which is the only one upon which I can inflict violence—violence is by definition directed towards the other. Enjoyment encounters "the elemental"—which is the worldly correlative to the subject's enjoyment. Enjoyment does not primarily have things as their objects, but *elements*. Elements are treated as things only in the economic relation to them (that is, when they are stored, used and counted, and so on). They are faceless; they are of course other than me, but this otherness is not radical, since I relate to them by consuming them. Levinas's description of enjoyment is a description of a world in which I am never interrupted by the other, a world without the ethical. Otherwise stated, it is a world that the responsibility for the other must interrupt. If there would be no justification for a metaphysics beyond ontology, this account of the economy of enjoyment would be the total and satisfying description of the world. In the same way as life as enjoyment is seen as "better" than the subjectless existence of the il y a,[110] philosophy as ontology is seen as the necessary break with a mystic communion with the elements. (Cf. EDE 231). Interestingly, this would sometimes cause Levinas to view Heidegger's radicalisation of ontology as a step corresponding to the anthropologist's descriptions of a more primitive mentality of Man.[111]

This life of enjoyment is not only individuation; it is isolation in the sense of being in contrast to the selfless openness to the other. There is, however an intimate otherness, which Levinas names "the feminine". Here, the feminine is not, as it was momentarily thought in *Time and the Other*, the absolute romanticised otherness; it is rather the aspect of otherness that helps me find a home—a shelter from the threats of the elements, and a resting place in which to plan work and enjoyment. The erotic relation is also described as a relation to the feminine. This does not mean that the others are separated into two categories, women who provide intimacy, and men who provide transcendence, but that these are different aspects of the same relation to the other.[112] Even if the relation to the other in its erotic and domestic declensions are also considered as *true* relations to the other, allowing for contact, it is only the ethical relation which corresponds to what Levinas views as imperative for philosophy to describe: the radical relation to the other as him- or herself (*kath'auto*). This is spelled out a little clearer in the chapter entitled "Phenomenology of eros", the aim of which is to show how the erotic relation presupposes (but never coincides with) the ethical. He writes: "It is necessary that the face has been apperceived for nudity to be able to acquire the non-signifyingness of the lustful." (TI 294; TaI 262).

The ethical relation is however differently structured than the erotic or otherwise loving relation. "If to love is to love the love the beloved bears me, to love is also to love oneself in love, and thus to return to oneself." (TI 298; TaI 266). Levinas does not mean to condemn the erotic or otherwise loving relation. There is nonetheless a suspicion towards the claim that love can be viewed as the root of morality.[113] Love can also be nothing more than a "dual egoism" (Ibid), it can entail the blatant disregard of the ones I do not love. Against this, one could argue that true love opens itself not only to the other, but to the world as a

[110] Infra, section 1.3.

[111] Cf. "Lévy-Bruhl and Contemporary Philosophy" (EN 49-63; ENO 39-51).

[112] This is how he proposes to read Ge 1:27: "...male and female he created them" (EI 61).

[113] Joel Backström has recently published a thesis with this claim, titled *The Fear of Openness. An Essay on Friendship and the Roots of Morality*, Åbo akademi, 2007. He deals with Levinas (pp. 182-192), who from Backström's point of view is claiming that love is "bad", and is thus pronouncing an injunction to hate the one one is helping. I suspect that the reason for this reading is that Backström sees Levinas as pronouncing ethics as guidance on how to live, whereas in fact Levinas is interested in the very possibility to discover something as ethical. As a guidance for an individual reader on how to live justly and happily. Backström's thesis might be a more advisable reading material than Levinas. The latter has a totally different aim, however, announced already in the "Hitlerism" article, namely to rehabilitate a discourse on the very humanity of Man—showing how this presupposes an asymmetrical relation to the other.

whole. This might be so, but how could this view not also be open for critique? Presupposing that one can truly and sincerely *say* that ethics must come from this true love means presupposing a position from which this loving community with the other could produce a true discourse. In discourse, however, we are already at a distance from ourselves, at a distance from the other. Thought in this way, discourse presupposes a fissure in the subject and between the subject and the other. Psychologically, it is doubtless the case that what qualifies as a good deed often springs from love. But Levinas's point of view, from which the ethical is the condition of possibility for critique—and as the possibility of a just politics—prohibits any easy switch from a psychological to a transcendental foundation. Even love must be critiqued, not because it is evil, but because critique is a moment of philosophical understanding. To put it otherwise, love is certainly good, but it is not *the* Good.

The ethical is described as a counter-current to, or as a rupture with, the happy and lustful enjoyment of the world. Suddenly, I am forced not to allow myself to enjoy—someone else needs me. The notion of the ethical presupposes, according to Levinas, the possibility of being for the other in spite of myself. Again, this does not mean that he *endorses* an ethics that implores all to forsake enjoyment. The aim is instead to *describe* ethics as a rupture with enjoyment, that is to say, Levinas explores the possibility of an ethics irreducible to the search for happiness and pleasure.

But if the ethical is this rupture with enjoyment, what is then the status of the pre-ethical ontology, of the pre-ethical I? Can one really uphold this strong divide between the ego's sphere of enjoyment and the other as absolute other? Will not the other human being be seen too much from her otherness opposed to my sovereignty? My suggestion is that Levinas's analytic of enjoyment should be read as an account of *what* encounters the other, from the vantage point of the encounter with the other. The egoist economy of enjoyment is recognised retroactively; only from the viewpoint of its rupture, can the economy be conceived as a totality. It is a mediation always already past.

The encounter with the face is the interruption of every economy. In both cases—in that of enjoyment and in that of the ethical relation—it is possible to say that the notion of the human is tied to an idea of deneutralisation, a search for the concrete that is not mediated by the "neutral concept". Both relationships are claimed to be immediate in the sense of preceding the theoretical subject-object dyad; as such they are relations that this dyadic structure must presuppose. Before the object is conceived as an object it is enjoyed as an element, and the objectness presupposes reflection which in turn supposes a critical stance, made possible only by one's relation to the other.

Levinas's claims remain unfounded, however, and some critical claims remain: could there not be many other ways of accessing being than in terms of enjoyment, other modalities equiprimordial to enjoyment, both mediated by and mediating the enjoying self? On a different register, we need to ask whether or not the description of the face-to-face relation is overdetermined by a Judeo-Christian tradition which shows its own theoretical particularity and thereby limits its universal import. Could one not understand this in terms of a mediation by tradition, and by implication question Levinas's claim appertaining to the *immediacy* of the face-to face relation? We will return to this problem in the last section of Part II (section 2.5).

As we have seen already, the claim of the immediacy of the face-to-face encounter—the relation to the *kath'auto* of the other (strange oxymoron)—is meant to support the claim that metaphysics can found ontology. Levinas does not want to voice this metaphysical access to the human in an essentialist language. On the contrary, it is rendered in terms of an "ethical metaphysics", a metaphysics of absolute alterity. In a sense, he takes up the trail that Heidegger provided. In the "Letter on 'Humanism'", as we saw earlier (section 1.5), Heidegger argues that humanism did not correspond to the human in its evental dignity (*er-eignete Würde*), binding Man to a metaphysics. Here in comparing Heidegger with Levinas, we must be attentive to a conceptual elision: what in the "Letter on 'Humanism'" Heidegger calls metaphysics, is named by Levinas ontology. Levinas believes that by tying the human to the ethical relation to the other he can inaugurate a philosophy of the human that escapes this binding to an essence. This philosophy he names "metaphysics". However, he intends to fill this syntagm with a different content than Heidegger.

Metaphysics is other than ontology. Yet, claims Levinas, it *founds* ontology. However, is foundation not already an ontological trope? Does it not already imply the assumption of a hierarchy of being? And what, in practise, are ontology and metaphysics—what distinguishes his discourse on the human, the face and the other from an ontological discourse? First, let us be reminded that Levinas does not condemn ontology. He does not have a quarrel with ontology as such; his objection is always first and foremost directed against what he calls ontolog*ism*, namely a philosophy subordinating ethics to ontology.[114] The problem is that his descriptions of the other, which are always the starting points of his philosophy, are themselves ontological. Whence the claims that the other is "the human par excellence", and Man is "being par excellence". Is this not then a metaphysical humanism in the very same sense that Heidegger was talking about? A humanism defined by a view of the human, locked to a certain metaphysics of the other?

Indeed, during this period, Levinas explicitly lets his philosophical project bear the title humanism. In *Totality and Infinity*, he attempts to systematise an anti-essentialist humanism, where the relation to the human is not ontological but rather that which founds ontology. The relation to the other as human is not

---

[114] Already discussed above, sections 1.2 and 1.6.

a relation to the human essence of the other individual (already considered as a member of the human species), a relation to the other as a part belonging to the genus humanity; it is rather the ethical relation to the other that constitutes the human. In his attempt at distancing himself from the ontological understanding of the human, however, he runs the risk of letting ontologism come in through the back door. It is as if there were a double foundation for his philosophy, that of the self-sufficient ego, and that of the other, providing a meaning for the subject's freedom (TI 83-88; TaI 84-89). In fact, the way in which he sets up the problem sometimes appears not to be so far from what Jean-Luc Marion called, in his descriptions of Descartes, a "double onto-theology".[115] On the one hand, "subjectivity originates in the independence and sovereignty of enjoyment" (TI 117, TaI 114); on the other, the reflective ego presupposes the encounter with the other, such that the other is the source of the condition of possibility for critique.

Levinas is wary of introducing such a dualist ontology. He does not want to claim that I and the other are absolute substances: "Relationship between separated beings would indeed be absurd were the terms posited as substances, each *causa sui*, since, as pure activities, capable of receiving no action, the terms could undergo no violence" (TI 247; TaI 223).

However, even if neither the other nor I are described in terms of a pure act, it is as if he has exchanged this with the purity of the ethical. He distils this hierarchical tendency in his own humanism in one sentence: "The true essence of man is presented in his face, in which he is infinitely other than a violence like mine, opposed to mine and hostile" (TI 323, TaI 290-291). Humanity is only truly presented in the face, which by definition is non-violent; it does not counter the violence of my freedom with another violence, but with a resistance that no longer makes me violent.

But how shall we understand violence? In "Ethics and Spirit" first published in 1952 (DL 15-26; DF 3-10), Levinas defines violence in the following manner:

> Violence is to be found in any action in which one acts as if one were alone to act: as if the rest of the universe were there only to receive the action; violence is consequently also any action which we endure without at every point collaborating in it (DL 20; DF 6).

From this he concludes that "nearly" every causality is violent, and so is the enthusiasm and delirium that neglects the cause or reason of one's actions. Here, the critical question is whether there can be a cause without violence. Levinas answers affirmatively: "Reason and language are external to violence. They are the spiritual order. If morality must truly exclude violence, a profound

---

[115] In *Sur le prisme métaphysique de Descartes*, PUF Épiméthée 1986, Marion finds Descartes's understanding of God and the ego as foundation for being (*Seiendes, l'étant*) as both matching Heidegger's description of onto-theology.

link must join reason, language and morality" (DL 21, DF 7).[116] This link, we could say, is the glue that he must hope for, in order for his articulations to stick. This amounts to a hope for a position outside of violence, a rupture with the sphere of violence. A location for such a rupture can be in conversation. Levinas writes: "The banal fact of conversation, in one sense, quits the order of violence. This banal fact is the marvel of marvels" (DL 22; DF 7). But it is of course an escape that never lands in a safe haven; in the face of the other my freedom is always judged arbitrary and violent (TI 83-84; TaI 55-56). This is not a question of mere perspectivism, which would hold that what I perceive as care the other might perceive otherwise as violence. On the contrary, the sensibility for the other means that I am never in a position to purge myself of violence, even though the demand not to be violent is inescapable. However, even if Levinas does not believe in a safe haven for the moral subject, exempt from violence, he is still committed to the "profound link" between reason, language and morality. This link is the irreducible bond by which his affirmation of a metaphysics is articulated. In *Totality and Infinity* this tripartite relation between rationality, language and morality is couched in terms of the relation to the face. The relation to the face is the only relation that can never be fully mediated by its thematisation, because it is the presupposition for all thematisation. It is described as the "ultimate situation", in which the other faces me "across (*à travers*) my idea of the infinite" (TI 80; TaI 81).[117]

This could be understood as a mere slip of the pen by Levinas—the face-to-face relation can of course not at once be immediate and come to pass "across" the idea of the infinite. However, there are other passages that repeat this motif: "Totality and the embrace of being, or ontology, do not contain the final secret of being. Religion, where relationship subsists between the same and the other despite the impossibility of the Whole—the idea of Infinity—is the ultimate structure" (TI 79; TaI 80). How should one negotiate a way through such formulations? First a reminder: by religion he does not mean anything like "belief that God exists", but precisely the possibility of relating to the other without including him or her in any proper totalisation. The human is also a key-word for a relation with the absolute which implies no mystical involvement of God; rather it pertains to the withdrawal of God: "Everything that cannot be reduced to an interhuman relation represents not the superior form but the forever primitive form of religion" (TI 78; TaI 79). God as the ultimate source of Being would threaten to become exactly the kind of neutral concept that would mediate and

[116] In our discussion of Derrida's critique (sections 1.10 and 1.11), the possibility of an outside of violence will be thoroughly questioned. Building on an interpretation of Levinas's later work, the notion of a transcendence from violence undergoes further complexification in Part 2.

[117] The "idea of the infinite" is Levinas's term, borrowed from Descartes' Meditations, defining a relation to a being totally exterior to the relation. For Descartes, this is the basis for the ontological evidence of God's existence—for Levinas, on the contrary it is the relation exceeding the ontological, being overflowed.

thus neutralise the other in his or her singularity. Does not this relation to the other as "the ultimate situation"—the other facing me "across" the idea of the infinite, "the ultimate structure"—repeat this (onto)theology, couched in the language of humanism? Levinas cannot be consistent in his intentions of transcending ontological language. Even if he would have taken more care to avoid these disturbing formulations, we may wonder whether it is not necessary for philosophy in its quest to transcend the particularity of statements to refer to these "neutral" structures. In *Totality and Infinity,* he does not have a systematic answer to these questions. But this is not to say that he is ignorant of the problem. Immediately after the above quoted passage he raises the dilemma in the following manner: "the same and the other cannot enter into a cognition that would encompass them; the relations that the separated being maintains with what transcends it are not produced on the ground of totality. Yet do we not name them together?" (Ibid). The fact that one can put the concepts together in a formal expression does not mean that one ultimately reduces them to a totalising function. "The conjuncture of the same and the other, in which even their verbal proximity is maintained, is the *direct* and *full face* welcome of the other by me" (Ibid). Thus, in this sentence (anticipating the concepts of the Saying and the Said from *Otherwise than Being*),[118] Levinas holds that the very conceptualisation, which allows the juxtaposition of the same and the other as categories, *is* a response to the other. The conceptualisation presupposes the critical attitude, "which is produced in face of the other and under his authority" (TI 80; TaI 81).

Now let us rehearse the problems we have found in *Totality and Infinity*: *Sovereignty and separation of the preethical ego*: A key term in the ontology of Totality and Infinity is that of separation. In order for the other to appear as absolutely other, there first has to be developed an entire sphere of the ego without the other, or with encounters with the other that are inessential inasmuch that they do not encounter the other in his or her absolute alterity.

Experience: The ethical relation to the other is understood in terms of an experience of the other's otherness. At the same time the otherness of the other is described as being beyond experience. This has the risk of connecting the other to the notion of experience, even if only negatively, such that the other receives its sense from his ultimate unknowability: the negative theology against which Levinas polemicizes transposed onto the human other.

Ontologisation: Levinas wants to turn the tables on Heidegger, claiming that metaphysics and not ontology must play the main role in a philosophy of the human. But in fact his descriptions of the human find sustenance in an ontologising language. This leads him to form ideas of the other as the *kath'auto*, which he takes as the essence of the human.

---

[118] These concepts will be introduced properly in Part 2.

Privileged discourse of immediacy: The access to the singular is assured by claiming metaphysics as a privileged, non-violent discourse, describing it as a "humanity without myths" (TI 75; TaI 77). This discourse takes recourse to the language of presence and experience, to an original "situation" (TI 9; TaI 24), a "gleam of exteriority in the face of the other" (TI 10; TaI 24).[119] The experience of the other is secured as immediate, unmixed with the violence of the economy of enjoyment. This experience of the other is *kath'auto*, and to be *kath'auto* is to be good (TI 200; TaI 183).

As already flagged in the beginning of this section, however, this somewhat uncharitable summary points only to a certain tendency in what is a very rich and multifaceted work of philosophy. In the same book, Levinas also says the following:

> The transcendence of the face is not enacted outside of the world [...] The "vision" of the face as face is a certain mode of sojourning in a home, or—to speak in a less singular fashion—a certain form of economic life. No human or interhuman relationship can be enacted outside of economy; no face can be approached with empty hands and closed home (TI 187; TaI 172).

With such a passage as this, would not the complexion of our understanding of Levinas's thought, at this point in its development, change somewhat? Would this not mark a break with the doctrine of separation? Does this not mean that the absolute otherness of the other is compromised? Indeed, to say that the "vision" of the face, i.e. the access to the other is "a certain kind of economic life" is a way of agreeing that the philosophical description of the face cannot be exempt from ontology, i.e. an admittance on the part of Levinas that the privileged discourse of immediacy is compromised. If this is so then what remains of the notion of the human as the point that opens up the possibility for the critique of both economy and of ontology? Subsequent to *Totality and Infinity* he would establish a better vocabulary for expressing this point of critique. It is to this that our attention will turn in Part 2.

One final remark before proceeding: the position of *Totality and Infinity* seems prone to the accusations that Heidegger made towards humanism in his *Letter*. Heidegger had written: "Every humanism is either grounded in a metaphysics or is itself made to be the ground of one." (WM 321; PM 245). Now, Heidegger's definition of course differs from Levinas's but Heidegger's warning, that humanism locks the understanding of the human to a certain understanding of a being, seems to be warranted. The human is defined as the Being par

[119] A philosophy leaning on a language of presence and experience to establish a language of metaphysics, brings to mind Jacques Derrida, who in *Of Grammatology*, John Hopkins University Press, 1974, p.49) described such a philosophy in the terms of a "metaphysics of presence". Derrida's coinage is inspired by Heidegger's critique of Platonism as the definition of Being as Presence (Anwesenheit).

excellence. A certain relation to this being is privileged over others, the ethical relation—this is the human relation above others. In the following years, Levinas would even more markedly give his philosophy the name humanism.

1.8
Return to Platonism

In an article entitled "Meaning and sense" (HAH 17-70; CPP 75-108),[120] published only three years after *Totality and Infinity*, Levinas explicitly names his philosophy both a humanism and a Platonism; it is a "return to Platonism" in a "humanism of the other man". *Humanisme de l'autre homme* was also the title of a collection of essays from 1972, in which the essay was republished together with two other articles, "An-archy and humanism" and "Without Identity". These two essays belong to a later period of his thinking, when the discourse of humanism had changed considerably, forcing him to become more sensitive to the problems of any humanist doctrine. They will therefore be treated in the second part of our investigation (section 2.1). Before doing so, sections 1.9–1.11 on the encounter with antihumanism and Derrida will provide the contextual backdrop, so as to better account for a notable turn in Levinas's engagement with a philosophy of the human.

Before all this, we shall treat in a little more detail the essay "Meaning and Sense", his most systematic defence of humanism. This essay was written in 1964 after studying Merleau-Ponty's *Signs*. In this way, the designator "contemporary philosophy", does not exclusively refer to Heidegger, but extends to include what were, at that time, new and developing trends in French philosophy.

Levinas starts by explaining contemporary philosophy's understanding of language, according to which there is no given which already possesses an identity. Otherwise expressed, there is no originally meaningless entity that gives meaning to meaning. Meaning is always metaphorical, figurative; it derives its meaning from other meanings. This modern view of language is described as an antiplatonism, since it implies that there is no first meaning: meaning is understood as being transferred only horizontally, never vertically.

For contemporary philosophy, the Platonist dream of an outside of language and culture is an error of thought; one never tires of clarifying that neither language nor experience is made up of isolated elements. As Levinas writes, in support of his contemporaries:

> One would be wrong to take the meanings which custom attaches to words that serve to express our immediate and sensible experiences to be primary

[120] Also in HO 9-44, translated by Nidra Poller as "Signification and Sense".

> [...] the meaning precedes the data and illuminates them (HAH 21-22; CPP 78).

In this form of antiplatonism, language antecedes experience; there is no experience outside of language. Understanding is creative, similar to an artistic process. Only through expressing being are we in contact with being.

With language and culture as the source of the appearance of being, the inextricability of language and culture from that which is to be understood is not a defect. On the contrary, "the intelligible is not conceivable outside of the becoming that suggests it" (HAH 30-31; CPP 83). The history that produces a meaning also produces its possibility to be understood. Levinas writes: "*[t]he access is part of the meaning itself*" (HAH 33; CPP 85). Conversely, he sees in Plato's separate intelligible world the belief that signification is anterior to both the language and the culture that express them. For Plato, it is possible to conceive a philosophical culture that "would consist in depreciating the purely historical cultures and in, as it were, colonising the world, [...] in redoing the world in function of the atemporal order of the Ideas" (HAH 31; CPP 84). This would be unimaginable for Levinas's contemporaries, for whom there can be no position outside from which to judge or evaluate different cultures. Levinas sees this latter insight as an ontology analogous with the political process of decolonialisation. Whereas this process is something that he presumably supports, he also finds the multivocity of cultural meaning, which such a view liberates, to imply an essential disorientation (HAH 34; CPP 86).

Against such a background, he can formulate his philosophy as the search for an orientation. Such an orientation can be given in many ways. One way of trying to find an orientation out of a morass of meanings is by way of an "economic" view, to which he will contrast his own. According to this, meanings must be fixed to needs: in technical and scientific culture, the ambiguity of meaning would be overcome when values and meanings are reducible to needs, society reducible to economic structures and the humanity of the human being to psychoanalytically exhibited complexes. The sense or the direction of meanings would always be found in needs, economy would be the first signifier. But Levinas finds phenomenology to have freed us from identifying reality with this univocalism of economy, showing this view to be only one of many modalities of culture. Every human need is always already culturally interpreted: only at a most basic level is the need univocal, where humans are reduced to living under sub-human conditions. The development of the new international society is not rightly understood as a satisfaction of needs. He writes:

> The forms in which this search for the unique sense of being on the basis of needs is manifested are acts aiming at the realization of a society. They are borne by a *spirit of sacrifice and altruism*, which no longer proceeds from these needs (HAH 37; CPP 87, my emphasis).

Levinas finds that one must learn from Plato's *Republic*, if, that is, one is to escape the false choice between a cultural relativism and a utilitarian universalism predicated on an economy of basic needs. Plato shows in the *Republic* how the State, which is to provide for the needs of all, is dependent on the philosophers' contemplation of the Good.[121] But, in the tributes Levinas gives to both the "spirit of altruism" and to the contemplation of the Good, is he going unnecessarily far? The way he phrases it, it might well be interpreted that he is waving off materialist explanations with, on the one hand, a rather naïve trust in altruism, and, on the other, an overestimation of the power of philosophical contemplation. As will become clear in later texts, however, it is not a matter of founding the discourse of morality on a spirit of altruism. Rather, it is a question of showing how discourse and morality both refer to a for-the-other, the very condition of possibility of both altruism and egoism. Levinas's most important point here is that materialism, like any ontology, points beyond itself. The very analysis that aims to map out the universality of an economy of needs implies a level that goes beyond the economy, at least for the analyst. If one could reduce every statement to its role in an economy of needs, the statement announcing the ubiquity of such an economy must be suspected of being a mere means to satisfaction. This is not per se a refutation of the practicality of the economic view, but shows that it has implications beyond itself, that it cannot be the last word.

Merleau-Ponty teaches that there is no completeness of being, no totality, only *totalities* shielded from any final judgement—being is historically determined. Any unity of being is only momentary, drawn out by way of the mediation between cultures. There could, as Levinas elegantly summarizes Merleau-Ponty's argument, be no Esperanto in which this unitary meaning could reside (HAH 39; CPP 88). Has one then not refuted the Platonic unique sense? Yes, but only by forgetting that understanding requires communication between me and the Other. Why does one bother learning a foreign language, or learning the customs of a given culture instead of just declaring it barbaric?

> One reasons as though the equivalence of cultures, the discovery of their profusion and the recognition of their riches were not themselves the effects of an orientation and of an unequivocal sense in which humanity stands [...], as though incomprehension, war and conquest did not derive just as naturally from the contiguity of multiple expressions in being [...] as though peaceful coexistence did not presuppose that in being there is delineated an orientation which gives it a unique sense [*sens unique*, meaning also one-way traffic] (HAH 39; CPP 88).

In spite of this lack of orientation, Levinas sees a "primordial event" in which historical life is situated as a dialogue with the other (*autrui*). He asks rhetorically: "Do not meanings require a unique sense, from which they derive their very

[121] Rep. 471c-541b.

signifyingness?" (HAH 40; CPP 89). One must therefore make a distinction between, on the one hand, cultural significations or meanings and, on the other, the sense and orientation of meanings. Cultural meanings take on their signification in communication to others, where the other *alone* has an original sense.

It is with this insight that Levinas takes leave of contemporary antiplatonism, becoming provocatively and unfashionably Platonist. Sense as orientation requires a step outside of oneself towards the Other. He does not want to renounce this horizontal meaning and understanding; rather he is looking for an orientation within it. He contrasts his view with Heidegger's, according to which Dasein exists in such a way that "its very existence is at stake in this existence." For there to be sense, there must be more at stake than this. Levinas means that the ego has a primordial orientation towards the absolutely Other. This orientation he calls a Work (*oeuvre*), which he also defines as "*a movement of the Same towards the Other which never returns to the Same*" (HAH 44; CPP 91), a generosity without expectation of gratitude. The work, defined in this way, cannot be reduced to the view of profit maximising. This does not mean that he denies that work thus conceived can be performed with a hope for profit, but that this hope does not help us see the purpose of the work *qua* work. Levinas is not giving a psychological description, but a conceptual definition of what a work is.

Even if one does not perform the work in hope for recompense, it is not a game of pure expenditure either, not an action into pure nothingness. Levinas does not believe in the absurd or nihilist *engagement*. Camus's absurd humanism is in fact not so absurd; in declaring itself a humanism it values the other human in the midst of all the disorientation and devaluation of values. And what claims to be pure nihilism is an egoism seeing to its own needs and valuing these needs as highest. Ideological positions which claim a complete lack of orientation are, if we follow Levinas, not trustworthy. The very notions of sense and work presuppose the relation to the other. A world of me and the others is already tilted in such a way that there is no stable ground upon which I can found the neutrality that the loss of all values presupposes.

The sense that gives an orientation to the work cannot be reduced to needs, which are egoistic, aiming at the happiness of the needing subject. Opposed to the movement of needs, there is the movement of what Levinas calls Desire. Quoting Dostoyevsky's description of Sonia's attitude towards Raskolnikov, he describes this desire as "an insatiable compassion", as a hunger from which we cannot be set free. The hunger itself, and not the subject, is nourished from it. Yet this Desire defines what it is *to be* a subject, to be responsible for the Other.

One might claim this relationship to be but one cultural construction among other possible constructions. Levinas agrees that the other person always appears within and by means of a culture, and that we can only understand her hermeneutically, as part of this cultural whole. But he also insists that this never exhausts the meaning of the Other. There is also a sense of its own in the appearance of the Other. The other person *is* sense. For only through her is meaning introduced into Being. The Other is not a creation of culture, she makes cultural meaning possible for us. The face of the Other does not represent a sense, but introduces sense, by letting us desire the good for the Other. In that way, morality is prior to cultural meaning. It is this priority of the ethical that enables one to judge, and critique, culture.

Contemporaries of Levinas saw themselves as departing from Platonism. But it was a departure hurried along the very same routes which Plato had provided: universalism. With a swift sketch, Levinas shows cultural relativism to be a descendant of, and dependent on, universalism.

> It is then that Platonism is overcome! But it is overcome in the name of the very generosity of Western thought itself, which, catching sight of the *abstract* man in men, proclaimed the absolute value of the person, and then encompassed in the respect granted to him the cultures in which these persons stand or in which they express themselves. Platonism is overcome by the very means which the universal thought issued from Plato supplied [...] (HAH 59-60; CPP 101; translation altered).

In the era of cultural relativism which Levinas describes, the respect for the person is overlaid with the idea of inherent and heterogenous cultural values. His fear is that the respect for the person is submerged (and possibly lost) in a respect for the culture in which she belongs. As a counter to this tendency, Levinas announces:

> To catch sight, in meaning, of a situation that precedes culture, to envision language out of the revelation of the Other (which is at the same time the birth of morality) in the gaze of a human being looking at another human precisely as abstract human disengaged from all culture, in the nakedness of his face, is to return to Platonism in a new way (HAH 60; CPP 101).

This is an announcement of a new Platonism, which is an "affirmation of the human" (HAH 60; CPP 101); a humanism aiming at the other man before his cultural belonging and historical situatedness. This Platonism is a new Platonism in the sense that it does not, as Husserl did, found the human in a transcendental and intuitive consciousness, but in "the straightforwardness of morality and of the work" (ibid). Both these point towards the other. The Other is not from the cultural sphere, not from our world at all; his face seems to open towards an outside. With this outside Levinas is not intending a *Hinterwelt* of eternal Platonic ideas; rather, alluding to Nietzsche and Heidegger, he shares their distaste for this form of metaphysics. The sense beyond meanings is not a highest meaning beyond the world, but the direction of meanings in the world. Levinas recognises the contemporary philosophical dogma of the context dependency of meanings, but shows a direction which gives a *sense* to the priority of language and expression, to the recognition of cultural pluralism. The direction is given by the other as being above and beyond my own production of meaning,

> that is, beyond every disclosure, like the One of the first hypothesis of the *Parmenides*, transcending all cognition, be it symbolic or signified. The one is "neither similar nor dissimilar", Plato says, thus excluding it from every even indirect revelation (HAH 62; CPP 102).

This beyond shows itself in the face of the other, which is "the unique opening where the signifyingness of the transcendent does not nullify the transcendence and make it enter into an immanent order" (HAH 64; CPP 104). The face does not represent, it expresses the Other. Levinas surprises us by saying that beyond being there is a third person who leaves a trace in the face. This third is what Levinas calls "il", it is abstractness, universality. However this term does not signify an impersonal abstractum, but it introduces a third *person*. This should not be confused with the concept of the third, which was introduced in *Totality and Infinity* (and reused in *Otherwise than Being*) as the political aspect of ethics—the fact that there never only is one Other to respond to, but always many, in fact a whole humanity. *Il* is here the very transcendence of the Other (the "fact" that he or she transcends), which signifies without being. This "*illeité*" goes beyond being (and the phenomenology or ontology that wishes to describe it), towards the infinite. Illeity is also described by Levinas as the divine, to which we can turn only through its traces in the other man. Just as with the Good for Plato, God cannot be defined in a meaning, but is that which lets signify. The trace of illeity is the "origin of alterity" (HAH 69; CPP 106), and by implication the origin of meaning. In the two later texts, included in the same volume, *Humanism of the other*, Levinas would take explicit care not to refer to an origin of meaning, but to an "anarchic" discourse of the human. But here, as it stands, the illeity is that which lets there be a sense to the multiplicity of meanings.

This is very much the interpretation that Heidegger gives to the Idea of the Good in "Plato's Doctrine of Truth": not only is the Good that which shines forth, it is that which lets shine forth. According to Heidegger, Nietzsche's inverted Platonism was nothing other than the fulfilment of Platonism, of Metaphysics. Here, Levinas does not explicitly refer to Heidegger. Nonetheless, it would not be too much of a stretch to say that his philosophy sets about to reverse anew the Heideggerian interpretation of Plato, to place Plato back on his feet once more. Levinas follows Heidegger's scheme of Plato as the paradigmatic metaphysician and the instigator of Humanism, with the difference that, for Levinas, this makes Plato the hero, not the culprit. His return to Platonism is in this sense an inverted Heideggerianism. Levinas's most important addition to this mixture is what he terms the de-neutralisation of being. Concepts are replaced by persons, and the Good can be sensed only in the direction of the Other. One way to describe this is as a concretisation of the Good through the face of the other.

"Meaning and sense" is where Levinas most convincingly argues for his philosophy as a humanism of the other man; in this sense he reaches the goals he had set in the 1930s, namely to establish the notion of the human in a new way. But there is a certain political naïveté in his philosophy of the human, couched here as a humanism. This goes hand in hand with the problem we discovered in *Totality and Infinity*, regarding the *status of his own discourse*. Recall that in *Totality and Infinity*, he seeks to claim access to the transcendence of the other in an ontology of immediacy (of enjoyment, of the experience of the face-to-face encounter). In the later text, the problem is how to salvage the universal from the antiplatonist affirmation of cultural specificity and value relativism. In what language might a *new* Platonism be couched that will not serve as a disguise for a new oppression of the other? Is a humanism of the other perhaps an oxymoron, in that it appeals to the singularity of the other at the same time as it aligns itself with the universalism of a humanism? At this time, Levinas seems to think he has found a discourse in which he can finally rest, a metadiscourse, which, by definition questions other discourses, but itself goes unquestioned. In this sense, it serves to provide a philosophical justification for a political discourse of humanism that does not question the supremacy of the West. At this juncture, what has temporarily fallen out of the picture is his early definition of the human as restlessness, which does not sanction either a metaphysical or a political complacency. In order to do justice to this notion, he will have to reconsider the notion of the human, such that the central question will have to be raised: should the problem really be posed in the language of humanism? In his later work he would paradoxically find the resources to answer such a question by passing through the antihumanist critique of the subject.

1.9
Antihumanism

If we ended the previous section by flagging a certain naïve disposition in Levinas's understanding of the human—landing in a complacent defence of the Western humanist project—then certain historical circumstances would contribute to dispelling such a naïveté. His attitude towards the notion of humanism became more hesitant during the end of the 1960s. This was a hesitancy very much in keeping with the times in France, which both theoretically and politically was ensconsed in a set of critical reflections about, to cite Derrida, the 'ends of man'.[122] In order to follow this development, a sketch of the philosophical climate surrounding Levinas at this time, will prove indispensable.

In reaction to existentialism and phenomenology, a notable set of French philosophers were to cast their philosophical itineraries in terms of an antihumanism. This movement has been associated with mainly three thinkers: Claude Lévi-Strauss; Louis Althusser and Michel Foucault.

1.9.1 Claude Lévi-Strauss and the Ambiguities of Antiplatonism

Lévi-Strauss's ethnographical project involved the collection of a vast data-set on the most diverse cultures of mankind, with the purpose of discovering the structures that give sense to a multiplicity of cultural practices, and to map out the invariant structural features of "the savage mind", those structures presiding over all human thought.

This affords him the possibility of criticising the humanism of the West as a naïve ethnocentrism. However, if classical humanism was thought to be the idea of an inalienable human essence undergirding all humanity, this position is perhaps not so far from structuralism as Lévi-Strauss would like to think. In one sense his structural anthropology can be seen as a reactivation of the Platonic dream of a universal science, with one notable revision, namely that ethnography replaces dialectics. Even though Lévi-Strauss sought to dissolve humanity

[122] Jacques Derrida, "The Ends of Man", in *The Margins of Philosophy*, trans. A. Bass, Harvester, 1982.

within the non-human,[123] this was to be achieved by first finding the universal human code, unconscious forms and structures that were the same for all intellects of all cultures and ages.[124] Despite an Antiplatonist agenda, such an argument is permeated by what is ultimately a Platonic discourse. Such is the case, when Lévi-Strauss explains how "understanding consists in reducing one type of reality to another [and] that true reality never is the most apparent".[125] Here, one might say, the aim is to arrive at a naturalism via an extreme formalism. The naturalist reduction, possible after further advances had been made in the natural sciences, is never performed by Lévi-Strauss. However, it is always left open as a promise. The role of the anthropologist is to gather specific data from observations of various human cultures and to trace the patterns they form; these patterns are then to be "integrated in a meaningful totality".[126]

Structuralism's subsumption of singularities, inscribing them in totalising structures caused a debate between Sartre and Lévi-Strauss, which is instructive for the purpose of relating Levinas to both thinkers. Lévi-Strauss had been a vociferous critic of the existentialist movement, insisting that the principle of all research must lie in the rigours of empirical ethnology based on all the peoples of mankind, and not in making spurious speculations about human subjectivity, seen from the perspective of one specific culture. The existentialist view of the human subject was to be given its due role, but as the expression of one particular culture.

Sartre had in his Critique of Dialectical Reason replied:

> The abstract point of view of *critique* can obviously *never* be that of the sociologist or ethnographer. It is not that we are denying or ignoring the concrete distinctions (the only real ones) which they establish: it is simply that we are at a level of abstraction at which they would have no place. In order to connect with them, one would need the set of mediations which transform a *critique* into a *logic* and which, by specification and dialectical concretization, redescend from logic to the real problems, that is to say, to the level at which real History, through the inversion which is to be expected of this abstract quest, becomes the developing totalisation which carries, occasions and justifies the partial totalisation of critical intellectuals.[127]

Of particular interest is how, in spite of Lévi-Strauss's accusation of Western chauvinism in Sartre's position, Sartre is unwilling to concede the moment of critical reflection to the categorizations of the ethnographer. Sartre insists—and in a way which runs parallel to Levinas—that his own description of the self-reflexive ego takes place on a plane above and before the ethnographer's catego-

---

[123] *La pensée sauvage*, Agora, 2009 [1962] pp. 294-295.
[124] *Anthropologie structurale*, Plon, 1958, s.28.
[125] *Tristes tropiques*, Plon, 1955, s. 62.
[126] *La pensée sauvage*, Agora 2009 [1962] p. 301.
[127] *Critique of Dialectical Reason*, Verso, 2004 [1960], p. 482.

rization of it as specific to a cultural horizon. The point here is that the very act of categorization presupposes for Sartre critical reflection. It requires of the ethnographer to reflect in a dialectical way on his own situation within a set of embedded practices and understandings, and to organise empirical data and construct typologies on this basis.

We have already observed in what way Levinas undercuts the contextualist's refutation of abstract man, by showing that its very logical structure presupposes the universalisation of Man. Unlike for Sartre, though, it is not the reflecting ego, which is to be salvaged from the accusations of cultural particularity. Rather, it is the face of the other which cuts through the layers of culture, and which makes critique possible in its disturbance of the complacency of the ego.

1.9.2 Louis Althusser and the Critique of Ideology

An understanding of science, much more to Levinas's liking, was developed by the Marxist thinker Louis Althusser. An exponent of a theoretical antihumanism, Althusser took issue with those thinkers claiming to be Marxist humanists,[128] finding in the early Marx resources to construct a fully-fledged socialist humanism. Althusser's position in this debate is important since in describing humanism as an ideology, he lays claim to a validity beyond the sphere of Marxism's internal debates in which he was directly engaged. He writes: "It is impossible to *know* anything about men except on the absolute precondition that the philosophical (theoretical) myth of man is reduced to ashes".[129] The danger of a Marxist humanism, for Althusser, lies in its illegitimate mixing of practical slogans and theoretical concepts. In practice, humanism can work as a slogan, as a hope for something better and more dignified for the human, but in theory it will only work to confound the real problems at stake. "Simply put, the recourse to ethics so deeply inscribed in every humanist ideology may play the part of an imaginary treatment of real problems".[130] One might use the word "Humanism" as a kind of a pointer, in order to give a practical direction, but the path in this direction can only be assured by a scientific approach to the problems at hand: "During this process we must make sure that no *word*, justified by its practical function has usurped a *theoretical* function; when it has served its practical function it must evaporate from the field of theory".[131] For Althusser, this means placing an emphasis on the later writings of Marx against the early works, the scientific approach against the ideological.

---

[128] After Stalin's death and the short-lived thaw under Khrushchev's government, it was for a period acceptable to promote an agency-oriented socialism, such as that of the Praxis group in Yugoslavia. Probably inspired by this movement, thinkers like Erich Fromm, Lucien Goldmann and Herbert Marcuse accepted the label of Marxist humanism.

[129] "Marxisme et humanisme" in *Pour Marx*, La Découverte, 2005 [1964], p. 236.

[130] "Note complémentaire sur l'humanisme réel'", Ibid [1965], p. 258.

[131] Ibid.

Althusser thus holds humanism to be an ideology, while Marxism is a science. He conjectures that "[a]n ideology as a system of representations differs from science in that its practical-social function defeats its theoretical function (or its function as knowledge)".[132] In order to understand the humanist ideology scientifically, Marxism must embrace a theoretical antihumanism, which could be complemented by a practical humanism. This reasoning presupposes that in science, ideology can be transcended, but practico-politically one forever remains within its snare.

> This is not an idea of ideology reducible to the cynical instrumentalisation of ideas for exploitative ends by the bourgeoisie. Rather, humanism as the bourgeois belief in liberty, equality and fraternity is the effect of practices embodied by *all* classes in capitalist society, but which serve to conceal and reproduce these practices *specifically* exploitative of the working classes.

But what does Althusser make of his concern with the exploited working class, which seems a *sine qua non* of Marxism? Does his identification with their plight come from him sharing the bourgeois ideology, which is to say, his practical humanism? Does this not lead to a vicious circle with regard to the suspicion towards ethics? In "Ideology and idealism", to be discussed later,[133] Levinas will claim that even the Althusserian critique of ideology (of which he approves) must presuppose the ethical sensibility that Levinas advances in his philosophy of the human.

1.9.3 Michel Foucault and the Historicity of Man

Whereas Lévi-Strauss and Althusser both believed in affirming a strong notion of science that would transcend the ethnocentrist or ideological entrapment of Western humanism, the position of Michel Foucault has a more complex relation to the concept of science. Foucault saw the philosophy and human sciences of the last centuries as accomplices to humanism. He claimed the notion of Man to be an "invention of a recent date", an invention that will soon perhaps disappear from our discourse. According to Foucault, the historical appearance of "man" in Western discourse dates from around the 18th century. The concept existed of course long before as a category for philosophical and scientific investigation. The novelty of the Moderns, however, was that they understood Man as the condition of possibility of all knowledge. With Kant, one important step is taken, since his Copernican turn shifts the focus from being to the transcendental subject. But the modern paradigm has, since the 19th century, taken this position one step further. It is no longer possible to separate empirical and

[132] "Marxisme et humanisme", p. 238.
[133] Cf Infra, section 2.3.1.

transcendental Man. Foucault writes accordingly: "Man, in the analytic of finitude is a strange empirico-transcendental doublet, since he is a being such that knowledge will be attained in him that renders all knowledge possible" (MC 329; OT 347).[134]

Here Foucault is drawn into a quandary of the modern episteme: the self-knowledge of the "analytic of finitude" can never become complete. For the knowledge of the knowledge must include the non-knowledge, or the unconscious, which is also a part of Man. Prescient to this paradox, Foucault asks, "[h]ow can man think what he does not think, inhabit as though by a mute occupation something that eludes him, animate with a kind of a frozen movement that figure of himself that takes the form of a stubborn exteriority?" (MC 334; OT 352) These questions lead Foucault to a radical conclusion: inspired by Nietzsche's announcement of the death of God, he declares the death of Man. This death is already transpiring: Man as a "strange empirico-transcendental doublet", writes Foucault, is already starting to percolate from our discourse.

For Foucault, this does not mean the end of philosophy—these insights on the contrary bring about the possibility for philosophy to wake up from its "anthropological sleep". "Anthropology and contemporary philosophy are tangled up in [...] a web of confusion and illusion".[135] Kant's anthropological and critical writings must be understood together; they "incline", he explains, towards each other:[136]

> [The] *Anthropology* finds itself doubly beholden to critical thought: as knowledge, it relies on the conditions that it sets and the realm of experience that it determines; as an investigation of finitude, it relies on the first, impassable forms that critical thought makes manifest.[137]

Whereas Kant's *Anthropology* was epistemologically and methodologically dependent on the Critiques, Foucault held that contemporary anthropology (meaning most likely the project of Lévi-Strauss) was trying to produce an anthropology that *assumes* the role of the critique, providing empirical answers to transcendental questions. The answer to this anthropological discourse is for Foucault to refrain from adumbrating a more truthful discourse (unlike Heidegger, who in his "Letter on 'humanism'" held that anthropological propositions might be "correct, but not true"). Foucault meant that one can only answer with a "philosophical laughter" at the "warped and twisted" anthropology (MC 353; OT 373); and work to change the order of discourse, rather than provide it with a better anthropology.

---

[134] But in Foucault's *Introduction to Kant's Anthropology*, Semiotexte. 2008, Foucault shows how already Kant's *Anthropology* "mimics the *Critique*", "gravitates around the *Critique*" (p.121). The empirico-transcendental doublet has its beginnings already in Kant.
[135] Foucault, *Introduction to Kant's Anthropology*, p. 121.
[136] Ibid, p. 19
[137] p. 119.

Changing the order of discourse in Foucault means most often privileging an historical account. Derrida had earlier[138] questioned Foucault's account of the history of rationality and madness from *Madness and Civilisation.* For Derrida, it is unclear with what writer's voice it is possible to write a history of rationality, the origin of the modern reason, which would mean the "historicity of history" (ED 68; WD 51). Madness per Foucault's definition is what cannot be said, yet "[e]verything transpires as if Foucault knew what 'Madness' means." (ED 66; WD 49)

In *The Order of things*, Foucault inevitably encounters the same structural problem, and discusses it himself. He treats it most thoroughly as the problem of the historicity of history, as it were, taking on Derrida's challenge. Beyond the histories of peoples, the history of means of production, of cultures, of meanings, one discovered the history of the views upon these, the history of philology, of ethnology, of economy. But these questions inevitably lead to the historicity of history, and the historicity of Man himself. Foucault describes this as a confrontation between historicism and the "analytic of finitude" (MC 384; OT 406), both seeking to encompass the other, though they are in reality different sides of the same coin. We have to tell the history of man's finite faculties, but at the same time show the finitude of the method that we use in order to tell this history. When Foucault discusses this confrontation between historicism and a philosophy of the finite subject, it might seem that he tells the story as if he were neutral to it, as if it were a game that his own work was not caught up in. But in dividing history into different *epistemai*, or world-views—such as the classic and the modern—he is himself practising a historicisation of being, the upshot of which is that the questions asked by the so-called analysists of finitude are left unanswered.[139]

Foucault does not think of his own philosophy in terms of an ethics, but explicitly claims that modern thought has not only been unsuccessful in proposing a morality, but is structurally incapable of it (MC 339; OT 357). He understands modern thought as a break with the only other (non-religious) ethical form of thought: Stoicism/Epicureanism.[140] Whereas Stoicism and Epicureanism were based upon the order of the world, deducing from that a code of wisdom or morality from which to live, in modern reflective thought Man is cut off from himself. Kant again provides the bridge beyond, since by means of the categori-

[138] In "Cogito and the history of madness" (WD 36-76), originally a lecture delivered at *Collège Philosophique* 4 March 1963.

[139] In "The Ends of Man", *Margins of Philosophy*, University of Chicago Press, 1985, Derrida would, without mentioning Foucault, again question the possibility of completely historising Man, without projecting Man as a *telos* in the sense of the philosophies of Husserl and Hegel. The end of Man can only be thought "from the vantage of the end of Man" (p.123).

[140] These are the traditions which he later, in *History of Sexuality*, would turn towards for revitalising a tradition of philosophy as care of self.

cal imperative, the subject discovers within itself its own law which is also the universal law (MC 339n; OT 373n-374n).

In lines that could be read as being directed against Sartre's humanism or Beauvoir's ethics (but which, in another sense, almost repeats them), Foucault writes:

> Let those who urge thought to leave its retreat and to formulate its choices talk on; and let those who seek, without any pledge and in the absence of virtue, to establish a morality do as they wish. For modern thought, no morality is possible.

And he continues in a Nietzschean tone:

> Thought had already "left" itself in its own being as early as the nineteenth century; it is no longer theoretical. As soon as it functions it offends or reconciles, attracts or repels, breaks, dissociates, unites or reunites; it cannot help but liberate and enslave (MC 339; OT 357).

Foucault's view that a philosophical ethics is made impossible by the emergence of the critical reflective thought of modernity is particularly interesting with respect to Levinas's further development. As we saw already in our analysis of *Totality and Infinity*, for Levinas the domain of the ethical is in a sense coextensive with the possibility of critique, the faculty which is perhaps the most characteristic of the era of modernity. Thus, whereas Foucault sees the epoch of critical thought as making a philosophical ethics impossible, in Levinas's understanding the opposite is true: the ethical is that which makes critique possible.

1.10
Derrida Listening to Levinas

The encounter between Levinas and Derrida is important for us for at least two reasons: firstly, Derrida presents a criticism that goes right to the core of the Levinasian project, and indeed it will be shown that this helped Levinas to see more clearly his main contributions to philosophy, forcing him to a sharper precision in his later texts. Secondly, in Derrida's reading of Levinas, there appears as it were an intersection, a particular philosophical language in its own right, irreducible to either thinker as an individual. This language will here be used in order to rephrase some Levinasian thoughts in a more systematic vocabulary.

Derrida is not a Levinasian. By the same token, he is not anti-Levinasian. In his sole text dedicated to Derrida, Levinas underlined the importance of their encounter. There he described the encounter as the "pleasure of a contact in the heart of a chiasmus" (NP 89; PN 62). With this metaphor Levinas wished to capture something both of the important and intimate contact with another philosophical itinerary, an itinerary which in many respects was otherwise so different from his own.

Commenting on this in a late interview, Derrida was hesitant to embrace the metaphor of the chiasm, but said that the encounter was for sure "going to the heart of the matter", "that which can sometimes take the form of a dispute, finds also its place inside me, between me and myself, between the Levinas in me and the Levinas outside of me."[141] And obversely, Derrida considered Levinas as also organising "a potent 'deconstruction' of ontology [...] of that which dominates occidental ontology.[142] [143]

A chiasmus consists of two lines intersecting at a junction (χ); two itineraries unchanged by the encounter. Is this the image Levinas wants to provide, and

[141] "Ce qui peut parfois prendre la forme de la dispute trouve aussi son lieu en moi, entre moi et moi, entre Lévinas en moi et Lévinas hors de moi." "Derrida avec Lévinas: « entre lui et moi dans l'affection et la confiance partagée » ", Interview with Alain David, *Magazine littéraire*, no 419, April 2003, p. 32.

[142] "une puissante 'déconstruction' de l'ontologie, [. . .] de ce qui domine la philosophie occidentale". Ibid.

[143] A discussion of his relation to Levinas is also found in "Från lag till rättvisa", comprising the proceedings of a seminar in which he participated at Södertörn University in the year 2000, later published in *Lagens kraft*, Symposion, 2005, pp. 97-120.

with which Derrida disagrees? I think if one is to make sense of this metaphor, it would be as two lines, both of which, even in the encounter with the other, are consistent in their own direction and aspiration, but which together form a meaning that signifies beyond the mere crossing of paths. After the encounter, the thoughts of either of the thinkers cannot be understood without those of the other. In the following two sections, I will therefore try to provide an account of the structure of this chiasmic constellation, rather than merely defending one path against the other.

In his first and most important text on Levinas, "Violence and Metaphysics", from 1964, Derrida takes up the most important issues from Levinas's work up to that point. Derrida challenges Levinas by following his own questions and continuing them in the same spirit. This is also how Derrida describes his approach:

> First, let it be said, for our own reassurance: the route followed by Levinas's thought is such that all our questions already belong to his own interior dialogue, are displaced into his discourse and only listen to it, from many vantage points and in many ways (ED 161; WD 136).

When establishing his interpretation of Levinas, Derrida's key term is the "economy of violence", which, it must be underlined, is not Levinas's own; Levinas speaks only of an economy of enjoyment. And, as we shall recall, enjoyment, in the sense that Levinas intends it, is not per se violent, since it is not directed towards the face. However, since pure enjoyment in this model would only be possible in a world without others, the idea of pure enjoyment can only be considered as a fiction. Instead, there will always be a conflict between the ethical and enjoyment. The ethical is from the start defined as a rupture with the economy of enjoyment. It is the ethical relation to the other, which *ex negativa* defines that which it interrupts as violent (i.e. the economy of enjoyment).

Derrida summarises Levinas in the following way: Levinas claims that without God/the holy/the face/the ethical[144] there cannot be anything outside the economy of violence, which is "the world of immorality" (ED 158; WD 133). But on the other hand of course, in order for violence to be recognised as violence, there must be the face. "With or without God, there would be no war. The latter supposes and excludes God." (Ibid). Derrida concludes: "God is thus implicated in the war (*mêlé dans la guerre*)" (Ibid). In this sense, God is part of the economy of violence. Later this is repeated in another way: God is inscribed in history (ED 170; WD). This shows, for Derrida, that, "in a language that our language—and Levinas's also—accommodates poorly, the play of the world precedes God" (ED

[144] It is important to note here, that although Derrida talks about God, he is not engaging in a theological discussion with Levinas. God, the ethical, the holy, the face, the absolute other all stand for the possibility to transcend an economy of violence, and God is the word that expresses this the most extremely and boldly.

158; WD 133). This would mean that the economy of violence is more ontologically fundamental than that which claims to transcend it. This seems to go beyond the implications drawn before, according to which Derrida says that God both transcends and is a part of the economy of violence, or, put otherwise, that He is a part of it by transcending it. This earlier claim, which is the one I shall seek to defend, thinks the economy of violence and that which exceeds it as co-originary. The latter (which, in the next section will find expression in those interpreters of Levinas that understand the just as a lesser violence) holds that the economy of violence precedes that which putatively transcends it, which amounts to saying there can be no real transcendence from the economy of violence.

Derrida claims to offer his interpretation simply by listening to Levinas and does so justly. At some points, however, Derrida himself declares a certain deafness: most notably concerning Levinas's claim that the alterity of *Autrui*, is an originality non-deducible from the egoity of the alter ego. Levinas says that there is a distinction between the singularity of the subject and the singularity of the other. When claiming this, Levinas often violently positions himself against Kierkegaard, who also revolts against the system, a revolt indistinguishable from egoism, however (Cf. TI 341; TaI 305). Contrarily, Derrida speaks up for Kierkegaard:

> Can one not wager that Kierkegaard would have been deaf to this distinction? And that he, in turn, would have protested against this conceptuality? It is as subjective existence, he would have remarked perhaps, that the other does not accept the system. The other is not myself—and who has ever maintained that it is? But it is *an* Ego, as Levinas must suppose [*supposer*] in order to maintain his own discourse (ED 162; WD 132).

As we see here, Derrida holds that Levinas must presuppose what he most of all sets out to refute: that the generality of the egoity precedes the otherness of the other! For Derrida this alterity must consist in *an* ego being *other than* me, in the sense of an *alter ego*. The egoity of the ego must be "supposed". For Derrida this seems to be an offhand remark, in need of no further argumentational support. But with this truncated movement, does Derrida not *sub-pose* the very structure which Levinas claims the asymmetry of the face-to-face encounter with the other must put into question?

By the notion of the alter ego, Derrida returns us to Husserl's fifth Meditation. Of course, Levinas cannot deny that the other is an alter ego, with its own irreducible perspective, similar to mine. His point is merely that this is not an exhaustive understanding of the other, but that there is a further, more radical twist that the idea of the alterity of the other can undergo. Not so Derrida. For him, since the other is always an alter ego, the egoity of the other must be taken into account before we start analysing the otherness of the other. Derrida denies

Levinas's claim of a radical asymmetry between the other and me: according to Derrida, this asymmetry must be preceded by a symmetry: the irreducibility of the other to the ego holds only because the other is also an ego for which I am an other (ED 184; WD 157): "It is [...] the transcendental symmetry of two empirical asymmetries." (ED 185; WD 157). This symmetry is what must be "supposed":

> That I am also essentially the other's other, and that I know I am, is the evidence of a strange symmetry whose trace appears nowhere in Levinas's descriptions. Without this evidence, I could not desire (or) respect the other in ethical dissymmetry (ED 188; WD 160).

This allows Derrida to state that Husserl's description of the other as an alter ego is less violent than Levinas's silence on the egoity of the other: "to gain access to the egoity of the alter ego as if to its alterity itself is the most peaceful gesture possible" (ED 187-188; WD 159-160). But this measure of violence "assumes", of course, what Derrida says that Levinas "has to assume", namely that the other is always already an alter ego, something which we should not concede too quickly.

Derrida cannot of course claim that his and Husserl's description of the other (nor any other, for that matter) would be absolutely non-violent. With the appearance of the other in his non-appearance, "with the phenomenality of his non-phenomenality", with the necessity of speaking *about* the other as non-thematisable, "this necessity from which no discourse can escape, from its earliest origin—these necessities are violence itself, or rather the transcendental origin of an irreducible violence" (ED 188; WD 160). No matter how one announces "this transcendental origin", the origin cannot be without violence. Derrida thus accepts the figure of an original installation of violence but draws out an extreme conclusion:

> this transcendental origin, as the irreducible violence of the relation to the other, is at the same time nonviolence, since it opens the relation to the other. It is an *economy*. And it is the economy which, by this opening, will permit access to the other to be determined, in ethical freedom, as moral violence or nonviolence. (ED 188; WD 160).

What Derrida reads in Levinas is how the relation to the other is the possibility of violence and non-violence, i.e. of the economy of violence. Derrida speaks about a "co-naturality of discourse and violence" (ED 189n; WD 404), of war being "congenital with phenomenality" (ED 190; WD 162).

However, this is tied to another instance of explicit selective hearing on Derrida's part: "let us confess our total deafness to propositions of this type: 'Being occurs as multiple, and as divided into Same and Other. This is the ultimate structure'(TI)"[145]. Against this, Derrida agrees with the Eleatic stranger from *The Sophist*, for whom alterity means only a relative negativity (ED 186; WD 158). Otherwise stated,

> [t]he other could not be absolutely exterior to the same without ceasing to be other; [...] consequently the same is not a totality closed in upon itself, an identity playing with itself, having only the appearance of alterity, in what Levinas calls economy, work and history. How could there be a "play of the Same", if alterity was not already in the same? (Ibid).

This is not only a lecture of logic, but concerns the whole story of the other that Levinas tells of me and the other (*autrui*), the same and the other (*l'autre*). Derrida's criticism of the way Levinas treats the couplets of self-other and same-other is the cornerstone of his disagreement with Levinas. He commends Levinas for showing how they have tended to be confused in the history of philosophy; Levinas has disclosed in his philosophising how the relation between *self and other* has often been subdued and subsumed under the logical categories of *same and other*. But Derrida accuses Levinas of not going far enough; Levinas just reverses the hierarchy (between the same-other and self-other), and in so doing leaves intact its structure of subordination, so that the self-other couplet replaces the position of dominance that the same-other relation had occupied. The corollary being that "there would be no interior difference, no fundamental and autochthonous alterity within the ego" (ED 162; WD 136).

Even if I am critical of Derrida's refusal of the originality of the asymmetrical relation to the other, I think that his second "deafness", to the substantialisation of otherness in Levinas touches an important problem. Levinas's focus on the concept of alterity causes confusion. For what Levinas is in search for is not really the "other" as in "other than", which is actually nothing but a relative negation. On this detail he had already made his motives clear in *Existence and Existents*:[146] his interest is with the notion of alterity as a quality opposed to ipseity. The other is for me the other in a sense that is irreducible to his or her being another I, an alter ego. Thus "intersubjectivity" is not the title that immediately translates the face-to-face, or what Levinas later would call "proximity", or "the-one-for-the-other". The notion of intersubjectivity brings with it the presupposition of two equal subjects, equal in their subjectivity. Questioning this does not mean questioning that the other is not also an I—but that it goes too far to say, as Derrida does, that one must "suppose" (ED 162;WD 137) this in understand-

[145] Derrida consistently refers only to the works as a whole without page references, even when explicitly quoting Levinas word for word. Somewhat speculatively, one could take this a sign of an extreme intimacy that Derrida developed to the movement of the Levinasian thought, such that it is difficult to see where the interpretation ends and the criticism begins. Even when quoting Heidegger in the same text, he gives page references.

[146] Infra section 1.3.

ing the other as other. This movement of "sub-posing" a subject that is first and foremost a subject—the very unquestionability of the primacy of a subject not first and foremost related to the other(s)—is what Levinas places in question. But for Derrida, at least in his criticism of Levinas here, identity and alterity can never be anything but relative attributes to already presupposed subjects. What Derrida means here is that one has to assume that the other is also a subject for whom I am an other, i.e. the reversibility of the I-you relationship. This cannot be questioned—at least not in philosophy,

> but in an inscribed description, in an inscription of the relations between the philosophical and the non-philosophical, in a kind of unheard of *graphics*, within which philosophical conceptuality would be no more than a *function*. (ED163; WD 138, Derrida's emphasis).

Derrida here writes in a very un-Derridean tone, as if he knew where the borders between philosophy and non-philosophy were, and were in a position to state that Levinas's pen tends to skid outside of these borders of the rules of philosophical writing, just as it can happen that a child out of mischief, or frustration, or due to lack of skill, draws outside the borders in a colouring book. One might assume that Derrida would be the first to agree that philosophy has always been redrawing these borders. Here, though, Derrida is doing something quite different, silently operating to reinstall the borders of philosophy that Levinas is trying to alter, all the while pleading deafness to the attempts to explicate how they could be redrawn. Could we not accuse Derrida of an attempt at a "Mastery of the limit", as Derrida himself characterised logocentric philosophy, the philosophy that claims to become master of the limits of its own domain?[147]

But on the other hand, no one is more attentive than Derrida to Levinas's struggle with philosophical conceptuality. As he notes, one way out for Levinas—defending him against his self-contradictions—would involve a protest against discourse itself, against the violence of discourse as such. But, as Derrida rightly says, Levinas has abstained from using this weapon—he does not claim that there is a pious (negative theology) or intuitive (Bergsonianism) relation that transcends discourse (ED 170-1; WD 144). For Levinas, only discourse can be just, yet the violence of the Same reigns in discourse. If this is the case, then, argues Derrida, "[t]his distinction between discourse and violence will always be an inaccessible horizon. The non-violence would be the telos and not the essence of discourse" (ED 171-172; WD 145). But if this is so, reasons Derrida, this peace is beyond discourse; it is in its future, not in its presence. What Derrida shows is that there is war in the heart of peace; nothing can transcend the economy of violence for all time, definitively. According to the way in which Derrida reads

[147] *Marges de la philosophie*, Minuit, 1972, p. i, transl. A. Bass as *Margins of Philosophy*, University of Chicago Press, 1982, p. x.

him, Levinas's discourse can at best be a lesser violence against a greater violence (ED 136n; WD 400n). In another passage, Derrida writes:

> Discourse, therefore, if it is originally violent, can only *do itself violence*, can only negate itself in order to affirm itself, make war upon the war which institutes it without ever *being able* to reappropriate this negativity [...] This secondary war, as the avowal of violence, is the least possible violence, the only way to repress the worst violence, the violence of primitive and prelogical silence, of an unimaginable night which would not even be the opposite of the day (ED 190-191; WD 162).[148]

This is a strong argument that the ontological violence performed by discourse is inescapable. What Derrida does for Levinas in this critique is to highlight the extent to which Levinas must always betray his own intentions in his anti-ontology, and do violence to the other. All the structures that Levinas produces in his critique of ontology are ontological, and the critique of violence, violent. This movement that Derrida perceptively tracks in Levinas's thinking will later afford an opening for what Levinas will call the Saying that both unsays and says the Said, showing how language both disrupts and establishes order, both approaches and distances the neighbour, both installs and disrupts ontology.[149]

One way of rendering Derrida's criticism of Levinas is as a version of Heidegger's criticism of humanism. Quoting Heidegger, he says that

> "What is proper to all metaphysics is revealed in its humanism." Now, Levinas simultaneously proposes to us a humanism and a metaphysics. It is a question of attaining, via the royal road of ethics, the supreme existent, the truly existent ('substance' and 'in itself' are Levinas's expressions) as other. And this existent is man, determined as face in his essence as man on the basis of his resemblance to God. Is this not what Heidegger has in mind when he speaks of the unity of metaphysics, humanism and onto-theology? (ED 210; WD 178).

Levinas is, according to Derrida, reducing the human to the face-to-face encounter, trying to forbid some metaphors and concepts and focus on others, and by

[148] This measuring of violence, the talk of a lesser and a greater violence has been interpreted as a Derridean position: the politics of lesser violence. We will treat this alleged Derridean position shortly.

[149] My (by no means original) claim that the notion of the Saying unsaying the Said is a response to Derrida's criticism is of course complicated by the fact that Levinas uses them already in the preface to *Totality and Infinity*, published with the book already in 1961: "The word by way of preface which seeks to break through the screen stretched between the author and the reader by the book itself does not give itself out as a word of honor. But it belongs to the very essence of language, which consists in continually undoing its phrase by the foreword or the exegesis, in *unsaying the said*, in attempting to restate without ceremonies what has already been ill understood in the inevitable ceremonial in which the said delights." (TI 16; TaI 30, my emphasis). But most important is here not if it is an actual response *caused* by the actual challenge of Derrida, but that it is a response that is *called for* by Derrida's question.

implication does not account for the original metaphoricity of language that philosophy must also speak. Derrida repeats one sentence from Levinas continuously: "The other resembles God" (ED 159, 210, 211; WD 134, 178) and asks if it is not the "original metaphor" (ED 211; WD 178), a violence of discourse trying to disguise its violence. Derrida ascribes a strongly hierarchic structure to Levinas's thought. Here he claims: "The face-to-face, then, is not originally determined by Levinas as the vis-à-vis of two equal and upright men. The latter supposes the face-to-face of the man with bent neck and eyes raised toward the God on high" (ED 158; WD 134). Here, even if not explicitly stated, one can read Derrida as accusing Levinas of subordinating human life to a theocratic understanding of the human in the image of God.

When Levinas names the face "substance", "*kath'auto*" and says that the live speech of the other is closer to the other, it is difficult to see, as we stated already in the reading of *Totality and Infinity*, how he is not returning to the ontologism that he himself set out to criticise. In this there can only be agreement with Derrida:

> In the return to things themselves where we find the common root of humanism and theology: the resemblance between man and God, man's visage and the Face of God. "The Other resembles God" (ED159; WD 134).

What we shall take from this reading of Derrida to the second part of our enquiry, and which coincides with the reading of *Totality and Infinity* laid out in section 1.7, are two things:

Firstly, even if I agree with Derrida that Levinas's infelicitous use of the categories sameness and otherness amounts to a subordination of this same-other relation to the self-other relation, I do not agree that this necessarily places into question the notion of the irreducible asymmetry of the relation to the other human being. Rather, Derrida's critique reveals clearly where the real contribution of Levinas lies: if there is an ethical otherness it cannot be interpreted as the "other than", which as Plato had already showed, is nothing but a relative negativity. It also forces Levinas to find a more radical formulation for his conception of asymmetrical responsibility, which will be discussed in section 2.2, in our reading of *Otherwise than Being*. The whole thrust of Derrida's work also leads Levinas to reconsider the phenomenological category of *experience* and switch attention instead to the discursive quality of ethics.

Moreover, I will draw on the notion of economy of violence, developed by Derrida in his reading of Levinas. According to Derrida, this economy of violence both presupposes and excludes the possibility of its being transcended. I will now develop this latter point through an exchange with another reading of Derrida, according to which, in his critique of Levinas, he develops a position where justice is couched in terms of "a lesser violence". This conflicting interpretation is an attempt to seal off any possibility of transcendence from this economy of violence. While we have focused on the way in which each thinker contributes to the other's thought, this other reading insists on a "disjoining" of the two, posing Levinas as the thinker of peaceful transcendence, Derrida as the thinker of radical immanence. In order to better understand how we might benefit from what we have described as a chiasmic encounter between Derrida and Levinas, it is instructive to contrast the reading being developed here with this other reading.

1.11 On the Notion of Justice as a "Lesser Violence"

exact knuckles chisel out
a neighbour
a practice in love
from hand to mouth
Mara Lee, *Hennes vård [Her care]*[150]

Once one has become accustomed to the notion of an economy of violence, internalising the logical structure that it entails, it will doubtless seem hard to question it. This must be the case for all philosophical systems, for which certain philosophemes and conceptual moves must properly be internalised for that philosophy to be structurally consistent. With this in mind we might want to step back for a moment and reconsider the justifiability of this model. Why should one wish to interpret everything in terms of violence? If, for example, I compose a song and sing it to others, why should this be seen in terms of violence? There are at least two principal lines of argument in defence of this model: The first one focuses on the fact that by seizing a possibility I deprive another of that same possibility. I here take into consideration that someone else could have been in my situation. Maybe I am taking the place of someone other, who would have procured the same enjoyment I am having. A second, stronger argument focuses on what I could have done instead. This brings in the Levinasian sphere of the other, the responsibility for whom I never can fulfil, and the other others (the third) who must be neglected if I turn only to the other. This would be violence by neglect. On this account, if we refuse this understanding of violence, we risk eliding the difference between responsibility and guilt (I did not do it, so I am not responsible); for Levinas's part, responsibility is precisely a responsibility without prior guilt ("Here I am for the other").

But if one can thus extend the notion of the economy of violence, it would seem that there is no outside to this economy. This poses a problem, however. How is one then to conceive of the ethical? The argument that I want to examine in this section holds that since life is nothing but an economy of violence, the

---

[150] My translation. The original, in Swedish, reads: "exakta knogar mejslar ut / en nästa / en övning i kärlek / från hand till mun". This section was largely inspired by this collection of poems. Her entire book discusses the problem of the violence of care. A key to the title is given by the author in one passage: "In some languages, such as Korean, the sounds l and r are allophones of the same phoneme" (Ibid, p. 51). Read in a Korean accent the title, *Hennes vård*, would be indistinguishable from *Hennes våld*, which would mean "Her violence", instead of "Her care". The arbitrariness of the choice between våld and vård in itself is an example of the violent care, nurturing violence at play in language.

ethical can be nothing but a lesser violence. This trope is used by Derridean thinkers such as Richard Beardsworth, Sara Ramshaw and Martin Hägglund, all of whom refer to Derrida's "Violence and Metaphysics" as their justification for thinking the just as a lesser violence. Their substantive claim is that to affirm the possibility of non-violence is to place this as a principle that exists outside of life. It would function as a transcendental norm used only to exact a punitive violence, a norm too abstract and thereby too insensitive to the vicissitudes and singularity of life itself.

This seems to be a much more far-reaching claim than Derrida's claim of war both supposing and excluding God, i.e. of the economy of violence, supposing and excluding that which transcends it. But as we saw in the previous section, Derrida's argument is riven by an oscillation that at times more than leans in this direction. Now, in order to trace this claim of a ubiquity of violence in life, we shall need to make a detour through Nietzsche, who (even if not referred to by these interpreters of Derrida) most clearly expresses an idea of justice as derived from violence. Nietzsche writes:

> To talk of right and wrong *as such* is senseless; *in themselves*, injury, violation, exploitation, destruction can of course be nothing 'wrong' insofar as life operates *essentially*—that is, in terms of its basic functions—through injury, violation, exploitation, and destruction, and cannot be conceived in any other way. One is forced to admit something even more disturbing: that, from the highest biological point of view, legal conditions may be nothing more than *exceptional states of emergency*, partial restrictions which the will to life in its quest for power provisionally imposes on itself in order to serve its overall goal: the creation of *larger* units of power. A state of law conceived as sovereign and general, not as a means in the struggle between power-complexes, but as a means *against* struggle itself, in the manner of Dühring's communist cliché according to which each will must recognize every other will as equal, would be a principle *hostile to life*, would represent the destruction and dissolution of man, an attack on the future of man, a sign of exhaustion, a secret path towards nothingness.[151]

Nietzsche's main claim is that there can be no justice in itself that stands outside of violence, since life in itself is violent. He replaces a hierarchy of justice and metaphysics with what one may call a vitalist hierarchy ("the highest biological point of view"). We must note, however, that it is its harm to the "future of Man", in the sense of a hostility to life that is his central concern. According to Nietzsche, the legal system must be seen as a state of exception in life, which is inherently struggle. The thought of a legal system that is not a state of exception, but universal, is hostile to life and humanity, insofar as it pronounces the right of absolute violence against all. From here follows his criticism of Dühring's stand-

---

[151] Nietzsche, *Zur Genealogie der Moral*, KSA 5, pp. 312-313; translated by Douglas Smith as *On the Genealogy of Morals*, Oxford University Press, 1996.

point of an original equality and a universal justice. For Nietzsche, this egalitarianism is nothing but nihilism. As we have seen, even if Levinas provides a somewhat different genealogy of justice, he also criticises the idea of an original equality, viewing justice and equality instead as exceptional, as breaks with an economy of violence, which is "levelled out" if it is taken as a state of nature (DEE 163-164; EE 99).[152]

From Nietzsche's main claim of the ubiquity of violence it follows that if everything in life is violence, then this must also go for every interpretation of life; ipso facto, Nietzsche's claim is itself a violent interpretation. Nietzsche would have no problem with that—"well so much the better",[153] he answered when conjecturing this reply. Life is in itself self-transcendent, and the violence of the interpretation can be a perfect example of its vitality. This will be an important point of reference for our discussion with the proponents of justice as a lesser violence.

Although not drawing upon Nietzsche, the Derrideans' suggestion that justice can be nothing besides a lesser violence is in fact nothing but Nietzsche turned upside down. Or rather, *ontologically* it is the same claim, but *axiologically* it is the opposite. It is *ontologically* the same claim, because Beardsworth, Hägglund and Ramshaw agree with Nietzsche in saying that there is nothing to life beyond the economy of violence. Martin Hägglund, who offers a particularly pointed formulation of the doctrine of justice as a lesser violence (and wrote with the explicit intent of separating Derrida from Levinas), writes: "a rigorous deconstructive thinking maintains that we are always already inscribed in an 'economy of violence'".[154] But *axiologically* the proponents of justice as the lesser violence perform the opposite of Nietzsche. Hägglund writes:

> If there is always an economy of violence, decisions of justice cannot be a matter of choosing what is non-violent. *To justify something is rather to contend that it is less violent than something else.*[155]

This lesser violence is for Hägglund also the goal of all political action. "If there were not the chance of less violence (and the threat of more violence) there would be no reason to engage in political struggle, since nothing could ever be changed"[156] From the standpoint of a closed economy of violence, it seems unclear why a lesser violence would be more just than a greater violence. Hägglund takes care to say that he is not holding "lesser violence" to be an objective norm. We cannot establish once and for all what is less violent, nor can we do it in a given situation.

---

[152] Cf. infra section 1.3, For the discussion of the "extraordinary", see below section 2.3.
[153] "nun umso besser", *Jenseits von Gut und Böse* §1.22, KSA 5, p. 37.
[154] Martin Hägglund, *Radical Atheism. Derrida and the Time of Life*, Stanford University Press, 2008, 82.
[155] Ibid, p. 83, my emphasis.
[156] "The necessity of discrimination. Disjoining Derrida and Levinas", Diacritics 34.1, spring 2004, p. 47-48.

He cautions therefore against interpreting lesser justice as an inherent good.[157] Against his lesser violence ally, Richard Beardsworth,[158] Hägglund states that deconstruction cannot make us better at practical political action. Every definition of violence is in itself violent, Hägglund argues, drawing the conclusion that we cannot establish the lesser violence as good. For Hägglund, however, the lesser violence is what guides us when we choose to engage politically. In his attempt to combine these two positions he cannot avoid contradiction. What Hägglund forgets is that when we choose something over an other we assume that which we have chosen to be better than the other. This is inherent to the very concept of choice, and does not mean that we have to pose something as objectively or permanently good. Thus, structurally, he clearly states that the lesser violence is better than the greater violence. Hägglund starts out from an incontrovertible epistemological claim, holding that we cannot objectively measure a lesser violence. But he misunderstands its implications, believing that such a claim necessitates the dissociation of lesser violence from value. Even if he is right to say that the difference between the lesser and greater violence only gains its meaning contextually, the claim that we always prefer the lesser violence introduces an axiological slant into the economy of violence. In order to make sense of such a slant, the economy must be measured by what escapes it.

The work of the feminist theorist Sara Ramshaw[159] offers an instructive example of how the concept of lesser violence by default suggests a transcendence from violence. In the conflict between feminism and patriarchy, she states, there can be no non-violent solution, for "there is no such thing as non-violence in a phallogocentric system; our only ethical choice is that of 'the lesser violence within an *economy of violence*'".[160] Here once more, the lesser violence is taken to be a guideline for political decision-making. Describing patriarchy as ruled by phallogocentrism assumes that society should be organized otherwise, for it already points suggestively to what is thinkable beyond a regime that inflicts injustice—passively and actively—against women and thus is an attempt to inspire a departure from phallogocentric violence.

The very idea of a lesser violence within an economy of violence is of course violent. It is violent in the sense of being a violent interpretation. It means viewing all the different aspects through the lens of violence no matter what other aspects there are. However, there seems to be no reason from this point of view to hold that lesser violence would be "the only ethical choice".

---

157 Ibid, p. 48.

158 Richard Beardsworth, *Derrida and the Political*, Routledge, 1996, xvi-xvii, 24.

159 Sara Ramshaw, "Monstrous Inventions: The Ethics and Trauma of Scientific Discovery", Thinking Through Gender and Science Workshop, Queen's University Belfast: http://www.qub.ac.uk/sites/QUEST/FileStore/Issue3GRFSpecial/Filetoupload,55420,en.pdf [Accessed March 4, 2010].

160 Ibid, p.8.

Nietzsche never made this mistake. He saw that if the violence of life is ubiquitous, life must still be affirmed, not because it is violent, but in spite of it. He affirmed above all a violent life not trying to hide itself as such. From Nietzsche's vigorous claim that life in all its expressions is violent one has slid almost seamlessly over to a thought about violence as the only relevant measure for justice. Granted, one can find this tendency sometimes (but not always) in Nietzsche. In reality, though, one has begun mixing this claim with a certain Platonism and interpreted it such that less violence always would be aimed at rather than much violence. In order for there to be such a preference, there must be a silent agreement that we hold violence to be bad and unjust: why else would we claim a lesser violence to be more just than the greater violence?

In contrast to the Nietzschean claim, this focus on the lesser violence is reactive—claiming the ubiquity of violence only in order to attempt to minimise it. If, then, peace as non-violence has been explained to be impossible, now it has merely been substituted by lesser violence as the measure for justice.

This position is of particular interest, because it corresponds to a certain contemporary predicament of the political episteme. On the one hand, one has internalised a certain disillusionment with a failed humanist project. On the other hand, one fears the excesses of a violent nihilism. This thought forgets that one can be cynical for the sake of justice, and that this justice then transcends the cynicism one displays.

Moreover, apart from being unconvincing, such an interpretation does not really seem to do justice to Derrida's own text. For Derrida the term of lesser violence is not a guideline for his own philosophy of justice but what one might end up with if one aims for a philosophy of non-violence, a philosophy which Derrida himself never endorses. He sees a tendency in Levinas of wishing to speak of the possibility of a relation to the other, through discourse, that can be exempt from violence. And Derrida's notion of a lesser violence is, in his eyes, the best a Levinasian philosophy can hope for: "No philosophy of non-violence could ever [...] choose otherwise than the lesser violence in an *economy of violence*" ((ED 136n; WD 400n). Derrida draws Levinas's attention thereby to the fact that discourse cannot be non-violent; it can only choose the lesser of two degrees of violence. The way I understand Derrida, is that this is the only possibility available to a would-be philosophy of non-violence, thus it is never a description of Derrida's own philosophy.

The problem that we have is that violence is not properly understood when it is only seen as opposed to a lesser violence. In order to conceive of violence at all, there must be something we want to protect from violence. Let us choose an example, seemingly untainted by humanism: cutting off one branch in order to let a tree live, is an example of the conception of lesser violence. If we can save the tree by moving a rock, thus making it easier for the roots of the tree to grow, this might seem preferable, because it is even less violent than cutting the branch. But why do we want to save the tree? Must we not care that the tree lives on in order for a treatment of it at all to be conceived as violent?

Let us readily agree that life as such is inherently violent. This is Levinas's own position, chiselled out by Derrida. But violence cannot be understood as such if there is not an approach that is other than violence, structurally opposed to violence. For Levinas, it is the relationship to the other as face-to-face which exceeds violence. This description, however, contains the problem that the face seems to be exempt of violence, while, as Derrida has shown, the claim to stand outside of violence would be the worst violence of all. I would like to suggest that violence cannot be conceived without something which structurally exceeds it. This something, we could call care. With care, I do not mean the Heideggerian notion of care, according to which all care is at the same time care for oneself and care for the world. On the contrary, the idea of care that I am entertaining would be sensitive to a difference between these modes of care, and ultimately a care that can be a care for the other in spite of oneself. This does not mean that care cannot be violent, or even that any care could be exempt from violence, but simply that, *seen* as care, it is *thought* in opposition to violence. The point I am raising here is that such an understanding of care is presupposed in the very concept of violence. Violence always implies that something or someone is being violated, approached in a manner that is harmful to its being; in order to measure this as such, one needs to compare it to an approach that is conducive to its being. Where no other approach is thinkable, one cannot speak of violence.

The value of scrutinising the argument for a justice as lesser violence is that we now see what is at stake in our own search for an understanding of the human beyond antihumanism. Indeed, we can contend that the way in which the thesis regarding justice as lesser violence is couched suggests that we are not yet beyond the conflict between humanism and antihumanism. The danger of a diluted antihumanism is that instead of radically questioning the humanist notion of justice as non-violence, it keeps it as a hidden transcendent provider of value: for why would justice otherwise be oriented towards the lesser, rather than the greater violence? And if violence is viewed apart from the care with which it must be co-original, can it really be violence? Rather, this view ends up in a neutralisation of violence, a domestication, since violence cannot be conceived as such if there is nothing that can be done violence to.

My point is not, then, that there is a possibility of remaining uncontaminated by an economy of violence. On the contrary, the perspective that life, discourse, and interpretation itself are always to some extent violent is methodologically very useful; and it is a perspective employed also by Levinas to a large extent. But in trying to make it the *only* perspective, the promoters of the closed economy of violence are in fact trying to avoid the real violence, the antithesis of care. Claiming that there is nothing beyond the economy of violence is just as much a case of the absolute violence as claiming that there is a point which is totally uncontaminated by it. In fact, one is trying to think an economy of violence as uncontaminated by care. But if care is co-natural with violence, a closed economy of violence is in fact an attempt to escape violence—a case of what the Swedish poet Mara Lee calls "killing the reference"[161]

It bears repeating that this does not mean there is a care, which is not in some sense also violent. Only that one cannot think violence, i.e. not understand what it is, without care. And justice cannot be understood from the notion of a lesser violence, but only from what we can call a distribution of care. This care is never uncontaminated by violence, but it is not the low quantity of this violence that justifies it, and transforms it into care. The doctrine of justice as lesser violence would give an unconditioned privilege to a reactionary politics, a politics that sees itself as violence and therefore sees all intervention as violent. It also gives an image of life and interpretation as a practice of damage control. This is, as we have seen, very far from Nietzsche, but it is also unconvincing as an interpretation of Derrida.

In the opening of "Violence and metaphysics", Derrida writes, "we will not choose between opening and totality" (ED 125; WD 104, translation altered). This refusal, which is the basis for his interpretation of Levinas, rests on Derrida's assumption that discourse is an economy of violence, both total and open, which allows for its own disruption, even if the disruptions will themselves constitute further violence. The notion of justice as a lesser violence would thus not be a "necessary discrimination", but a suppression of violence's other and thereby a metaphysical closure denying an outside of violence, a "mastery of the limit", as we have already cited from Derrida's *Margins.*[162]

As we shall see in the following, Levinas develops a new dyadic structure between the Saying and the Said in *Otherwise than Being*. This is his response to Derrida's opening gambit in "Violence and Metaphysics", where the necessity of seeing discourse as both opening and totality was introduced. In order to restate the notion of the human as transcending the economy of violence, one must also hear the violence by which it is said.

---

[161] Mara Lee, *Hennes vård*, Vertigo, 2004, p. 60.

[162] *Marges de la philosophie*, Minuit, 1972, p. i, translated by A. Bass as *Margins of Philosophy*, University of Chicago Press, 1982, p. x.

1.12
Ethics of Suspicion

> It is the superlative, more than the negation of categories, which interrupts the system,
> (AE 19n; OB 187n, translation altered)

When Hägglund presents his radical elaboration of Beardsworth's thesis about justice as the lesser violence, he does it in order to criticise a trend in interpretations of Derrida, which have often sought an alignment of Derrida and Levinas. For Hägglund, whereas Levinas represents ethics as a permanent transcendence from the economy of violence, Derrida expounds the permanent inscription of any ethical and political injunction within the economy of violence. Whence the catchy title of Hägglund's paper, "On the necessity of discrimination. Disjoining Derrida from Levinas". The interpretations targeted on this occasion are in particular those of Robert Bernasconi and Simon Critchley. These interpretations are however not only groundbreaking as readings of Derrida, but as treatments of Levinas also. Robert Bernasconi's "The Ethics of Suspicion" (ES) provides a model for the reading of Levinas here presented, in that it shows (in the terms here established) how Levinas provides a model of an economy of violence which ethics (in Levinas's understanding) transcends—even if this very transcendence is re-inscribed within an economy of violence once more, which compels us to transcend it anew.

Hägglund, who uses Levinas as a foil with which to contrast the position of Derrida, describes Levinas as wanting to provide a permanent transcendence from the economy of violence. Bernasconi had in fact shown (albeit in other words) that this was not the case. He writes: "Levinas has more in common with the contemporary suspicion of ethics than with the ethical tradition itself. Indeed Levinas's response to the hermeneutics of suspicion is to insist that its suspicion of morality has an ethical source" (ES 8). Referring to the many repeated formulas of exclusions, such as "the saying without the said", which Levinas uses throughout his work, Bernasconi gives the following interpretation:

> A saying without a said, a desire without a need, a love without eros, a gift without expectation do not represent extreme cases, exceptions in a world dominated by the said, by need, or eros. The logic of Levinas's "without" seems to suggest rather that there is no saying without a said, no desire without a need, no love without eros, (DVI 112; CPP 164), no gift without thought of some reciprocity because, as embodied, we live in a world dominated by the said, eros, economics and so on. The saying without a said, the desire without need, the love without eros, the gift without some return are enig-

> matic in terms of the system, *never free of that order which they interrupt but irreducible to it.* (ES 14, my emphasis).

We could add, considering our discussion in section 1.11, that there is *in this particular sense*, no non-violence without violence. However, that the non-violence is not free of the economy of violence which it interrupts, does not mean that the interruption is negated. Each of these figures introduces a certain economy that is exceeded and interrupted. Bernasconi adds another figure: "an ethics without an ethics". The first ethics would be an ethics of suspicion, and the second would be what passes for ethics in a particular society; i.e., what passes as the right thing to do, the rules to which one can adhere that set one's mind at ease.

Building further on Bernasconi, we can emphasise that the interruption need not be real in the sense that it intervenes directly as a force in the economy that it interrupts; it need not appear even as a temporary dysfunction or an anomaly of that economy. The interruption need only be thinkable, even as an impossibility. The interruption of a given economy is the very possibility of opening the perspective from which the economy is viewed as a contingently constructed totality. Without this thinkable interruption, the economy could not be visible as such. In order to see what is at stake, we can recall the broken tool in Heidegger, suddenly letting that which was only practically manoeuvrable as ready-at-hand (*Zuhandenheit*), become theoretically graspable as present-at-hand (*Vorhandenheit*),[163] or the bracketing of the natural attitude in Husserl, allowing the reflexive distanced view of the noematic givenness of the world.[164] This interruption of the economy is the possibility of critique, the birth of critique for Levinas. In *Totality and Infinity*, this was described as a quasi-experience of the other, eluding thematisation. The face of the other shows my freedom to be at fault and thus opens it for critique. The face is "the unique openness in which the signifyingness of the trans-cendent does not nullify the transcendence and make it enter into an immanent order" (HAH 64; CPP 103). In *Otherwise than Being*, as we shall see, this critical turn will provide the very structure of the subject.

Bernasconi's doubling of ethics makes it possible to sort out certain statements of Levinas's which do not fit with this picture, assigning them to a second order ethics—the ethics of which the Levinasian ethics is suspicious. By way of this doubling, the disturbance that some of Levinas's expressions cause can be relieved. This includes Levinas's call for a "return to Platonism in a new way" (HAH 60; CPP 101), his insistence that ethics must be able to judge culture, his reference to "norms of the absolute [...] norms of morality [which] are not embarked in history and culture" (HAH 61; CPP 101). They can be viewed as ex-

[163] Martin Heidegger, *Sein und Zeit,* Niemeyer, 1993 [1927], pp. 74-75.
[164] Edmund Husserl, Ideas Pertaining to a Pure Phenomenology and to a Phenomenological Philosophy, First Book, General Introduction to a Pure Phenomenology,
trans. F. Kersten, Martinus Nijhoff, 1982, 313-314, 332.

pressions of a more naïve ethics that is not part of the Levinasianism to which Bernasconi sees himself faithful. Bernasconi writes: "That there is such an ethics in place in his works is as inevitable as the fact that there is an ethics in place in society." (ES 9). He puts this ideological and complacent ethics up against what is Levinas's real contribution, "the ethics of suspicion".

But the question is whether this figure of excess and interruption, which Bernasconi maps out, is not precisely what Levinas means by the absolute, and by Platonism. And why would not "the morality judging culture" be precisely the ethics of suspicion (ethics judging ethics) that Bernasconi develops so convincingly?

We must at least be sensitive to the risk of an infinite regression here. For, if the ethics of suspicion will judge any ideologically infused ethics, we must pose a new question: who will judge the ethics of suspicion? Of course, neither Levinas nor Bernasconi are ignorant of this problem. Another way of viewing Bernasconi's criticism of Levinas is to say that he is engaged in a self-reflexive mode of critique. He turns Levinasianism against itself, not only in the sense of divining the correct from the errant in Levinas, pitting the better part of Levinas against its more questionable features. Rather, for a critique to be effective it must go all the way down and interrupt the very discursive economy of Levinas's philosophy, according to which the interruption effected exegetically becomes part of a new economy and which will, in its turn, call for interruption, ad infinitum. "The ethics of ethics" that Bernasconi locates in Levinas corresponds to the Saying of the Said, which we will discuss in section 2.2.

The figure of an ethics criticising an ethics is used also by Kierkegaard. In his *Book on Adler,*[165] he writes of the confusion that appears when one realises the insufficiency of the ethics of society. Kierkegaard suggests that one needs a second ethics. He describes its function by comparing it to how one masters vertigo. In order to overcome vertigo, one needs to fix one's attention on a point on the horizon. In the same way, on an existential level, the human being, deprived of all foundation for his existence, might look for support in a second ethics.[166]

Of course things are quite different with Levinas, where the ethical is no longer a question of looking for foundation and support, but of unsettling and disturbing foundations. How, though, does a culture establish such a self-critical ethics without entering a new level of self-complacency? The prospects of self-reflection will be examined further in the light of the historicity of Levinasian thought, to which we will turn in section 2.5.

---

[165] *Book on Adler, Kierkegaard's Writings*, Vol. 24, Princeton University Press,1998.

[166] This interpretation is indebted to Pia Søltoft, who elaborates this in *Svimmelhedens Etik—om forholdet mellem den enkelte og den anden hos Buber, Lévinas og især Kierkegaard*, Gads forlag 2000, where she tries to bring Kierkegaard closer to the idea of an ethics of the other.

Part II

Otherwise than Humanism and Antihumanism

In the first part, I gave a description of the early development of Levinas, which traced a course through his search for a new point of anchorage for the notion of the human. But this search was from the beginning plagued by a dilemma. On the one hand, his descriptions of Hitlerism in "Reflections on the Philosophy of Hitlerism" show the danger of refusing the notion of the human, of dissolving this figure into the forces of history. On the other hand, the philosophical attempts at *founding* the notion of the human had carried with them the threat of capturing the human in a stale and politically complacent form, disarming the radicality with which Levinas wanted it to be filled.

When trying to preserve a sense to the notion of the human without landing in this potentially conservative understanding, Levinas looks to the idea of the beyond, trying to free this idea from the associations of foundation and origin. Already in his article on Maimonides, discussed above (section 1.2), we find him reluctant to affirm the idea of the origin in the form of Aristotle's *primus movens*. This dissatisfaction led him to further his quest for a notion of the human. Only with respect to the other, and not the subject, would the idea of the human gain its full intelligibility and purposefulness. In *Totality and Infinity*, this move beyond is couched in terms of the face-to-face encounter with the other. But as I had claimed in the first part of our investigation, by committing himself to such an experiential understanding of the ethical, Levinas is at risk of slipping back into an ontologisation of the human, the very philosophical move which he is otherwise criticising.

In this second part, I wish to show how, in his later writings, Levinas alters the phrasing of his position, partly as a response to Derrida's reading of his own work (discussed in section 1.10), and partly in reaction to the antihumanist critique of the subject (1.9). I will develop this discussion in five steps: first (2.1), I shall discuss Levinas's re-evaluation of the critique of humanism in the two last essays of *Humanism of the Other*, where he uses this critique in order to reconceive the notion of the human; second (2.2) I will show how this development continues in *Otherwise than Being*, where he more systematically lays out the subject in terms of responsibility; in the third section (2.3), I shall discuss and develop the notion of critique in relation to Levinas's understanding of the political; in the fourth section (2.4) I shall apply this understanding to the question of

Human Rights; and finally (2.5), I shall discuss his view of humanism as a tradition, in the conflict between what we could preliminarily call the universalism and the particularism of his thought.

It would be wrong to think that his later thinking represented an irreversible break with his earlier thought. As such, not all the ideas expressed in this part must be understood as the direct effects of the encounter with the so-called "antihumanist" philosophers of the 1960s and with Derrida's interpretation of his work. On the contrary, most of the ideas had already been expressed at a more or less developed stage. Of course the same can be said both of thinking more generally and the ideas of antihumanism specifically. One should not trace antihumanism to a specific eruption in French thought, empirically datable to a single event or a given period of time. Correspondingly, it is possible to plot many of the antihumanist ideas along a course of the history of philosophy that would pass through the work of Heidegger, Freud, Nietzsche and Marx, and all the way to the beginnings of philosophical thought itself. Nevertheless, it is only with the later work that his new understanding comes to *explicitly* take in these influences.

The aim of this part is to give a systematic account of the most mature expression of Levinas's philosophy from the 1970s. Where earlier works express particular details more clearly, I have seen no reason not to use them here.

What, then, is the most important shift occurring in the later work? In an interview published in 1988, he comments: "*Totality and Infinity* was my first book. I find it very difficult to tell you, in a few words, in what way it is different from what I've said afterwards. There is the ontological terminology. I have since tried to get away from that language (PM 171)". Of course, he saw himself grappling with this problem already in *Totality and Infinity*, expressed in the figure of metaphysics going beyond ontology. What the quote clearly shows, however, is how later he considered these attempts not to be entirely successful.

As we saw in section 1.7 on *Totality and Infinity*, Levinas's description of the ethical relation to the other in terms of experience harboured much ambiguity. On the one hand, he evokes the notion of experience by way of emphasising the face-to-face relation; on the other hand, he claims that the relation is beyond experience. When, in "Signature", a short autobiographical piece, he summarises the most significant outcomes of *Totality and Infinity*, he writes: "the fundamental experience which objective experience itself presupposes is the experience of the other. It is experience *par excellence*" (DL 437; DF 293). Thus, in a truly Platonic gesture, Levinas claims that which transcends experience to be the experience *par excellence*. But now, he finds this gesture deeply problematic. In the brief summary of his work after *Totality and Infinity*, he writes:

> The ontological language which is still used in *Totality and Infinity* in order to exclude a purely psychological signification of the proposed analyses is

> henceforth avoided. And the analyses themselves refer not to the experience in which a subject always thematizes what he equals, but to the transcendence in which he answers for that which his intentions have not encompassed [*mesuré*] (DL 440; DF 295).

By the way Levinas here chooses to highlight the notion of experience we can see that he finds it to be the vehicle by which the problems of *Totality and Infinity* come to light. The new task is to find a notion of transcendence not dependent on experience. This does not mean that it is "beyond experience" in any mystical sense of the word. The problem, as the above quote intimates, is that the subject will always thematise itself (or, "what he equals") in terms of experience. This could lead one to draw the wrong conclusions, namely that the transcendence of experience augments a negative theology. But the transcendence is *not* a hyper-experience or the *Aufhebung* of experience; it does not receive its sense through transcending experience, rather from its positively ethical signification.

In this brief auto-biographical comment, Levinas is struggling for words. The point of this awkward phrasing—saying the subject "thematises what he equals" (*ce qu'il égale*) rather than saying "thematises what he is", or simply "thematising himself"—is, I would suggest, that, in the very thematising, Levinas sees an activity, a movement, that fails to account for the subjectivity which he identifies with a "*response* to that which his intentions have not encompassed". When Levinas sets himself the goal of thinking subjectivity otherwise than as experience, this does not mean any kind of denial of either a first person perspective, or of the justification of a phenomenology of experience. What he does deny is an idea of the experiencing subject as the origin from which all philosophy must draw its justification. This will be spelled out more clearly in the next section.

For now, we shall settle on considering Levinas's later philosophy as an endeavour to think the subject in a way other than through experience. This means that although the subject understands itself in terms of experience, another story can be told. This story lies, as the above quote says, in the *response* to that against which the intentions of the experiencing subject have failed to measure up.

2.1
An-archic Youth

Between Levinas's two main works, published in 1961 and 1974, his most important texts for our investigation are the three small texts collected in the relatively little discussed volume, *Humanism of the Other*, published in 1972. The first of them, "Meaning and sense", was first published already in 1964, and can be ascribed to the earlier period of Levinas's development. The present section deals with the remaining two essays, "Humanism and an-archy" and "Without Identity", (published in 1968 and 1970, respectively). We shall also consider the preface to the three texts. The theme of humanism ties these three essays together. In the exposition that follows, however, my reason for treating "Meaning and Sense" separately from the two later essays and the preface will become evident.

Even if Levinas will later judge the "ontological language" of *Totality and Infinity,* and other works from this period, as problematic, neverthless this book remains the most important point of reference for his later philosophy. Some important moves are nonetheless made in *Humanism of the Other*, a work all too often neglected in the secondary literature. In the preface, Levinas refers to his efforts in this small book as stages of an "untimely meditation (*consideration inactuelle*) that is not yet or no longer frightened by the word humanism" (HAH 7; HO 3, translation altered).[167] This is an allusion to Nietzsche's *Untimely Meditations.* But even if there are some scattered remarks on Nietzsche in these texts, there are other reasons for using this epithet.

The reflections are untimely, firstly in the most obvious sense of being atypical for his time. Levinas takes up once more the over-used and, in progressive academic circles, already derided syntagm, humanism; humanity is "not deemed worthy of the attention of philosophers" (HAH 11; HO 6), he notes. But these reflections are *in-actuelles not* only because they brush against the grain of present opinion. They are *in-actuelles* in a second sense. Levinas proposes a subject

[167] The three main essays that serve to comprise *Humanism and the Other* had already been translated as separate articles by Alphonso Lingis in *Collected Philosophical Papers*. The book *Humanism of the Other,* however, only exists as a complete volume (including the important preface) in Nidra Poller's translation from 2003. I have a predilection for Lingis's translations of the individual articles, and have therefore consistently used his translation except for in the preface, where no other translation exists. There I have instead used Poller's translation, altering it whenever deemed necessary.

beyond the being-in-act with which the subject had been identified in the history of Western humanism.

In the preface to *Humanism of the Other*, Levinas sketches a short history of the subject as actuality. A fundamental moment for transcendental idealism is, according to Levinas, Kant's transcendental apperception, by which one is to understand that the manifold of the given is always accompanied by the "I think that..." of the transcendental ego. Thus understood, the subject has a gathering function. This "thinking" is not an act in the psychological sense, it is not an act of the psyche. For Kant, as well as later for Husserl, a sharp distinction is made between the transcendental subject and the psychological subject. Levinas writes:

> It is not because the unity of transcendental apperception—or understanding—is spontaneous in the psychological sense that it is action. It is because it is the actuality of presence that it can become spontaneity of the imagination, that it can have a grip on the temporal form of the given, and call itself act. The *I* is posited by the *timeless* exercise of that actuality, the necessarily free *I* of classical humanism. (HAH 8; HO 4, Levinas's emphases, translation altered).

For transcendental idealism—which for Levinas is an attempt at providing a philosophical justification for classical humanism—the actuality of presence is timeless. This might seem a contradiction. With Husserl, there are two developments of the understanding of the subject, both of which Levinas affirms: firstly, the subject is now, from Husserl onwards, (HAH 9; HO 4) a living subject. The subject is described in terms of personality, historicity, embodiment, and so on. The conditions of possibility of given noemata are not only the categories and *Anschauungsformen*, but implicate the whole of the subject as a lived personality in a life world. Secondly, Husserl has taken an important step in describing the subject as "irreducible passivity" through the passive synthesis, defined as the pre-intentional gathering of the temporal stream of consciousness, underlying the unity of the subject. This notwithstanding, in its very synthesising, Husserlian intentionality maintains, according to Levinas, the structure of "the actuality of presence" from the Kantian tradition (HAH 8; HO 4). "Subtle analyses of the ante-predicative still imitate, under the denomination of passives, the models of syntheses of the predicative propositions" (HAH 9; HO 4). A "predicative proposition" is for Husserl an object for an act of doxic positing;[168] it can be a statement like "the table is green", founded in the simple presentation of the green table. We can here interpret Levinas as repeating his earlier criticism that the analogy between doxic positing and all other acts of constitution is the model for all intentional consciousness in Husserl.

Through these analyses of the ante-predicative, the phenomenologist would try to demonstrate how the horizons of intentional acts determine the structure

[168] *Formale und Transzendentale Logik*, Martinus Nijhoff, 1974, §45.

of being. Transcendental subjectivity discovers itself by a reflection inwards towards the noesis—it discovers itself *as* reflection.

But classical humanism's notion of the subject, by which phenomenology comes to a sort of perfection, is self-effacing. Levinas writes:

> [I]f the free subject—where the man of humanism placed his dignity—is nothing but a modality of a "logical unity" of "transcendental apperception"—a privileged mode of actuality that must be an end in itself, should we be surprised that, following on Husserl's scrupulous formulation of reduction, the Ego disappears behind (or within) the being-in-act that it was supposed to constitute? (HAH 9, HO 5)

Is not Levinas contradicting himself? He claims that the subject becomes alive with Husserl, and yet, at the same time, he states that the ego disappears from view. What I take him to mean here is that the more scrupulously one's investigation into the transcendental subject proceeds, the less there remains of it as a living ego. It is a notion that makes itself disappear in the system of reductions. The subject and the system mutually signify each other. In his dissertation, Levinas had commended Husserl for reaching the concreteness of Man through the phenomenological reduction. Now, his judgement is that in Husserlian philosophy, which so strongly revived the notion of the transcendental ego, this notion was brought to its limit in a way that would fashion its own philosophical demise. Alluding to the Heideggerian turn in (or from) phenomenology, Levinas continues:

> The thinking subject [...] interprets itself henceforth, despite its industrious research and inventive brilliance, as a detour taken by the system of being for its own needs (HAH 10; HO 5).

For Levinas, this means subordinating the subject to the notions of being and truth. "The rest of what is human remains foreign to it." (Ibid)

Up to this point, Levinas has described the development of subjectivity as "being-in-act". But now he proceeds to lay out his own agenda: "'Intelligibility' and 'relation' have a different meaning in the studies collected here. "They are still alive with the memory of patricide that cornered Plato" (Ibid). Levinas is here referring to the Eleatic stranger's contention, *contra* Parmenides in the Sophist, that even non-being in some way is, in the sense of otherness. "Without that violence," Levinas continues, "relation and difference would just be contradiction and adversity" (Ibid, translation altered). It is interesting that he should refer here to the introduction of both relation and difference within the philosophical nomenclature as a violence breaking with the Parmenidean order. In *Totality and Infinity*, otherness would always be related to non-violence. This passage seems to be a concession to Derrida's critique—namely, that the very philosophical move, which makes it possible to speak of otherness, is always already in itself violent. Yet, it is only "in a world of total presence or simultaneity", says Levinas, that difference appears as violence (Ibid). This puts a slightly different inflection on things, and affords another way of viewing difference. Levinas will speak of difference as going beneath (*en-deçà*) presence, where he finds the 'non-indifference', or 'proximity' of the neighbour. With the terms of proximity and neighbour (*proximité*, *prochain*) he is looking for a new formulation to frame the relation to the other, such that it no longer hinges on the face-to-face encounter framed in a language of experience.

Thus Levinas expresses himself more clearly on a point which, in *Totality and Infinity*, was riven with ambiguity. Even if the relation to the other in the earlier book was described as beyond experience, the concept of experience was employed nonetheless to describe this relation. And the construction of the relation to the other in *Totality and Infinity* is as face-to-face: the situation of immediately and ethically experiencing the other. But once Levinas introduces the notion of *proximity* of the neighbour (*prochain*),[169] it is not a matter of a new kind of ethical experience, rather "*it means casting doubt on EXPERIENCE as the source of sense*" (HAH 11; HO 6, Levinas's emphasis and capitalisation).[170]

This questioning of experience as the source of sense could be seen as a couched defiance against Derrida's assertion that Levinas has difficulties in balancing the demands of a strict empiricism with a system philosophy. On Derrida's interpretation, Levinas's notion of ethics relies on a notion of experience beyond any systematic comprehension. In this sense, Levinas, on Derrida's reading (a reading that for the most part we assent to here), is dependent on a system philosophy in order for his notion of experience to make sense. Now here, Levinas's claim is that the system and the subject refer to each other; empiricism and system philosophy are interdependent, although both fail to describe the aspect of the human which he now names proximity.[171] No longer letting experience be the ultimate source of sense has vast philosophical consequences, which Levinas here expresses, though with some opacity. For Levinas, such a break means "the limit of transcendental apperception, the end of synchrony and its reversible terms; it

[169] It is of course not the first time he uses the concept of neighbour; already from "Enigma and Phenomenon" (BPW 65-78) onwards, it is the neighbour, rather than the stranger, that is the term that gives meaning to the other.

[170] This puts a question mark to John E. Drabinski's hands-on scheme according to which Levinas's in *Totality and Infinity* is a "phenomenology of alterity as excessive presence" and *Otherwise then Being*, still a phenomenology of experience, "is a book of absence", withdrawing behind the phenomenon (*Sensibility and Singularity. The Problem of Phenomenology in Levinas*, State University of New York Press, 2001, pp. 216-217). This is true at a surface level of text. But the important thing is that Levinas wants to move away from an experiential source of sense. In *Otherwise than Being* he also writes: "It is the superlative rather than the negation of the category that interrups the system" (AE 19n).

[171] This complicity between empiricism and system philosophy would be treated more elaborately in Otherwise than Being (AE 206-211; OB 131-134).

means the non-priority of the Same" (Ibid). The idea of a system that can contain the idea of presence, which the transcendental experiencing subject had offered, was fundamental to the notion of transcendental apperception. The implosion of this context means the end of presence as the key to subjectivity, "it means the end of actuality as if the untimely (*intempestif*) came to disturb the concordances of representation. As if a strange weakness caused presence or being-in-act to shiver and topple" (Ibid, translation altered). Levinas advocates a philosophy for which subjectivity is no longer reducible to presence, experience and actuality. This understanding of subjectivity he now compares to tears, to a "swoon (*défaillance*) of being fainting into humanity, not deemed worthy of the attention of philosophers" (Ibid). Thus, the notion of the human becomes Levinas's marker for his understanding of the subject as opposed to the subject as the vehicle of apperception, and as opposed to the notions of force and awakeness. It appears that only when we no longer understand the subject as transcendental apperception, can we access the notion of humanity.

Levinas continues: "But the violence that would not be this repressed sobbing, or would have strangled it forever, does not even belong to the race of Cain; it is the daughter of Hitler, or his adopted daughter" (Ibid, translation altered) This is one of the most obscure sentences in the whole of Levinas's oeuvre. "This repressed sobbing" must refer to that which went before: the movement of being fainting into humanity, i.e. to the movement that makes us understand the subject and the notion of the human as defined through a certain passivity, rather than activity. But what does it mean to claim that the violence suppressing it is not of the "race of Cain", but is perhaps the adopted "daughter of Hitler"? It seems that the violence forever extinguishing the humanity of the human would be of modern origin, a cruelty unforeseen by the tellers of the tale of Cain slaying his brother Abel. With the expression "the daughter of Hitler", Levinas signals it as a problem for a post-Holocaust philosophy. One could take him to mean that a modern persistence in understanding the subject as actuality, which—after the Enlightenment had shown its obscene underside—has become untenable. The most extreme experience of this would be the image of Hitlerism masquerading as a humanism. Here Levinas seems to engage in hyperbole in order to cast his critique in the starkest possible terms. But it need not be read as such. Instead of regarding it as a violent accusation waged against the history of the West, one could rephrase it like this: the fact that what was seemingly one of the most civilised cultures (the bearer of "humanism" with philosophers as the "functionaries of humanity") could become the administrator of the Holocaust has made any naïve understanding of the human subject philosophically implausible—which is to say, a humanism of a "good" subject as actuality and presence is no longer possible. To persist with such reveries after Hitlerism is to enact its own violence, suppressing as it does another understanding of the notion of the human, to which Levinas wishes to give voice.

In-actuality, not being in act, not being reduced to its presence, is one of the ways in which the subject is not its own origin. This he names an-archy. One could say that in-actuality is the temporal expression of an-archy. "An-archy" is not firstly to be read with its political connotation but as a negation of the principle and the origin, of the *arche*. In this sense Levinas is in keeping with the critique of humanism of his time, which targeted for critical scrutiny an idea of the subject thought as its own origin and principle. Its achievement was to expose the autarchic subject as a phantasm, which served to offer a mere illusion of autonomy.

Levinas does not merely want to draw our attention to the realm of the ethical.[172] He is claiming that this realm cuts through all that we know as subjectivity.

> The contestation of the priority of the act and its privilege of intelligibility and significance, the rupture in the unity of "transcendental apperception", signifies an order—or disorder beyond being, before the place, before culture. (HAH 11; HO 6).

In "Meaning and sense", discussed earlier, (section 1.8) Levinas had claimed that the notion of the human could not be reduced to a cultural phenomenon—understood as a product of an economy of needs—for it was "borne by a spirit of altruism". Here, in the preface, this claim undergoes modification:

> We recognize the ethical. We can distinguish in this contact anterior to knowledge, this obsession by the other man, the motivation of many of our everyday tasks and great scientific and political works, but my humanity is not embarked in the history of this culture that *appears*, offering itself to my assumption and making possible the very liberty of that assumption. (HAH 11-12; HO 6-7, translation altered).

What we may recognise as a description of the ethical—where what appears as ethical in our culture coincides with greatness—is insufficient to account for the human. The notion of the human is perhaps neither the cause nor the effect of

---

[172] And not as Richard Cohen says in his introduction to the English translation of Humanism of the Other, an encouragement of care for the ethical self. Cohen writes: "Care for the other trumps care for the self, is care for the self" (HO xxvii). The latter is not Levinas's, but Heidegger's position. Care for the self can only be justified as care for the other, says Levinas, which means exactly the opposite to what Cohen is saying. The specificity of Levinas's position lies in the very meaningfulness of a care for the other which is not a care for the self, an orientation of the world that is not directed towards a care for the self. Possibly the reason for Cohen's misreading is that he takes the self as a moral category in a strict sense in Levinas. He writes, further down on the same page, that "the dignity of the self arises in and as an unsurpassable moral responsibility to and for the other person". This is not wrong, but it is not only the dignity of the self, but the self and the subject per se, that arise as moral responsibility. Thus, Levinas's philosophy is not primarily, as Cohen tends to read him, an imperative to become more moral, to nurture one's "moral self" (ibid), but a description of the structure of subjectivity.

what appears as great in any given culture. "The spirit of altruism", which in "Meaning and sense" Levinas found in the cultural context of the emergence of the international community[173] would presumably from his later point of view be a part of that which "appears". Now Levinas is going further; equally plausible is if the notion of humanity can signify a relation that does not appear. This non-appearance should not be mistaken for a non-fathomable appearance, as religious mysticism might relate to God or to nothingness. The point is that "the face"—which since "Is Ontology Fundamental" signifies the non-consumability of my relation to the other—"is not confined in the form of its appearance" (HAH 12; HO 7). Of course the face appears to me, and I experience the face of the other. But the signification of what Levinas speaks as a face is not confined to this appearance. Again, Levinas believes my concern for the other does not spring from an experience. Here, Levinas says that "The 'I speak' is understood in all 'I do' and even in the 'I think' and 'I am' (HAH 13; HO 7). Kant and Descartes thought that the subject constituted itself as acts of thought, and in later philosophies this had been extended to other acts as well (Husserl: doxic act; Heidegger: understanding of Being). Levinas is challenging this, claiming that the identity of the subject lies in its speech.

But this speech is not seen as originally a free act. Being a subject is not a free choice; it means as Levinas puts it, being "elected", given a responsibility. This election or bestowal of duty is neither act nor experience, it is an "imprescriptible duty surpassing the *forces of being* [...] from beneath all rememorable present, an-archically, without a beginning" [HAH 12; HO 7]. Thus the duty precedes the subject in every other sense of the term: the subject speaking itself already has the duty, is defined and marked, "traumatised", "accused" by it. Levinas often deploys the example of the French "me voici"—similar to the English "it's me"—in which the subject announces itself in the accusative, "like a sound audible only in its echo" (HAH 13; HO 8). Whereas the nominative "I" can bear the illusion of a pure act—of a substance to which predicates can positively be ascribed—the accusative "me" is already marked by the other, and is not the protagonist of the proposition.

That subjectivity no longer finds its origin in intentionality, in experience or presence by no means supposes the death of the subject. What it does mean is that "my contingent humanity" has become conferred"identity and unicity" (HAH 11-12; HO 7). This identity and unicity comes from being marked by responsibility, elected as the one who is responsible.

Thus, what has happened here is that the relation to the other is no longer conceived (as in *Totality and Infinity*) as an event tearing the subject out of its sphere of enjoyment, but as a duty from which the subject appears as such. We will use the two later texts of *Humanism of the other* in order to find out in more detail how Levinas construes subjectivity.

---

[173] This is discussed earlier in section 1.8.

The second text we will treat in this section, "Humanism and an-archy", takes as its starting point the purported crisis of humanism that was discussed at the end of the 1960s. First, Levinas accounts for it as an outpouring of disappointment in the capacity of humanity, in the possibilities of politics and technology to create a happy and just society. He paints a picture of an intellectual climate where the intellectuals no longer put any trust in the notion of rational man. This performs, in a sense, a rationality distrustful of itself. One might ask how this can be a rational and true position to hold; can one reason at all with a position, which does not believe in the power of reason? But Levinas dismisses this standard "refutation". This would already presuppose an undamaged rationality that can make present the rational and the irrational statements in order for comparison to be possible. But Levinas does not believe that this can be taken for granted. Here he agrees with the antihumanist critique—insofar as it targets a politically naïve rationalism. As was the case in the Hitlerism text, Levinas perceives threats coming from two sides: on the one hand from a philosophy that substantialises and reifies man (HAH 77; CPP 130), and on the other from a philosophy that would let the subject be devoured by the structures of being. But the strategy adopted is not the navigation of a middle path between these two possibilities. Rather, he detects a complicity between the two positions, according to which both transcendentalism and antihumanism lead to an anonymous understanding of the human.[174]

This can be exemplified by his dissection of the notion of the rational animal: "the *rational animal* as *animal* is founded in nature; qua rational it pales in the light in which it leads to manifestation Ideas, concepts that have come back to themselves, logical and mathematical chains and structures" (HAH 78; CPP 131). The notion of the rational animal thus becomes the metonymy for the ontological positions neutralising the human, allowing it to drift into anonymity, either by a reductive naturalism or by a universalistic idealism. Both these approaches involve the belief in a foundation that will ground (idealism) or replace (reductionism) the human. Levinas is instead searching for the human beyond foundation.

As he mentions in the preface to *Humanism and the Other*, one of the standard attempts of providing a philosophical foundation for the human was as activity in the present. The subject is understood as beginning. Beginning is the possibility of action, which is the possibility of existing other than as a mere "repercussion of energy along a causal chain" (HAH 79; CPP 131). Beginning "is the wonder of the present" (Ibid). Beginning and the present take place in consciousness, *as* consciousness. Being conscious of something means discovering its origin, making it present in consciousness.

---

[174] The formally analogous constellation in the Hitlerism text is that the traditional Western philosophy has a concept of the subject that becomes so watered down that it actually paves the way for what seems to be its antithesis.

> All contents of consciousness were received, were present and consequently are present or represented, memorable. Consciousness is the very impossibility of a past that would never have been present, that would be closed to memory and history [...] Nothing can enter fraudulently, somehow smuggled into a conscious ego, without being exposed to avow itself, being equalled in the avowal, becoming truth. (Ibid).

This quote recalls Husserl's time analyses, according to which the future and past are both understood from the starting point of their presence in consciousness, building horizons of future and past through what Husserl calls protention and retention. From Levinas's viewpoint, this becomes an imperialism of the present, where the fact of consciousness signifies the impossibility of the past. In both *Time and the Other* and *Totality and Infinity*, Levinas aimed to provide a plausible account of the existence of a future that does not conceive the subject in terms of possibility, but of passivity. Now, analogically, he is searching for an understanding of the past that does not pass through recollection in the present. In all of these works, the quest is for a time outside the grasp of actuality.

The problem with the idealist account of subjectivity (of which Husserlian phenomenology in this respect is a descendent) according to Levinas, boils down to this: the rational subject depends on the possibility of returning to itself, of reflexivity. Levinas writes: "[A]ll rationality comes down to discovery of the origin, the principle. [...] The reflexivity of the ego is nothing other than the fact of being the origin of the origin" (Ibid).

The antihumanists deny this possibility of returning; for them there is nowhere to return to, whereas the humanism (a term now referring to both Husserl and German Idealism) that Levinas is depicting above sees the human as rationality, and rationality as the process of returning to the origin. But even though Husserl would agree that this return can never be fully accomplished, he sees philosophy, as the care for humanity, as the ever renewed path towards this rationality as self-transparency. This makes the very concept of the human precarious. Levinas seeks a way behind this opposition and asks himself: "might not humanism have a meaning if we think through the way being relies on freedom?" (HAH 80; CPP 131). This calls for a new sense of passivity "beneath" (*en-déca*) consciousness, knowledge, action, beneath the *arche*. How are we to understand "beneath", if Levinas is not merely to introduce another principle of principles? That it is beneath these beginnings means that it does not have its origin in the beginning of the subject. Again, this does not mean that he wants to dispose of the subject. His task is to find another understanding of the subject than that of consciousness as beginning in the present. Subjectivity as the possibility to begin in the present was generally viewed from the perspective of the ego in isolation. But the ego can be questioned by others. Levinas goes so far as to say that the others "obsess" the ego, that they take it "hostage". This means that at the basis of the rationality with which the ego identifies there is already a relation to others beyond rationality. This is the nature of the subject in-itself. As an in-itself it is already for-the-other. Subjectivity is thus—before presence, before consciousness—for-the-other. In this way, Levinas sees himself writing "contrary to Fichte and Sartre, who think that everything that is in the subject, even the subject itself, devolves from a position due to this very subject." (HAH 120n; CPP 134n). This does not mean that he says that the subject is not free. Levinas's relation to Sartre is ambiguous; he also sees himself as writing an addendum to Sartre: "Sartre has spoken of the subject *condemned* to freedom. The following pages describe the meaning of this *condemnation.*" (Ibid). The subject must be free in order to have a relation to its determination "for-the-other".

When Levinas uses the term "for-the-other", he is working to transform the Hegelian notion of for-the-other already altered in Sartre. Being-for-the-other has in Hegel firstly a logical meaning. A thing, taken in itself, is an empty abstraction if one does not grasp it through its being-for-an-other. Every definition, every quality of a thing, which is needed to flesh out its thingness for itself, is a for-the-other.[175] But in Hegel's *Phenomenology* this operates also on the level of the development of the human subject. For Hegel, the identity of the subject as for-itself can only be grasped as understanding oneself as a being-for-the-other, according to which the other is another consciousness who understands the first subject as thus defining its own existence. The subjects must mutually recognise each other in order to realise themselves as autonomous subjects. Were it not for the State, Hegel assumes that the subjects would be unable to settle this otherwise than through the struggle (described in section 1.4 above) in which each subject seeks to force the recognition of the other. The relation of mutually recognising consciousnesses can ultimately only be fulfilled by the State, where the relation is sublated; consciousness can realise itself as for-itself recognising the others under the laws and institutions of the State.

This was adapted by Sartre as the consciousness encountering another consciousness, and therefore never being merely for-itself, but always also for-the-other. But for Sartre, as we saw (section 1.4), there can be no reconciliation between the two positions: for-oneself is never for-the-other. In the eyes of the other, I am no longer for-myself.

For Levinas, the preposition "for" in the "for-the-other" is transformed. "For" means now not only "defined by", "posed by"; first and foremost the "for" means "for the benefit of". Thus, being-for-the-other no longer merely means that I am heteronomously defined. It means that I am, as a subject, corporeally and teleologically, for the other. For Levinas, this means that the identity of the self proceeds in being for the other, in responding to the other's needs. This is also described by Levinas in terms of being seized by the Good; it is a determination "overflowing choice" (HAH 85; CPP 135). For "[t]o be dominated by the good is

[175] This is laid out in *Wissenschaft der Logik*, Band 1, Ch.2Ba: "Etwas und ein Anderes".

not to choose the Good out of a neutrality before the axiological bipolarity" (Ibid). Being condemned to freedom in this sense means that freedom is never valueless, that nothing is arbitrary. On the contrary, "[e]verything is grave" (HAH 87; CPP 136), writes Levinas. If the subject, as the existentialists say, is defined by a fundamental anxiety, it is not over my mortality or over the meaninglessness of the world. My responsibility for the others, my anxiety over the mortality of the others, means that the world is already meaningful. At this juncture a particular point bears repeating: Levinas does not intend the subject's responsibility to the other to be cast in terms of an ontological altruism, a statement of the original goodness of the subject. His purpose is to show how, in its very movement, philosophy must presuppose a concern for the other. The concern may of course be non-existent, but it must be presupposed as a possibility in order for there to be any sense to the statements of philosophy.

Levinas names the relation to the other an-archic since it is anterior to the autarchic subject, the subject understood as being its own principle. On the one hand (and unlike in earlier texts), he advises against calling this an-archic relation religious, for fear of creating a new theology.[176] But on the other hand, one cannot gloss over the fact that the name of the value, which directs the subject is God. As we saw already in his early text on Maimonides, Levinas does not use the word God to name the first principle, or the supreme being. On the contrary, "God" signals the "an-archic", the sense in which there is no ultimate beginning or principle. Since God as the Good is before choice, the Good is without an antivalue. Evil is not an equal to the Good, but appears in the tension between an inescapable egoism, "being persevering in being", and one's "responsibility, despite itself, for the refusal of responsibilities" (HAH 89; CPP 137). To find the good in the human subject as reason discovering itself (Husserl) or freedom choosing itself (existentialism) is thus a dangerous misconception of subjectivity. The universalism growing outing of such a view could easily become an imperialism. Agreeing with the worries of his contemporaries, Levinas writes: "Modern antihumanism is no doubt right when it does not find in man understood as the individual of a genus or of an ontological region, an individual persevering in being like all substances, a privilege that would make of him the goal of reality." (HAH 89-90; CPP 138).

The question is whether Levinas is not fashioning for himself a caricature of his philosophical opponents as promoting an unethical philosophy. Does he not risk confusing universal human faculties which are to be deployed for the uni-

[176] Levinas's demarcations towards the religious sphere can seem half-hearted, and sometimes inconsistent, at least in its terminology. In "Is Ontology Fundamental?", he wanted to call the relation to the other religious, "without uttering the word God or the word sacred (*sacré*)" (EN 19; ENO 7-8). What he consistently rejects, at least as descriptions of his own project, are the terms theology and mysticism, denoting modes of thinking based on the knowledge or the experience of the divine, respectively.

versal human good with the egoism of a subject demanding the Good for herself? As the text stands, one could easily dismiss Levinas for simply confusing the singular with the universal. Is it really egoistic to aspire to the rational? It would be quite untenable to uphold such a claim. What can be said instead is that rationality is always situated. The problem thus appears when one claims a strict identity between what one holds to be rational with the Good. From the viewpoint of the philosopher, the problem comes to light when reason appears for itself (in Husserl's words)

> as rational, knowing that it is rational in wanting to be rational, that this implies an infinity of living and striving towards reason. Reason means exactly that which Man *qua* Man wants in his innermost self. For it is that alone, which can satisfy him, bring him bliss. (Hu VI, §73, p. 275, my translation).[177]

For Husserl, rationality has become closely linked to both the aim and desire to be rational. This is what, starting from Husserlian premises, constitutes the essence, the very humanity, the salvation of Man.[178] From a Levinasian viewpoint, however, the circle is broken. The humanity of Man cannot be defined by the rationality of the subject, referring back to itself as rationality. In order to receive its meaning, it must refer to the Good as for-the-other. To describe the subject as self-discovering rationality is not only insufficient, but carries, as we saw, the danger of committing the violence of suppressing the preceding (and the defining) relation to the other.

Levinas thus agrees with the antihumanist deconstruction of the human subject, but not with its eradication. The last sentence of the essay spells out his opposition: "Modern anti-humanism is perhaps not right in not finding in man, lost in history and in order, the trace of this pre-historical and an-archical saying." (HAH 91; CPP 139). The saying (which will gain its full perspicacity in the following section) refers to the responsibility for the other, a responsibility which is pre-historic and an-archic in the sense that the ego, responsible for the world as a whole, cannot relate back to anything in history which put it in this situation, nor to a principle of consciousness. The responsibility does not date from any historical event or internal principle of the ego; it can be reduced neither to the animal nor to rationality. It is, Levinas states, "prior to Being and beings, not saying itself in ontological categories" (Ibid). "Not saying itself" as an ontological category is presumably not the same as not *being* an ontological category. I interpret this as a category that in itself does not carry its full meaning as an ontological category, but as ethical, in its saying. The key for Levinas is "to find a

---

[177] "als vernünftig verstehende, verstehend, daß sie vernünftig ist im vernünftigseinwollen, daß dies eine Unendlichkeit des Lebens und Strebens auf Vernunft hin bedeutet daß Vernunft gerade daß besagt, worauf der Mensch als Mensch in seinem Innersten hinaus will, was ihn allein befriedigen, „selig" machen kann".
[178] This will treated more extensively in section 2.5.

meaning in the human without measuring it by ontology" (HAH 90; CPP 138). This recalls the ending of the preface, where Levinas found the identity of the subject in the voice saying "I". How are we to understand this identity? Or can it be identified?

"Without Identity", the third and final text of *Humanism of the Other*, also takes up a position in the widespread announcements of the end of humanism. This time Levinas has one eye on a certain common ground between Heidegger and contemporary human sciences[179]. Both Heidegger and the human sciences doubt the agency and the "interiority" of the human subject.

For the human sciences, says Levinas, it is from the beginning a question of method. In order to study in a scientific manner, the object of study must per definition be able to be viewed in an objective manner, from the outside. And the facts thus viewed must be formalised so that they can be manipulated with logical operators. This methodological principle then grows into an ontology: "The whole of the human is outside" (HAH 97; CPP 142), say the human sciences. The common denominator of these theories is their propensity to explain away human agency, be it through logico-mathematical (positivism), psychical (psychoanalysis) or economic (Marxism) structures.

Where the structuralists dispel the subject with logical formalism, Heidegger does so by equating man with the welcoming of Being. Human Being as a receptacle for Being, as messenger of Being, is always on the receiving end, and that which it receives stands out in the open. The view of a free ego, with a free will, and the power to freely reflect upon itself is contested. The subjectivity that Levinas wants to defend, however, is as we have seen not that of the ego reflecting upon itself in confinement or the ego as the source of activity.

Levinas can therefore endorse Heidegger's critique of the Cartesian subject. But he senses a new ominous role for man in Heideggerian philosophy. Alluding to Heidegger's rhetoric of the 1930s, he writes: "*Being requires man as a native land or a ground requires its autochthon*. The foreignness of man in the world, his stateless condition, is taken to attest to the last spasms of metaphysics and to the humanism it sustains" (HAH 100; CPP 144).[180] Man receives an external purpose as the "messenger and poet" of Being (HAH 101; CPP 144).

So how does Levinas formulate his alternative to Heidegger? Rather than seeing alienation as a sign of a time out of joint, of a subjectivism caused by a

[179] "Sciences humaines" is by Nidra Poller in *Humanism of the Other* (HO) translated as "social sciences" which normally would not be wrong. But considering the topic that Levinas is treating, the notion of the human, a more literal translation is more suitable—keeping in mind that the French term has a somewhat different connotation: it is for example never the project of Dilthey and his modern disciples, to formulate a *Geisteswissenschaft* at par with a *Naturwissenschaft*, which Levinas is targeting here, but typically the work of Lévi-Strauss and his criticism of Sartre.

[180] Cf. our reading of the "Letter on 'Humanism'" in section 1.5 which affirms Levinas's interpretation.

forgetfulness of being, as an indication that one must seek a nearness to Being, Levinas sees it as integral for the constitution of the subject. The other has slipped into the subject already before the beginning of the subject. He writes, using Rimbaud's famous dictum, the "'I' is an other". The problem with the notion of the subject, which was rejected as a philosophical concept by Levinas's contemporaries, was that it was thought exclusively in terms of the act. As in the preface, and in "Humanism and an-archy", Levinas claims that this is not the whole story of the subject:

> Everything human is outside, say the sciences of man. It is all outside, or everything in me is open. Is it certain that in this exposedness to all winds subjectivity is lost among the things or in matter? Does not subjectivity signify precisely by its incapacity to shut itself up from inside? (HAH 103; CPP 145, translation altered).

Levinas claims that the subject is qualified by openness, a definition which aligns itself with a whole array of philosophical tropes. In order to describe what he means by this, he differentiates it first from Kant, who said that every object is opened to all other objects.[181] Secondly, he differentiates it to Heidegger, for whom openness signifies Dasein's ecstasy in being, the clearing which is the name for Being's consciousness of itself. Levinas sees Heidegger's position as related to naturalism, for which consciousness is an "avatar" of nature. But in the third sense, which he suggests, openness can mean a "denuding of the skin exposed to wound and outrage, [...] suffering for the suffering of the other" (HAH 104; CPP 146). This notion of openness he names vulnerability. One should note here that the notion of suffering is related to that of passivity. The understanding of the subject as passivity was prepared by Heidegger and before him Husserl. Passivity was already in Husserl or Heidegger, of course not understood in the mere sense of not being active, in the way things merely are. What Levinas adds is that the passivity that makes out the subject is suffering, *pathein*. I suffer the suffering of the other, I am vulnerable to it. "Every love or every hatred of a neighbour as a reflected attitude presupposes this prior vulnerability" (HAH 105; CPP 146). Being vulnerable means already being outside of oneself, without identity in which one can rest, already being for the other. "The humanity of man, subjectivity, is a responsibility for others, an extreme vulnerability" (HAH 109; CPP 149). To suffer for and by the other is to care for and "bear" the other. For this relation, Levinas evokes a Hebrew word for compassion—*rakhamin*, which has a reference to the uterus, and to maternity. In the most extreme relation of exposition to the other a mother bears a child within herself; she cares and suffers for the other within herself and in spite of herself. Levinas is advanc-

[181] This refers to the third analogy of experience in Kant's first critique (A211-218), according to which all contemporaneous substances are in constant interaction.

ing a philosophical claim, according to which my subjectivity is to be conceived from this moral suffering, as a being-for-the-other.

By understanding the identity of the subject as being-for-the other in the form of a vulnerability to the suffering of the other, he is transforming the Hegelian concept which had also been used by Sartre. For them, this also meant that the subject received its identity from outside. But whereas in the case of Hegel this meant that the subject comes to consciousness through the encounter with others, and for Sartre this meant that the subject received its identity in the gaze of the other, for Levinas it takes on a different significance: subjectivity receives its meaning in its vulnerability to others.

The relation to the other, which comes to define the subject, is also named responsibility. Man "is stitched by responsibilities" (Ibid). Levinas dislocates the notion of responsibility from the discourse on the autonomous subject, and makes it the centre of his own definition of the subject as vulnerability. Responsibility is thus no longer understood as the ability to respond, but as the inability not to respond. My obligation to respond is lived as the exposedness to the suffering of the other. In this sense, responsibility is vulnerability.

This openness to otherness, which is the very stitching of the human subject, cannot be reduced to causality; I am not made vulnerable by the other, but I am already this vulnerability. It is not the case of a free ego being affected by an external causality, but of a subject whose freedom is already formed by the passivity of the self. This is a distinctly altered picture compared to both *Totality and Infinity* and *Time and the Other*, where the subjectivity was first constituted in a sphere of free enjoyment, a sphere which was then to be broken by the other. Therein we read how the other interrupts an already constituted subject in its enjoyment of the world. Hereafter the very subjectivity of the subject is its vulnerability for the other. But is vulnerability a new transcendental concept? Although Levinas does not use this expression, with its heavy philosophical baggage, one could nonetheless ask nonetheless if vulnerability is not transcendental in the sense of being the condition of possibility for all relations to the other. This will be discussed further in section 2.3.

Vulnerability is sincerity—intellectual sincerity also depends on exposing oneself, being exposed, finding oneself defenceless before the other, the subject communicating before the truth and the information that it can communicate. Herein lies the hope for philosophy, for critique. The beginning of philosophy (not *arche* as foundation) is an-archic; it derives from vulnerability, it is a saying to the other. Levinas also refers to this as "youth", a term he never defines, but which stands for the possibility of beginning anew, or, in the terms already established in our investigation, the transient transcendence of an economy.[182]

[182] In the end of Totality and Infinity, a similar movement is performed by the concept of fecundity, allowing a passage beyond presence and beyond possibility understood from the activity of the subject. Fecundity, just as youth, leads the way to a transcendence beyond pres-

Levinas says that philosophy loves this youth. He gives examples like "the One without being" of Plato's Parmenides, "the Kantian unity of the 'I think', before its reduction to a logical form that Hegel would bring to the concept", "Husserl's pure Ego, transcendent in immanence", "the Nietzschean man shaking the world's being in the passage to the superman" (HAH 106; CPP 147). All these are examples of existents before their specific determination in existence. "Youth is authenticity", he declares. In articulating "youth" with "authenticity", it appears that Levinas is reintroducing the sovereign subject, untouched by being, back into his philosophy. But this is only the case, prima facie. Levinas is precisely trying to disconnect the notion of the subject from that of sovereignty. Instead, the purity of youth is to be found in the passivity of the subject in its relation to the other. Accordingly, Levinas sees the role of the philosopher as returning "to language to convey, even if in betraying them, the pure and unsayable" (HAH 106; CPP 148; translation altered).[183]

This now leaves us in a position to describe more specifically the function of the notion of youth, as it comes to be deployed in Levinas's essay, "Without Identity". First I think it right to see the introduction of this term as serving to qualify what in the end of Part I had been discussed as a transcendence of the economy of violence. As we saw there, this transcendence can never be exempt from begetting a new violence—it is a transcendence which cannot be assured a permanence. In the terms just introduced by Levinas, youth must become aged, the skin wrinkled. This finds a parallel in the fate of the word human as a rhetorical trope. In the beginning of the essay, Levinas quotes Maurice Blanchot: "To nobly say the human in man, to think the humanity in man, is to quickly arrive at a discourse that is untenable and, how can it be denied, more

ence which is not a permanent transcendence (the latter can in fact be nothing other than prolonged immanence). In fecundity, this passage beyond presence goes hither and beyond the ethical, leading through concepts as filiality and parenthood to the concept of the family, also transposed to a monotheist view of the whole of humanity as brothers under God our Father. Levinas in Totality and Infinity feels that he needs this in order to secure that the ethical is not only becomes a disappearing moment in the subject, but gains a prolongation in time, through the view of humanity as a family stretching out over time. The danger with such a view, apart from Levinas's unflinching adoption of the paternalist diction of the Bible, and his disregard for non-monotheist culture, is that it threatens to re-establish the permanence of presence and the cult of activity which it sought to overcome. No longer is it the will of the subject, but it is a hidden will of monotheist culture re-establishing itself over time. With the notion of youth, Levinas attempts not to open a concept which is before and beyond the ethical, and does not allude to the passage of generations of the sons of Abraham.

[183] Couching the philosophical task in this manner, Levinas cannot avoid but returning to the difficult question of access; namely how can the philosopher access the pure and the unspeakable? The pure and unspeakable, which for Levinas is to be accessed, is of course for Levinas the relation to the other. It is true that we can be guided by his qualification of the relation to the other in "Is Ontology Fundamental?" as speech, as communication. It is only in *Otherwise than Being*, however, that Levinas, through the categories of the Saying and the Said, will be in a better position to offer a systematic treatment of this possibility. For the time being we must settle for anticipating the logical moves that Levinas will need to make, but leave the mechanisms by which this solution comes to light in abeyance.

repugnant than all the nihilist vulgarities" (HAH 96; CPP 142). It is as if not only the humanist transcendental subjectivism, but also the humanist rhetoric is self-defeating, divesting itself of its value whenever it is used. Later, Levinas quotes Blanchot again:

> "It may be", Blanchot also wrote, "that, as one is pleased to declare, man is passing. Man is passing, has even always already passed, in the measure that he has always been appropriated to his own disappearance... This then is not a reason to repudiate humanism, as long as it is recognized in the least deceptive mode, never in the zones of inwardness, power and law, order, culture and heroic magnificence..." (HAH 110; CPP 149-150).

Levinas interprets Blanchot as (in the first quotation) capturing the notion of the human from the perspective of age, but (in the second quote) still being open to the youth of the concept in its very decay, in its "passing" (passivity). Here Levinas seems open to the possibility of a non-deceptive philosophy of the human, one that does not merely become a vehicle for ideology. But why is this not just another ideology? What distinguishes his "humanism of the other man" from an ideology? Levinas seems to anticipate the critical question, when he writes: "It is not something constructed only in philosophy; it is the unreal reality of men persecuted in the daily history of the world, whose dignity and meaning metaphysics has never realized, from which philosophers turn their faces" (HAH 110; CPP 150). But the fact of being persecuted can surely be no guarantee that one will act responsibly—in reality, the opposite is most often the case. This could only make sense if Levinas is speaking on a transcendental level, in the sense that he is saying that this is a responsibility in spite of persecution. Still, Levinas is vague on this point. One could read it as a reference to the suffering of the Jewish people such that he takes the message of infinite responsibility in spite of all suffering, from Judaism. But in what way would this liberate this humanism of the other man from being a "philosopher's construction", an ideology? Would the history and memory of suffering be the condition for becoming a responsible subject, a precondition for the becoming of the human?[184] If the realisation of this responsibility becomes dependent on the suffering of a particular culture or movement, then how can it at the same time be a claim on how the philosophical subject is realised? If we choose to read Levinas as merely giving an example of how subjectivity implies responsibility *despite* persecution, we will have available a more consistent reading, and one which also fits better with his description of responsibility in *Otherwise than Being*. In the final argument of this book, Levinas returns to the critique of humanism, showing how that critique performs a similar operation to what he is proposing in the form of a new understanding of subjectivity. The "Nietzschean word" of antihumanism

[184] Robert Bernasconi reads it this way in "Strangers and Slaves in the land of Egypt: Levinas and the Politics of Otherness", *Levinas and Justice: Commentaries on Levinas and Politics*, eds. Asher Horowitz and Gad Horowitz, University of Toronto Press, 2006.

cuts through both the humanist contexts and sedimentations, which serve to obfuscate the responsibility of the other. Levinas reasons not so much in opposition to the critique of humanism (as practiced by Foucault, Althusser and Lévi-Strauss (cf. above, section 1.8)) but rather lays out its preconditions: no matter how formal and disenchanting these approaches to the human of the human science are, they are also evidence of the inescapable importance of the human, "that man has not ceased to count for man" (HAH 113; CPP 151).

In "this Nietzschean word" he finds what he earlier labels "youth", and now equates with authenticity in the heart of antihumanism. In the movement of 1968, "in the fulguration of some privileged moments, quickly extinguished by a language as conformist and garrulous as that it was to replace" (Ibid), Levinas finds an illustration of this youth as authenticity. If by youth one is only emphasising a transitory state, a passing away, one could be forgiven for thinking Levinas's reflections as erring on the side of pessimism. But this is not what he intends. Rather Levinas uses youth as a way of framing the very promise of critique, of philosophy. And this is where one can, as he says "surprise" the subject—capture it in its moment of transcendence.

The essay ends with what can be seen as an allusion to "Reflections on the philosophy of Hitlerism", written forty years earlier:

> Able to find responsibilities again under the thick stratums of literature that undo them (one can no longer say "if youth only knew"), youth ceased to be the age of transition and passage ('youth must pass') and is shown to be man's humanity. (Ibid).

"Man's humanity", *l'humanité de l'homme*: these words draw to a close both "Without Identity" and *Humanism and the Other* as a whole. Thereby Levinas repeats the ending phrase of "Reflections on the Philosophy of Hitlerism" (treated in section 1.2), published forty years earlier. On that occasion Levinas announced the question of "the humanity of man" as what is at stake in the conflict between Western civilisation and Hitlerism. In both texts Levinas is steering a path between a Scylla and Charybdis. In his early essay on Hitlerism he presents it as a choice between an aging Western civilisation that formulated its ideals too abstractly and a "Hitlerism" abandoning all ideals of transcendence, emphasising force and ethnic belonging over universal ideas of the human. In that text both his antipathies and his sympathies were clear, but he never provided the foundation for the notion of the human he felt that Western thought had failed to buttress. In "Without Identity", the relation between the humanist and antihumanist philosophy is much more complex. It seems it is mainly through the antihumanist critique that one should approach Levinas's notion of the human. In the end, he has managed to smuggle the antihumanist critique into the core of the humanist conceptuality, that of the human subject: the subject *is* this "Nietzschean word", this youth.

In the final refrain of this essay it seems that he answers the question carried over from his early text by positing humanity as youth. Nevertheless, critical questions remain. Does not subjectivity as youth signify a repetition of the subject as beginning in the present? How else are we to understand what he says about the authenticity and "fulguration of certain privileged moments of 1968" (Ibid)? It would be wrong to see him claiming the foundation for which humanist thought has searched in vain. Youth is not necessarily understood as a beginning in oneself, in consciousness. These fulgurant moments are born not in consciousness, but in the exposedness and responsibility towards the other.

The notion of youth opposes itself to foundation. He chooses the term youth because of its air of promise; when Levinas says that youth "stopped being the age of transition of passage", it is because it cannot be reduced to being a passage. It is also a way out. Levinas was impressed by his contemporary, Jeanne Delhomme, who described the modality of philosophical thought as "without continuity in itself, without continuation of itself" (HAH 106; CPP 147). A philosophical comparison which Levinas himself would perhaps be less likely to favour is the connection of youth with the Heideggerian notion of *Anfang*, beginning, often translated as "inception": *Anfang*, *Anfänglichkeit*. This term by no means captures something as "early in history", as "already the Greeks". When he returns to the Greeks, it is because he holds that they were able to think in a more "inceptual" way, more in touch with the concepts they used. Furthermore, *Anfang* does not denote an ever-existing principle, but the possibility of possibilities, of thinking how something can begin. Analogously to the way Levinas thought that the notion of the human must be thought from the notion of youth, Heidegger would find the notion of the human in its *Anfänglichkeit*, inceptually.

In the *Letter of Humanism*, already discussed above, Heidegger contemplates Heraclitus's "*êthos anthrôpôi daimôn*", translating this as "the (familiar) abode for humans is the open region for the presencing of the god (the unfamiliar one" (WM 356; PM 271). This for Heidegger becomes a possibility to experimentally rename his philosophy as an original ethics:

> If the name 'ethics', in keeping with the basic meaning of the word *ethos* should now say that 'ethics' ponders the abode of the human being, then that thinking which thinks the truth of Being as the inceptual [*anfängliche*] element of man, as the one who ek-sists, is in itself already the original ethics (Ibid; translation altered).

But just as Heidegger does not want to call his thinking a humanism, and no longer wants to call it a fundamental ontology, his thinking cannot be regarded as an ethics either; such a term will always be thought as operating within the metaphysical tradition, not open for the *êthos* in its inceptuality. To think man in his inceptuality is for Heidegger to think him as "existing in the truth of being".[185]

Heidegger's thought of philosophy as original ethics in the "Letter on 'humanism'" really sets the projects of Levinas and Heidegger up against one another. When Heidegger said that his philosophy can be understood as an original ethics he does it with some hesitancy, feeling that this notion will be misunderstood just as his notion of fundamental ontology was misconstrued—misinterpreted as the most fundamental ontology rather than the fundamental *questioning* of ontology. It is of course the risk of all notions constructed in order to create new byways for thinking that they might be read along old well-trammelled paths. Heidegger was aware of this, continually reinventing his concepts, for the sake of the movement of thinking itself. "The thinking that tries to advance thought into the truth of being brings only a small part of that wholly other dimension to language" (WM 357; PM 271). From this point of view, for the sake of thinking, it is better to forsake terms such as ethics, ontology or humanism, for fear of being misunderstood. Otherwise the readers will understand these notions "imagined through terms maintained in their usual signification" (Ibid).

Now in this extreme vicinity of questions—of "an originary ethics", of an understanding of "youth" or "inceptuality"—we can begin to discern the distinct difference between Levinas and Heidegger. For Heidegger, the largest concern is for thinking not to become untrue to itself in its penetration of the "wholly other dimension" (Ibid) that it seeks to articulate (*zur Sprache bringen*). Levinas's concern regarding the subject's communication of philosophical thoughts, is not first and foremost how thought is to be true to itself in its discoveries. In relation to this, truth, even understood as revealing, is not the central concept. Rather, for Levinas, it is secondary to critique, founded in the one-for-the-other. Of course, for Heidegger also, thinking is a practice that cares for the openness for something other, for "a wholly other dimension" (above). But this otherness is conceived in terms of divinity: "presencing of the god (the unfamiliar one)" (WM 356; PM 271), and in explicit contrast to the ethical in any other way than the opening for the daimonic, the immense, the divine. Levinas, by contrast, claims that any relation to God can only be made meaningful in terms of the ethical in the sense of the secular concern for other human beings. For him, the

[185] "The truth of being", must be understood from Heidegger's critique of the philosophical concepts of truth from Plato to Nietzsche, for whom truth according to Heidegger is conceived as correspondence. The correspondence theory of truth is not per se wrong, but is limited to the viewpoint of the subject as distanced from the world, as not being in the world. It conceals the more originary (inceptual) being-in-the-world as the discovery of being. Truth as correspondence is derivative from truth as *alêtheia*, which always already occurs. The mistake of taking truth as correspondence as originary is for Heidegger possible only because man ex-ists in the world, as both distant from and in the world and himself. Man can therefore see himself and the world as two spheres the correspondence of which one can compare.

scene to which one has always to return is an interhuman concern, which must always pass through communication. This is not because this encounter between me and the other is more truthful—such that it depicts the original goodness or altruism of the subject. As I understand it, philosophy must return to this scene, because it is the scene of philosophical justification. It is for others that I must give account of my philosophical thoughts. This does not mean that philosophy is nothing but this. But to the extent that philosophy justifies itself, it does mean that this justification is a *social* event. The result of this priority is not to privilege the spoken over the written word, as Derrida accuses Levinas of doing in *Totality and Infinity* (ED 151; WD 127). Rather, the written word, the 'text', is no less a social phenomenon. In this respect the scene of the social is fundamental for all language.

This social setting is retrievable of course not only from the early Heidegger. It is a scene that, since the dialogues of Plato, has been a typical way for philosophy to understand itself, the "natural" medium by which philosophy communicates. What Levinas adds to this conception is his particular understanding of the responsibility and vulnerability of the philosophical communication to the other.

As we have already seen, Levinas is often seen as an antiphilosopher, preferring prophetism over philosophy. This accusation is sometimes delivered in a tone of respect. Badiou writes about the "intimate movement" of Levinas's thought, its "subjective rigour", which holds itself outside of philosophy. We already quoted him in the introduction: "In truth Lévinas has no philosophy—not even philosophy as the 'servant' of theology. Rather this is philosophy [...] annulled by theology, itself no longer a theology".[186] Recall also Derrida (section 1.10, infra) who claims that Levinas's questioning of the reversibility of the I-you-relation cannot be performed within philosophy, but only in an extra-philosophical "unheard of graphics" (ED 163; WD 138), and Marion, who finds that Levinas's criticism of Heidegger's privileging of Being over beings has a certain sense outside philosophy, in a "language of the prophets".[187] There is a certain truth to these descriptions, in the following sense: Levinas is not satisfied to operate within any pre-given rules of philosophy, but asks how philosophy can justify itself. But rather than being extra- or antiphilosophical, one can say that his contemplations are, to the extent that they go "beyond" philosophy, metaphilosophical. And arguably, philosophy has always been this; it must radically question itself in order to remain philosophy.

In fact, Levinas trusts the philosophical concepts and our capacity to read them more than Heidegger does. Heidegger's move is always to distance himself from the traditional terms of philosophy, soon also displacing the concept of philosophy, letting the word thinking denote his own philosophizing (cf. WM

[186] Badiou, *Ethics*, Verso, 2001, p. 22-23.
[187] Marion, *L'idole et la distance*, B. Grasset, 1977, p. 278.

364; PM 276). Levinas's strategy is instead to show how fundamental concepts of philosophy (e.g. "ethics", "the subject", "the good", "the human") already point toward the relation of one-for-the-other, which is the prime concern (*die Sache, to pragma*) of his philosophy.

This digression has been taken as an attempt to find a resonance for the term "youth" in the work of Heidegger. Let us now immanently found the term in our interpretation of Levinas. If we use our discussion of an economy of violence, developed in Part 1, so as to frame our present preoccupation with the idea of youth, as discussed in "Without Identity", we can make the following articulation: youth is the violent exit from an economy of violence, which, on the one hand, is passing, transient—in the sense that it will be re-inscribed within an economy of violence—but, on the other, cannot be reduced to this transience, to this non-permanence in being. This allows us ultimately to see how Levinas's notion of the human is a revolt against the temporal hierarchy which devalues youth as ephemeral, a deliberate provocation aimed at those voices, which, with an air of condescension, utter "youth must pass" (HAH 113; CPP 151).

The untimeliness or in-actuality of the Levinasian considerations mentioned at the beginning of this section, is a reflexive notion. It refers not only to the temporal modus of the subject as the content of his philosophy; in-actuality is the very temporality of the critique revealing this content.

But does not this interpretation then lead us back to a self-complacent humanism? Concomitantly, will not Levinas's philosophy merely lead back to revealing and then justifying its own mode of philosophising? Perhaps—if his inquiry were to stop at this point. However, this is not where he ends: "Not to philosophise is already to philosophise", sometimes Levinas paraphrases Aristotle in order to refute him vehemently. This is a significant twist. For where Plato, Aristotle, Husserl and Heidegger in different respects spoke of philosophy (or "thinking") as a care for the self in that it more elaborately repeats the movement that is always already there in the self, Levinas wants to break with what he regards as a self-complacency. By way of reference to the Nietzschean word, he finds an unexpected ally outside of the phenomenological tradition. For Nietzsche, as well as for Levinas, philosophy is critique, a critique that is ultimately not for the sake of philosophising ego, but for something other. Nietzsche names this other "life"; for Levinas, this critique points towards a concern for the neighbour.

We have now reached a stage where this particular section of our investigation can be brought to a close, and accordingly, where we can recapitulate the central moves that are accomplished in the essays "Humanism and Anarchy" and "Without Identity", as well as the prefatory note that accompanies them. First, in these short texts, Levinas has taken a big step towards understanding the human subject, not from experience and presence, but from the relation to the other as saying. This relation is defined in various ways, and by way of different statements. These statements must however be seen as having a significance beyond themselves; they serve as reflections also on the very means by which such statements are communicated. This is the movement that Levinas will call unsaying, by which he seeks to capture the reduction from the said to saying.

As we have now gathered from *Humanism of the Other*, we can read Levinas as claiming the following: antihumanism did not negate the human subject but unsaid it, opening the ground thereby for it to be resaid. "The Nietzschean word" is youth, and in an exemplary manner performs subjectivity, which Levinas will articulate with the human. The philosophical critique must, in order to live up to the standard of the Nietzschean word, perform the saying of subjectivity. This is a move acted out by Levinas through the conceptual couplet of unsaying and resaying. Unsaying stands for the discontinuity, how the saying must always betray the said. Resaying, obversely, stands for the insistence on a notion's revitalisation in communication. Unsaying and resaying are two aspects of philosophical communication rather than two different processes, aspects that both oppose and presuppose one another. Resaying can only take place if the concept is unsaid also, otherwise the aspect of self-critique would be lost. Unsaying can however only take place for the benefit of renewed concepts to be communicated, concepts to be resaid. The notion of resaying positively emphasises that the said, the concept, must be understood as a gift from the saying. This in contrast to the notion of unsaying, which, in its negativity, emphasises that the said entails a loss of the element of saying.

The philosophical resaying and unsaying occurs in several ways throughout Levinas's work. In the texts from the time of *Totality and Infinity* it is often described on an experiential level. This situates the relation between the resaying and unsaying dialectically, according to which the relation to the other finds its gravity in experience, only for this experience to be negated as experience. In *Humanism of the Other*, it is clear that both the saying and unsaying occur on a conceptual level, dislocating philosophical concepts or notions, and tying them to a sphere of responsibility and vulnerability, and to the very discourse of saying. This will be developed further in our reading of Levinas's second major work, *Otherwise than Being*, presented in the next section.

2.2
Resaying Subjectivity
(Otherwise than Being)

In the preliminary note to *Otherwise than Being*, Levinas sets out his intentions clearly, declaring it to be a work on subjectivity. Building on his discussion in *Humanism of the Other*, he is now ready to formulate a radical transformation of the tradition's understanding of subjectivity. The aim of the book is, he writes,

> to catch sight, in the substantiality of the subject, in the hard core of the "unique" in me, in my unparalleled identity, of a substitution for the other; to conceive of this abnegation prior to the will as a merciless exposure to the trauma of transcendence by way of a susception more, and differently, passive than receptivity, passion and finitude (OB xlvii-xlviii).

"More passive than receptivity", he writes. Indeed, sometimes he even says "more passive than passivity". Levinas insists on these hyperbolic formulations. Statements such as these operate on two levels. First, they awaken the imagination of the reader (starting from more or less known concepts, such as receptivity, passion and finitude) but at the same time by speaking in the comparative ("more x than y", or even "more x than x") they force the imagination to yield. This way of forcing and frustrating the imagination is consistent throughout the work. Another peculiarity of Levinas's writing at this stage is the horizontal arrangement of his concepts. This is to say, rather than building a traditional philosophical structure where one concept is shown to be logically anterior to another, Levinas's concepts arrive, so to speak, alongside each other. Even if the joining copula is avoided, these concepts appear to be associated with each other, often seeming to be synonymous with one another. Separate key concepts such as "subjectivity", "one-for-the-other", "proximity", "sensibility", "hostage", "persecution" are used for fragmented sketches of what appears to be the same subject matter. Here also, Levinas forces the imagination to join together these images of alterity, yet does not provide the synthesis that the sketches hint at. Both these traits of his writing point towards an abstraction, towards a beyond, which can find adequation neither in a thematic description, nor in an attitude of the subject.

The human as the one-for-the-other is now Levinas's expression for the possibility of interrupting—he could probably no longer say: escaping—what

Derrida calls the economy of violence. But even in his earlier texts, where he explained transcendence in terms of an escape, Levinas would always insist that in its transcendence the subject retains a foothold in being. The later position therefore is not so much a rejection of this goal of transcendence, but a more rigorous interrogation of the condition under which it appears.

In *Otherwise than Being* this transcendence is produced as a structure in the subject. Even if Levinas is critical towards the traditional view of subjectivity, couched in terms of autonomy and autarchy, his work is nonetheless a defence of a philosophy of the human subject. The word "human" is now used almost interchangeably with the formula "one-for-the-other", which is Levinas's preferred way of describing the subject as the relation to the other, and not only a term in this relation. Here "the human" does not denote a certain experience in time; rather it signifies the very constitution of the subject as the one-for-the-other of responsibility.

Levinas shows that previous conceptions of the subject—as consciousness of being, as life force, as expression of will to power, as engagement—presuppose another understanding of the subject. To criticise the notion of subjectivity as theoretical consciousness is of course in no way original. Much of the accomplishment of 20th century philosophy has been to show that what a subject is is inextricably tied to its existence in a culturally and historically determined world; the subject both receives and creates the world that it lives in and interprets. As we have seen, Levinas has from the start acknowledged and affirmed this understanding of the subject; but for him, even the understanding of subjectivity as being and acting in a world presupposes a more radical understanding of subjectivity. For him, being a subject means to be vulnerable to the wounds of the other, a definition which always also implies the responsibility for the other. Central to Levinas's understanding of subjectivity is responsibility thought precisely as vulnerability to the other, a thought that can also be reversed: the vulnerability for the other as responsibility. Here, the notion of vulnerability is coupled with the notion of passivity. Repeatedly, Levinas speaks of a "passivity more passive than passivity" (e.g. AE 31, 85, 116, 277; OB 15, 50, 72, 180). This allusive hyperbolic claim can, for sure, be read in many different ways. However, I would like to emphasise two functions:

Firstly, it is a question of isolating a passivity that precedes the dichotomies of both activity and passivity and of freedom and non-freedom. This means it is neither a matter of a subject, by its own will, choosing to be responsible, nor is it a matter of some God or other forcing the subject to be responsible. Rather, as a subject it is an-archically, or to use a Heideggerian formula (that often seems to shape much of Levinas's thought) it is always already responsible. Understood this way, this passivity must be a passivity other than that of pure matter, since this meaning lies precisely in an inability to escape one's own responsibility towards the other (AE 277; OB 180).

Secondly, this formula emphasises the sense of excess characteristic of many of Levinas's descriptions of the subject. The subject cannot be a match for the demand responsibility entails. One's responsibility cannot be met once and for all, in the sense of a deed done, a mission accomplished; responsibility is infinite. The reason for this is not that there is so much that I can do for the other, nor that there are so many others before whom I am responsible. The responsibility is not infinite in the sense that it is immense; neither does it find adequation in the humility of the subject (AE 25; OB 11).[188] Rather, responsibility is infinite in the sense that it cannot reach a limit. This means that the more I meet the demand, the more I will sense it. The shouldering of responsibility does not finish it off but awakens it all the more strongly. Moreover, responsibility does not aim towards my salvation, or even my satisfaction; it is not the case that the responsible life is necessarily a more fulfilled life. Levinas is aiming for a level of responsibility for the other in which the other concerns me whether I want it or not. It is a "desire of the undesirable", an "obsession"; the subject is the other's "hostage". This does not mean that self-abnegation is a measure for the goodness of an act either, but rather that Levinas is interested in this very possibility of going against oneself; this is the movement that he chooses to call ethical. The ethical is sometimes described as the journey upstream, as the movement against the conatus, or put otherwise, as an internal rupture of the ego. The trope of subjectivity as rupture is not new to modern philosophy. But whereas Levinas locates the rupture as integral to the subject, philosophical discourse has often thought the rupture as external, that is, as a rupture of the subject with the world.

In the case of the latter, subjectivity is the event without which the existence of the world could never be articulated. Nonetheless, this articulation entails a distancing from that which it articulates. It is not the sensed but the sentient, not the willed, but the will, not the understood, but the understanding. In the early Levinas, the hypostasis of the subject from the *il y a* played this role. In his later work, however, there is yet another rupture implied in subjectivity, a rupture with oneself. For Levinas, a subject is as such always in division.[189] In the core of its identity and unity as self, he writes, the self is torsion, fission, a detachment of oneself from oneself. In this sense, the self is, in its innermost, a departure from its interiority, a break with itself—it is the one penetrated by the other, a vulnerability, a pain without sense or meaning. The subject is *for the other*. This "for the other" does not operate on a superficial level of the subject, reducible to a more fundamental principle. It cannot for example be reduced to intentionality

[188] The mention of humility could be seen as a dig at Heidegger, who sometimes depicted his thinking along the lines of humility—for Levinas the language of humility is but a reversal of the language of power, that thereby doesn't manage to leave this idiom—cf in section 1.5 our discussion of the "unscheinbare Furchen" in the "Letter on 'humanism'".

[189] This point has been advanced most famously by Rodolphe Calin in *L'ex-ception de soi*, P.U.F., 2005.

as a modality of "consciousness of ..." or to commitment (*engagement*), in the ways he understands Husserl and Sartre, respectively. Nor is this break with itself a lack in a subject otherwise autonomous and stable. The subject is always already both term and relation—one-for-the-other. It is defined through this affective responsibility for the other. Levinas describes this by the term accusation, taken in both meanings of the verb *accuser*: the subject is held responsible and the subject is brought forward, its structures made more acute; the subject is acutely brought forward *as* responsible. This is not something that occurs to an empirical ego already in the empirical world, somehow becoming better at opening itself up for the other, and thereby more responsible for the other. All that Levinas gathers in order to think subjectivity coheres around the *sub-jectum*, "supporting the whole of being [...] responsible for everything" (AE 183; OB 116). Subjectivity as the centre of everything is to be re-interpreted not as a principle of foundation, but a principle of responsibility. He writes: "The unity of the universe is not what my gaze embraces in its unity of apperception, but what is incumbent on me from all sides, regards me in the two senses of the term, accuses me, is my affair" (Ibid).

Another defining characteristic of this responsibility is, as we have mentioned already in Part I, its asymmetrical structure. The asymmetry of the intersubjective relation is perhaps the key concept of *Totality and Infinity*, and remains a precondition for the whole discussion in *Otherwise than Being*.

Here, Levinas develops his description of the responsibility for the other one step further. The notion of responsibility is fully understood only if it includes the responsibility for the responsibility of the other. This is a statement of Levinas's so often the cause of provocation, as if he were offering nothing less than a megalomania of the subject, a view of the ethical subject as enveloping all responsibilities of all others. There is no real argumentation for the responsibility for the other's responsibility provided in Levinas's text, but in order to make his position more plausible, let us consider some mundane questions that could seem very far from the concerns of Levinasian discourse: How much responsibility should we give our children? How do we prepare former criminals for a life as responsible citizens? To what extent should we take on a responsibility of care of another when, with the onset of old age, it is adjudged such a person can no longer take care of herself? No matter where one chooses to draw the line in these questions, such examples entail the same restrictive problematic. It is a problem of deciding how much of this responsibility for the other's responsibility it is, in a given situation, right to act upon. These deliberations can only be understood as taking place against the background of a fundamental responsibility for others, including their responsibilities for others and for me. In the cases of finding others incompetent to take responsibility in a given situation, it is *my* responsibility to decide whether to assume responsibility or not.

For Levinas, this responsibility for the other goes even as far as the responsibility of the persecuted for her persecutor. One might speculate on why he decides to emphasise this aspect of responsibility for the other's responsibility. I view this as his response to Derrida, who in "Violence and Metaphysics" claimed *contra* Levinas that the other must also be an alter ego. In earlier writings, this egoity (or subjectivity) of the other is often placed within brackets. The assumption that the other is also a subject with responsibilities might be seen as already making a move outside the original asymmetry of the I before the other. But if Derrida's interpretation in section 1.10 was shown to merely reinsert the ego in the other (as an alter ego), for Derrida this was deemed "less violent" than Levinas's claim appertaining to an originary apprehension of the other without its egoity. The notion of the responsibility for the responsibility of the other is therefore Levinas's way of incorporating Derrida's objection to his own account.

True, the other also has responsibilities for me, and for my responsibility for him or her. This creates a "vortex" of reciprocal responsibilities, seemingly pulling one into the infinite. However, Levinas is clear in stating that this vortex always "stops at me" (AE 186n; OB 196n). Thereby Derrida's assumption of the originality of two symmetric asymmetries (infra section 1.10) is put into question; the symmetry is postponed. For if there is such a symmetry as an "origin" or perhaps as an ethical ideal, it will, whoever I am, be *my* responsibility to uphold this symmetry.

> The notion of responsibility for the responsibility of the other, which is meant to encompass even the responsibility for one's persecutor, is bound to be viewed as provocation. This is most probably due to a persistence in reading Levinas as a moralist, as a thinker laying out a normative ethics. But this is not his intention. His aim is to provide a phenomenology of the ethical, describing how the ethical can take on a meaning for the subject.

This understanding of the subject as responsibility, claims Levinas, is irreducible to ontology (cf. AE 219; OB 140). This dogged rejection of ontology might after Derrida's critique be dismissed as naïve. Is Levinas not merely replacing one ontology with another? But he is not unaware that his descriptions of the subject—defined as responsibility, vulnerability, passivity, and so on—are also ontological. What he claims instead is that the subject is not *first and foremost* an ontological concept. This can be read in two ways. Firstly, to be a subject is not primarily to be ontological, in the sense of being a receptacle for being, to be that which understands being, that for which being is. Secondly, it is a statement about how concepts function; as noted, Levinas uses many terms (e.g. "subjectivity", "humanity", "proximity") as if they were more or less synonymous. But what are synonyms? Different names for that which *is* only in one and the *same* way? This would arouse the suspicion that they describe an underlying substance, a suspicion which however I find to be misleading. According to Levinas, words establish the "this as that" in the already said (AE 62; OB 35). They refer to one another in non-arbitrary ways, and never to an underlying substance.

Levinas's central undertaking is an intervention in the discourse on the human. With auxiliary notions such as proximity, obsession, trauma et cetera, new associations are created around subjectivity that are, as I have said, not arbitrary, even if such associations are unaccustomed for the philosophical tradition. When the ontological concepts are viewed through the lens of this condition of asymmetry, they show themselves to be "overdetermined" and gain an ethical meaning (AE 181; OB 115). This overdetermination means that it is not the abstract subject's responsibility of an abstract other, but my responsibility for a concrete other, which ultimately determines the sense of these concepts. Without this emphasis, the asymmetrical relation of responsibility loses its meaning.

Written words are elements of a communicative relation between a writer and a reader and a philosophical text is no exception. This highlights the very aspect of discourse Levinas captures by the conceptual dyad of the Saying (*Dire*) and the Said (Dit).[190] Saying is always addressed to someone, and this address is at the very core of signification. The Saying is the linguistic side of what is otherwise described by Levinas as responsibility and vulnerability, i.e. the principle that justification has its footing in responsibility. Some interpreters, possibly misled by speech-act theory and by the gerundive used in the English translation, have assumed that what Levinas is expressing is the distinction between a process and its end-effect.[191] But the infinitive *Dire*, which Levinas uses, expresses the notion that speech is always in some sense an address to someone, as opposed to the *Dit* of the articulated world, whether as process or result. The said, the *logos*, is for Levinas linked with presence. It constitutes the sphere for comparing, measuring, interpreting and understanding. The saying is that which makes all of these activities possible but is at the same time that which is suppressed by them.

But what is speech? If speaking were nothing but transportation of signs, argues Levinas, then the signs would already be within me, and I would be for-myself, by-myself. The subject of saying does not give signs, but makes itself into

[190] Let us use an example: in a discussion on subjectivity, in which he has just claimed that "I" cannot be reduced to the ego, Levinas adds: "The conceptualisation of this last refusal of conceptualisation is not contemporaneous with this refusal; it transcends this conceptualisation" (AE 202; OB 127).

[191] See for example Simon Critchley's description of the Saying as "a performative *doing* that cannot be reduced to a propositional description". "Introduction", p.18, in Critchley & Bernasconi (Eds), *The Cambridge Companion to Levinas*, Cambridge University Press, 2002. I think Critchley is right insofar as a propositional description is an element of the Said. But to talk about the Saying as an "enactment" and an "ethical performance" seems to mean understanding it from the realm of activity, presence, synchrony; all of which Levinas relates to the Said. In *Ethics of Deconstruction*, Edinburgh University Press, 1999, however, Chritchley provides a much more adequate and productive account of the saying and the said (cf. especially pp. 162-182).

a sign; it "becomes an alliance" (AE 82-83; OB 49). In saying, the subject communicates itself as attached to the other, as responsibility. Communication would be impossible if it were to start from a free subject wanting to put everything under its power, or if one were to open up to communication only in search for recognition. The subject is already a welcoming of the other. The problem of other minds is secondary, deriving from the quest for certainty embarked upon by the Cartesian ego in its hypothesised solitude. Merely inverting this, claiming it is the said that communicates in saying (Heidegger: *die Sprache spricht*) would be tantamount to letting the subject disappear in the said, missing thereby the very moment of communication. Nor is the subject founded in a preceding dialogue of understanding (Buber, Gadamer). The problem with the latter view is that dialogue already presupposes speakers. It is this precarious communication, and not a dialogue of mutual understanding that constitutes the I. Communication is also a resignation for the risk of miscomprehension. I am involved with the other before I know who she is (AE 189-191; OB 118-120).[192]

Since the relation to the other is never described in terms of knowledge, but always as responsibility, Levinas is sometimes understood as offering only a negative description of the other.[193] But in fact, there is in his work, (as mentioned in section 1.7, above) an on-going polemic against a thinking based on negations, which is to say a "negative theology". Such a polemic is necessary since Levinas tacks a course that comes dangerously close to this line of thinking, especially in the emphasis he places on the other as interrupting all thematisation. The difference with negative theology lies in the "positivity" that Levinas ascribes to the relation to the other—the relation referred to in this work as the-one-for-the-other, or the human. This means, as Levinas had already stated in *Totality and Infinity*, that "[t]he sense of our whole effort lies in affirming not that the Other forever escapes knowing, but that there is no sense in speaking here of knowledge or ignorance." (TI 89; TaI 89) The definition of the otherwise than being is not that it is unknowable. It is approached in a way other than knowledge. Even if it is beyond our knowing, it is nonetheless a condition of possibility for knowledge. Already in the preface to *Otherwise than Being*,

[192] Catherine Chalier seems therefore to exaggerate when she claims that Levinas's philosophy "requires that the subject knows how to distinguish between the brutal heterenomy of the tyrant" and the ethical heteronomy of the other.(*What Ought I to Do? Morality in Kant and Levinas*. Translated by Jane Marie Todd. Ithaca: Cornell University Press, 2002, pp. 78-79). On the contrary, Levinas's claims that the communication with the other is a "dangerous life, a fine risk to run" (AE 190-191; OB 120). This means that the sensibility for the neighbour cannot be conditioned by a prior knowledge of the other or of the outcome with my meeting with the other.

[193] Cf. Søren Overgaard, "On Levinas's Critique of Husserl" in Zahavi, et al (eds), *Metaphysics, Facticity and Interpretation*, Kluwer, 2003, who speaks of Levinas emphasising the "essential inaccessibility of the other" (p. 116).

Levinas describes the task he sets for himself, as an attempt to gain "access" to the beyond (AE 10, OB xlviii).[194]

How is this access to the singular philosophically performed? In the introduction to *Otherwise than being*, Levinas says he learned from Husserl how every movement of thought contains an element of naïveté. In opposition to the Hegelian claim to include the real in thought, Levinas affirms the Husserlian movement of philosophy as a reduction of naïveté calling for ever new reductions. For Husserl, as Levinas describes him, this means effacing the trace of one's own steps—an infinite process. The movement of reduction must be led by the idea of an "original impression", for "without the impression, consciousness is nothing"[195]. This *Ur-Impression* cannot be totally retrieved, made present, even if it is the recovery towards which phenomenological reduction strives. The distance to cover in this act of recovery is a distance of time. But it is not a time that is external to consciousness; it is always the time of time-consciousness, stretching backwards to that which is to be (re-)established. Time is always the time of time-consciousness re-establishing a presence. Time-consciousness assembles the unity of identity. Situating phenomenology's "hermeneutic turn" already in Husserl's texts, Levinas reads this as a linguistic process; identification is an establishment of a "this as that". Being discovers itself as already articulated, as the already said coming to itself. Levinas elaborates this process in the following way: "The entity that appears *identical* in the light of time *is* its essence in the *already said*. The phenomenon itself is a phenomenology." (AE 65; OB 37, emphasis by Levinas). Through this articulation of being, being is laid out synchronically. It is on such a basis that the philosopher can understand the subject as a "being of truth". Here we are not covering any new ground; we have already seen how Levinas objects to this understanding. The difference now shows itself in the way in which Levinas develops the figure of the human in terms of the Saying. Thus, he writes: "If man were only a saying correlative with the logos, subjectivity could as well be understood as a function or as an argument of being." (AE 66; OB 37).[196] Otherwise put, this philosophy subjects the thinking of the human to the paradigm of understanding. This is part of the movement that for Levinas has its logical consequence in the (post-)modern tendency of viewing the human as only epiphenomenal to the play of being (AE 269-270; OB 175). This is of course projected backwards from Heidegger's definition of man as

[194] In an interview in German with von Wolzogen Levinas describes the function of philosophy, of his philosophy, as above all accessing the singular. Here he names this access "the human", and uses this as an occasion to position himself against Husserl's idea of the philosopher as the "functionary of humanity" (IEA 134).

[195] *The Phenomenology of Internal Time Consciousness*, trans. James S. Churchill, Indiana University Press, 1964, p. 142.

[196] This in many sense repeats his insight from "Is Ontology Fundamental?", discussed in section 1.6, above.

the guardian or recipient of Being. However, Levinas sees Husserl as pointing already in the same direction.

Levinas maintains that if philosophy is to defend its claim of "separating truth from ideology" (AE 77; OB 45), it must open up for diachrony, to a trace of something that was never present. This absence is not the result of a lack in the subject (lack of memory, repression); it is rather the portent of a positivity in the form of the ethical. Bernasconi (ES 16) describes this claim as an example of Levinas's naïveté, as if he were claiming to have accomplished this separation through his philosophy. Even if there is some justification to this interpretation, I think it more productive to read Levinas as saying that this separation between truth and ideology is something that philosophy can never claim to have accomplished, yet a desire of which it can never relieve itself. Philosophy is a never-ending process of trying to validate truth claims. Any notion of truth must be dependent on an experience of being or some other kind of access to being. Husserl believed in an analogy between the theoretical and the practical or what he otherwise put as the axiological access to phenomena. The practical can only be understood with knowledge as a model. (AE 106-107; OB 65-66) According to Levinas, this is a prejudice. The sensation underlying experience cannot be reduced to a "clear idea" abstracted from experience. The inadequacy of such an idealism becomes apparent when examining the phenomena of taste and smell. In the field of the senses, the cognitive aspect is not primordial; the senses let me enjoy and suffer. Enjoyment and suffering are not just a pre-cognitive information, as input to statements about being. Nor is a mood first and foremost a way in which we gain access to the world. Even if Levinas thinks that Heidegger positively contributed to a liberation of our view of the subject as primarily having a theoretical access to phenomena, in Levinas's reading at least, Heidegger too ultimately privileges knowledge—this is the sense in which the clearing (*Lichtung*) lets that which is come to light. Levinas reads Husserl's "consciousness of…" and Heidegger's descriptions of the access to Being as amounting to more or less the same gesture. In contradistinction, Levinas means that there is an element of subjectivity that goes deeper than the access to being. He writes: "The notion of access to Being, representation and thematization of a said presuppose sensibility, and thus proximity, vulnerability and signifyingness." (AE 110; OB 68).

In order to understand something, in order for this something to have meaning, we must be able to set it in relation to other things and other things must be able to refer to it. But for there to be meaning at all, there must be the psyche, or subjectivity. Levinas refers to the subject as *signifyingness par excellence*. In a sense he is in agreement with the Heidegger of *Being and Time*, who in §18 showed that all meaning is related to a certain human praxis, which itself always refers back to the life of Dasein itself. The difference here being that whereas Heidegger in *Being and Time* primarily understood meaning from Dasein's preoccupation with itself, for Levinas the subject is constituted as sensibility for the other. This is of course not all the sensibility there is—there is also the sensibility to the elements of the world (the enjoyment, joy of eating, drinking, of taking in the world, etc).[197] Vulnerability can only be thought in reference to an I already characterised by enjoyment.[198] The one-for-the-other is an interruption of the enjoying of life, of life enjoying itself, a joy of the world and oneself in this world.[199] This is not a denial of the experience of enjoyment; Levinas is careful, however, not to use the term "subject" for this realm, saving it for that which represents a *break* with enjoyment. He transforms the notion of the subject: from the transcendental subject of idealism, denoting the gathering unity of experience, to the transient rupture with the conatus of enjoyment.[200]

There is thus an ambiguity about the human subject's relation to the immanent and the transcendent; and this ambiguity is a condition of possibility for this vulnerability itself; the possibility of sensibility to coil up towards itself is the possibility to turn towards the other. As already stated, Levinas is not claiming that there is an original state of altruism. He is describing the prerequisites for there to be altruism and egoism at all.[201] Nor should his writings on the ethical be reduced to an appeal to altruism. Levinas's descriptions of the human have nothing to do with a normative ethics;[202] what he calls ethical is the very possibility of

---

[197] Enjoyment is given a more elaborate description in *Totality and Infinity*. Levinas here talks of this as an animal joy (Ibid). The word animal is not said haphazardly—Levinas makes a special point that it is a dog which recognises Ulysses returning home to claim what is his.

[198] Cf. also the extensive discussion of enjoyment in TaI 122-142, dealt with in section 1.7 (infra).

[199] But at the same time as it is an interruption of enjoyment, it is a condition of possibility of the libido, of erotic proximity. In *Totality and Infinity*, the erotic relation to the other was conditioned by the ethical in the sense that the ethical relation provided the transcendence that was necessary for the erotic relation not to be a consumption: Even the disrespectful playfulness of the erotic presupposes the face (TI 294; TaI 262). Since Levinas writes very little about the erotic after *Totality and Infinity*, it is not clear if the new description of the subject somehow altered his position on the erotic.

[200] This explains for some misunderstandings. The Christian theologian John Milbank (http://www.theologyphilosophycentre.co.uk/papers/Milbank_Metaphysics-LevinasBadiou.doc; [accessed 15 dec. 2009] for example, reproaches Levinas for not being able to see the desire for the other in terms of the "fulfilment of erotic aspiration for communion", and speaks of the self "locked within the secure *cogito* of enjoyment" (p.9). Levinas does not deny this aspect of desire, only that it is more than negatively constitutive for the subject—i.e., the subject is thus *defined* as going against this desire.

[201] "Altruism and egoism are posterior to the responsibility that makes them possible" (AE195n; OB 197n27). This can be seen as a direct challenge to Heidegger's claim from "On the Essence of Ground", according to which the statement: "Dasein exists for the sake of itself" gives "the condition of possibility of man being able to comport 'himself' *either* 'egoistically' *or* 'altruistically'" (WM 157; PM 122). Levinas thus seeks to replace the Heideggerian care for the self with the responsibility for the other as the condition of possibility for morality and immorality.

[202] He is not claiming that "I should subject myself to the other", which, as Martin Hägglund argues in *Radical Atheism* (p. 90), would be converted to the tyrannical "you should give everything to me", given the indexicality of the expressions "I" and "you. The problem is that Hägglund ignores the asymmetry of the Levinasian ethics, and reads Levinas as trying to formulate a new normative ethics, new rules for human behaviour. But this misreading is to

taking an interest in how such an ethics should be constructed or whther at all it should be constructed.[203] Between altruism and egoism there is also the love and the joy of sharing love, described at length in *Totality and Infinity*.[204]

Levinas's philosophy of the human has implications far beyond the discourse on ethics, though; what is at stake is also the very possibility of discourse questioning itself, the possibility of critique. Critique can be given different foundations. The foundations for critique most popular around the publication of *Otherwise than Being* were of course Marxism and psychoanalysis. But there was already a sense of incredulity towards these foundations. We should recall Foucault, quoted already in the introduction, expressing this in his characteristic tone of optimistic despair:

> There is no longer any orientation [...] We must start over again from the beginning and ask ourselves what we can base the critique of our society on in a situation, in which the previously implicit or explicit foundation of our critique has broken away. We must start again... start the analysis, the critique all over again."[205]

Levinas proposes nothing less than this orientation for a critique. The sensibility for the other is for Levinas the birth of critique, and thereby of knowledge, science and philosophy. Indeed, he makes the question of the human, thought as the otherwise than being, into the most central point around which a philosophy can enquire into its own possibility. The thematisation of what is otherwise than being, performed by philosophy, will always harbour a betrayal, but this is a betrayal that philosophy must work to reduce. We have described this reduction as a movement that passes from the said to the saying. In this sense, philosophy must prioritise the saying over the said. On the one hand this establishes a hierarchy, since the saying is emphasised over the said; on the other hand, saying is an-archic, beyond both foundation and hierarchy.

There is therefore a tension between the notion of the an-archic and a certain hierarchical tendency in the work of Levinas. This finds perspicuity in the chapter V.1.d of *Otherwise than Being*:

> The implication of the one in the one-for-the-other is [...] *not reducible to* the way a term is implicated in a relationship, an element in a structure, a struc-

---

some extent productive: in his systematic endeavour of reading Levinas against the writer's own intentions, Hägglund's uncharitable interpretation provides a kind of a contrast that shows where one could end up if one tries to apply Levinas as a normative thinker of ethics.

[203] In fact, such an ethics would rather seem to appear within the realm of the political for Levinas. Utilitarian considerations about whether it can be right to sacrifice one for the good of many others, would in this sense not by default be rejected by Levinas, it could be seen as taking place on a political or metapolitical, rather than an ethical level.

[204] Levinas's later description of the subject as traumatised, as obsessed by the other, does not deny this.

[205] Michel Foucault, "La torture, c'est la raison", Interview with K. Boesers, December 1977, *Dits et écrits III*, Gallimard 1994, p.397-8.

> ture in a system, which Western thought in all its forms sought as a sure harbor, or *a place of retreat*, which the soul would enter.

And without a pause—like the exhalation after inhalation—Levinas starts the next chapter (V.1.e), describing the one-for-the-other as

> *foundation of theory*, inasmuch as it renders possible the relation and the point outside being, the point of disinterestedness, necessary for a truth that does not want to be pure ideology (OB 136, AE 214, translation altered, my emphases).

The same concept is thus at once the foundation and that which does not allow for a place of retreat! However, if we understand it as the human, as youth, it is no longer a contradiction. The transience of youth, considered in section 2.1, does not mean that it cannot be serve as a foundation. It is a foundation which is not a place of retreat, but on the contrary the possibility of a beginning. It must also be remarked here that the idea of a "point outside being", addressed in the quote above is not to be understood as non-being. Rather, it must be understood as the non-totality of the economy of being, as the possibility of a rupture. The notion of the human, or as he says here, the one-for-the-other is at once that which does not allow the subject a resting place, and at the same time that which must justify all theory as the possibility of critique.

Levinas writes: "Pure criticism does not lie in the thematization operated by reflection on the self, nor in the simple look of the other that judges me" (AE 147, OB 92). Reflection is in this sense not self-igniting; "its spontaneity [...] permits it to take refuge in this very eye that judges it" (AE 146, OB 90). Reflection is not enough for critique, unless its movement is already vulnerable for alterity. Nor is the experience of the other's judgment sufficient (as he, in fact, was arguing in *Totality and Infinity*). I must already be a one-for-the-other, "obsessed". One can compare this with Levinas's interest for the stubborn and recurring re-emergence of scepticism in the history of philosophy. Levinas means that the sceptic cannot be refuted, as it is often tried, with the claim that the very statement of scepticism is self-refuting. Scepticism does not care whether it is self-refuting. This is because it does not accept the rules of the game of reason, demanding the consistency of the statements of an argument. Scepticism can "take refuge" in one statement and not be sensitive to the fact that it contradicts the other statements it implies. Rationality already presupposes that statements are not closed to other statements. It supposes that we can synchronically assemble statements and judge them together. Scepticism will deny this possibility, and rationalism will take it for granted. When Levinas claims therefore that critique is born out of vulnerability, he claims to show the foundations of rationality. But this is not meant as a final refutation of scepticism. What Levinas says instead is that a philosophy beyond scepticism must presuppose the vulnerability for the other.

The very incentive for one glance, one view, one statement to go outside itself and open itself to comparison is not explained by rationality and reflexivity itself; they presuppose the sensibility for the other.

So how do we conceive Levinas's view of philosophy? In his influential book, *Ethics of Deconstruction,* Simon Critchley produced the thesis that deconstruction is a practice of ethics, ethics in a Levinasian sense. And he interprets Levinas's later work as moving towards a more deconstructive approach.

> The real advance of [...] *Otherwise than Being* [...] is that he incorporates the Derridean problem of closure into his attempted articulation of the ethical [...] If there was an underdetermination and a certain philosophical naïveté about the possibility of an ethical language in *Totality and Infinity*, then it is completely transformed in *Otherwise than Being* where the aporias entailed in the attempted expression of the ethical in the language of ontology become, arguably, the central preoccupation. Levinas's real innovation in *Otherwise than Being* is the model of the Saying and the Said as a way of explaining how the ethical signifies within ontological language.[206]

Performing the chiasm from both directions, Critchley does not only interpret Levinas with the help of Derrida, but also Derrida with the help of Levinas. Quoting Derrida, Critchley writes that "Deconstruction is justice"[207], explicating this as justice being "the undeconstructable condition of possibility for deconstruction". In a late text, published after the first edition of Critchley's *Ethics of Deconstruction,* Derrida commented on this reading of deconstruction as an ethical task, fearing

> the constitution of a consensual euphoria or, worse, a community of complacent deconstructionists, reassured and reconciled with the world in ethical certainty, good conscience, satisfaction of service rendered, and the consciousness of duty accomplished (or more heroically still, yet to be accomplished).[208]

Derrida did not refer to Critchley here, but the gesture forced Critchley to write an appendix to *Ethics of Deconstruction,* trying to respond to this. This is particularly interesting since Critchley here summarizes his dual claim that deconstruction can be said to be ethically motivated, and that Levinasian ethics can be said to be a deconstruction. Derrida names that which is highlighted by deconstruction as *différance.* This is in a sense for him the core subject matter of philosophy, but at the same time is that which cannot be contained

---

[206] *Ethics of Deconstruction*, Edinburgh University Press, 1999, p. 259.
[207] *Force of Law,* Routledge, 1992, p. 15, 21.
[208] *Passions*, 'L'offrande oblique', Galilée, 1993, p. 13-15, "Passions. 'An oblique Offering'", transl. David Wood, in *Derrida: A Critical Reader*, ed. D. Wood, Blackwell, 1992, p. 37-41. Cited in the appendix to the later edition of *Ethics of Deconstruction*, 249-250.

by philosophy's closure. Différance is deferral in the sense of the deferral and production of difference. Critchley reads *différance* as a "metaphysical name for the unnameable" and deconstruction as a practice that "affirms the unnameable" [...] without giving in to Heideggerian nostalgia or Heideggerian hope".[209] Invoking the notion of justice is thus, according to Critchley, not to be understood as an appeal to a self-complacent understanding of the deconstructive practice, but from the effort of doing justice to that which is seen as merely contextual, "the effort to take this limitless context into account".[210] Philosophy tries to free itself from its context and the deconstructive reading shows this movement of closure.

According to Critchley, philosophy à la Derrida and the later Levinas is "a practice attentive to the aporias of closure", "a perpetual wakefulness of thinking, taking place as the interruption of consensus".[211] This is a formulation that indeed balances on the limit between Levinas and Derrida, and implies an interpretation of Levinas which I can nothing but endorse. But when Critchley lays this out he refers only to Derrida, and defines this practice further as the affirmation of the unnameable.[212] The effort of drawing the context into the text is a continual affirmation of the unnameable. If this is to be seen as the general imperative of deconstruction then perhaps this is where we are to index the difference between Levinas and Derrida. Of course, as Derrida himself notes,[213] Levinas also practices a deconstruction of sorts. But in Levinas, it is not the unnameable or the context as such, which gives the direction to deconstruction. Of course, already the notions of the "as such", and that of "the" direction (as if there were only one) are questioned by Derrida. Even so, in his affirmation of the contexts marginalised by the concepts of the tradition, Derrida's deconstructive project is still (which he would not deny) negatively determined by the very concepts it questions. What inspires Levinas's project, however, is irreducible to a deconstructive privileging of the margins; it is inspired by a certain urgency of the human relation, always thought as exceeding the bounds of deconstruction. Even though it can, and must, be deconstructed, the deconstruction would for Levinas be led back (re-duced) to the relation to the other. Levinas is aware, especially after Derrida's intervention, that his language for describing this relation is never untainted by the tradition that supposedly stands to hide it. But philosophy can constantly renew itself and find new ways back into discursive renderings of this relation. And the tradition is also constantly shown not only to be hiding, but also revealing this relation. Even if this relation cannot be exhausted by its denominations, there is an urgency of the name. As much as it is true that

[209] *Ethics of Deconstruction*, Edinburgh University Press, 1999, p. 263.
[210] *Limited Inc*, translated by S. Weber, Northwestern University, 1988, p. 136.
[211] *Ethics of Deconstruction*, Edinburgh University Press, 1999, p. 261.
[212] *Margins of Philosophy*, Chicago Press, 1982, pp. 26-27.
[213] Cf. "Derrida avec Lévinas: « entre lui et moi dans l'affection partagée »", *Magazine littéraire*, p. 32.

names and words deceive, there is no time to exist in the nameless, as Heidegger demanded, and with whom Critchley's Derrida would seemingly agree.

Whether or not this is a summary that does justice to deconstruction we can here leave open. Our focus should be on whether this holds as a description of what we learn from Levinas. We can at least see that our interpretation of Levinas lands close to this description, but that it also differs in an important respect. For one thing, Levinas has no interest in affirming the nameless. Indeed, he always gives a name to the interruption of closure, to the transcendence from the economy. Here, we are focusing on the name of the human—there are texts where he prefers the name God for this gesture. This act of naming is, as Critchley also emphasises in his interpretation of the Saying and the Said, always a betrayal, but a necessary betrayal. The difference is a matter of emphasis. For Levinas there is an urgency of the name for there to be a direction for the Saying over the Said.[214]

[214] Critchley's preference for an ethical affirmation of the unnameable returns in another fashion in *Infinitely Demanding*. There it appears in the shape of the formality in the contentless ethical statement. That which is sensed as a demand is a statement, but since it is not given what the content of the statement to be affirmed might be, Critchley's own act lands in an affirmation of the adherence to a statement, as it were, an odd privileging of the said over the saying (Cf. Infra section 2.5).

2.3 Ideology, Hypocrisy and Critique

> ... to understand on the basis of the supreme abstractness and the supreme concreteness of the face of the other man those tragic or cynical accents, but always that acuteness, that continue to mark the sober description of the human sciences...
>
> (AE 99; OB 59)

By allowing the name of the human, so suspect of ideology, to take a central place in his philosophy, Levinas situates himself in the debates on humanism waged in his time. How is one to understand Levinas's own philosophical endeavour against the background of his view of the notion of the human and the subject? And what is the role of philosophy and the human sciences in general from this background?

One might think, and indeed it has even been claimed (e.g. by Husserl), that a (transcendental) anthropology would have a privileged role among the sciences, on account that "all that is thinkable passes through human consciousness" (AE 96; OB 57, translation altered), or if you will, all that occurs, in one way or another, occurs in the "lifeworld" of the human. But Levinas paints a picture of a time and age that has increasingly understood that "nothing is more conditioned than the alleged originary consciousness and the ego" (AE 97, OB 58). In the age of the hermeneutics of suspicion, it seems that there are no facts about the human upon which a science of the human could be built.

Levinas seeks to place himself in a position, which claims that nothing is less conditioned than the human, all the while assenting to the antihumanist dismissal of beginning with consciousness as a pivotal point for philosophical inquiry. What Levinas calls "the human", "the proximity of the neighbour", is not based on facts about humankind. Factual explanations such as the sociological, ethnographic, historical or biological accounts of the human can be proffered, each equally plausible. But there is something restrictive in all these perspectives. While all of them take, in one form or another, the human as their object of inquiry, they offer no account of the human as the condition of possibility for these inquiries. The human, as understood by Levinas, is not to be thought as a category in which the other and I fit in as specimens. By way of a contrast to his understanding of the human as intrinsically a social event, Levinas, in both his major works, makes brief reference to the Greek myth of

Deucalion. In this myth, the god Deucalion throws rocks behind his back, which later transform into human beings, as pieces of the same rock, chips of the same block. (TI 236; AE 247; TaI 214, OB 159). In "The Prohibition against Representation", this is described succinctly as the "[e]vent of sociality prior to all association in the name of an abstract and common 'humanity'" (AT 131, AyT 127).

All the mistakes and ideologies of the human scientists and transcendental anthropologists do not alter this understanding of the human, which in this sense is the "least conditioned" (AE 98; OB 59).[215] On the contrary, only because others can matter to me, can a human science have both relevance and importance. This is what motivates the human sciences, in spite of "the incessant discourse about the death of God, the end of man and the disintegration of the world" (AE 99; OB 59), behind which concern for the human is dissimulated.

Levinas out-manoeuvres antihumanism in a way that will allow him to retain its prescient insights at the same time of undercutting the thrust of its rejection of the human. This leaves him in a position in which he can claim antihumanism to be true beyond the reasons that it itself provides. When it denies the primacy of the subject, it has done away with the idea of an ego which is its own goal, an ego "which is still a thing, because it is still a being" (AE 202; OB 127). It has "cleared the place" for Levinas's own position, and for a notion of critique that does not start with a philosophy of human consciousness. "Humanism has to be denounced only because it is not sufficiently human" (AE 203; OB 128), Levinas says, thus echoing but altering Heidegger's *Letter*[216] The turn from the discourse on the human to that of the openness of the movement of Being Levinas sees as a perfectly sound reaction to the lofty exaggerations of existentialism and humanism. All the same, he finds that this position is incomprehensible without the notion of a beyond being which serves as the very possibility of critique. And this beyond being is again the human, understood as one-for-the-other. In a sense, we can describe Levinas as trying to intervene in the discourse on the human in order to change it from its function as an element of an ideology (which antihumanism reduced it to) to the possibility of an internal critique of ideologies (which, in spite of itself, antihumanism must presuppose). This does not mean that we are prompted to believe in a beyond in the sense of a position beyond ideology, secured by Science, Religion or Philosophy. These different ways of culturing the human, from which Levinas has taken much inspiration in his formulations of the beyond, always run the risk of providing a false sense of security. This should be overcome by the restlessness of the human, a restlessness also proffered by these very movements.

[215] This claim, around which I see all of Levinas's philosophy cohering, will be reinvestigated with respect to its historicity and critically discussed in section 2.5.
[216] Cf. above, section 1.5.

2.3.1 "Ideology and Idealism"

> Here we find the premises of a non-Marxist reading of philosophy as ideology
>
> Jacques Derrida (ED 145; WD 121).

A central text for developing an understanding of Levinas's notion of critique is "Ideology and Idealism" (1972). In this text (which Badiou, Žižek and similar critics seem conveniently not to have read) Levinas defends Althusser's notion of a critique of ideology, as a relentless critique of ethics. The philosopher to whom Levinas is immediately responding is Claude Bruaire, who had firmly criticised the notion of a suspect reason. From Bruaire's rationalist position, the critique of ideology seems to hold reason to be suspect merely because it has not provided the right proofs. In Bruaire's eyes, it appears as a weakness, a philosophical surrender. Bruaire argues that philosophy as suspicion of ideology is a self-contradiction. On its own terms philosophy can be nothing but ideology[217] Levinas's rebuttal takes the following form: if reason implies thinking the world as ordered, then one need only look at the problems in our society (ecological crisis, social and economic injustice, the alienation of industrial society) to say that reason understood in this way is suspect of ideology. If reason is deaf and blind to these injustices, it does not deserve its name. In this sense, the rationality of science hinges on it partaking in a critique of society. This can only be justified in the contributory work for a better society, and in nurturing one's own sensibility toward injustice. For Marxism, the typical concretion for injustice is the proletarian, the other. Human science, in order not to be ideology, is driven by a restless worry (*inquiétude*) of not being open to the other. Any society that is not examined by this kind of science threatens to become totalitarian. Totalitarianism claims to have access to the true and the good for humanity, and thus has a world-view which makes vulnerability for the other impossible. But this is also a universal problem of human science, a thinking wherein everything is thought to be ordered according to the same model—according to which the human is also subsumed. Even if originally inspired by a sensibility for human suffering, science will necessarily imply a certain kind of reduction of the other to the same, a certain insensitivity before the other. Thus, any politically informed human science will constantly have to view not only society at large, but itself, as suspect of ideology. This implies a precarious balance between the hypocritical[218] and the truly critical. On the one hand the ethical disturbance that is the

[217] Cf Bruaire, *Pour la métaphysique*, Fayard, 1980, pp. 116-126.
[218] John Llewelyn has in his interpretation of Levinas developed a concept that he calls hypocritical diction (cf. Llewelyn, "Levinas critical and hypocritical diction", *Philosophy today*, Supplement 1997, pp. 28-40), that seems to go in the same direction as mine.

motor of political and scientific thought must be voiced in a conceptual language. On the other hand, this voicing will appear for science in the shape of ideology.

The notion of the human, or the one-for-the-other, is the name for the possibility of being vulnerable to the other. It carries with itself the possibility of not settling down, be it in a system, an idiom or a morality. Critique can only remain such if it also implies a suspicion of the reality of its own hypocrisy.

2.3.2 Politics After?

Levinas's late text "Politics after!" (ADV 221-228; BV 188-195) opens up for a further elaboration of his notion of critique in the realm of the political. Although in the title Levinas proclaims "Politics after!", I think it best to avoid Derrida's interpretation[219]—sometimes expressed by Levinas himself[220]—namely, that ethics is the foundation for politics, as if there would be an ethical sphere that is not already political. The notion of the human should rather be seen as founding the resistance to foundation. There is no purely ethical structure, which could found a purely political structure. Already in *Totality and Infinity*, Levinas writes: "In the eyes of the other, the third looks at me...The epiphany of the face qua face opens humanity"[221] (TI 235; TaI 213). This is Levinas's way of saying that there is nothing ethical that is not also political, nothing political that is not ethical. The ethical and the political are different aspects of human relationality, namely the relation to one and the relation to many. Through the promise of justice, the trace of the ethical dwells in the political. In order for justice not only to be the impartiality of a reason claiming to be blind, it must embrace the signification that has motivated it (AE 146n; OB 193n). In one sense, seen separately from one another, politics and ethics are abstractions. A movement claiming to be only political will have no way of forming the direction of its rationality, whereas the ethical must acknowledge its movement into politics in order to transcend a purely hypocritical self-righteousness. Levinas's notion of justice rests on these two poles. On the one hand, the an-archic responsibility for the singular other; on the other, the comparing and measuring rationality which must be introduced because there is always more than one neighbour. Justice must receive its meaning from the notion that everyone and anyone can be my neighbour.

So it is not the political per se that is being questioned in "Politics after!" What is put into question is rather a particular view of the political, which often

---

[219] Cf. *Adieu*, Galilee, 1997, pp. 133-134.

[220] Cf. (to only mention one of numerous examples) the interview with François Poirié, where he speaks about the notion of justice as "deduced" from the face-to-face, *Is it Righteous to be? Interviews with Emmanuel Levinas*, ed. Jill Robbins, Stanford University Press, 2001, p. 54.

[221] It must be noted that "humanity" in this quote points towards the universal, where as it other times can be used synonymously with "the human".

is referred to as political realism—typically associated with thinkers like Machiavelli and Hobbes. Political realism builds on the assumption that power is the final end of all political action, and that political agents—whether they be individuals, institutions or states—do everything that they do in order to maximise their power. For political realism, which views politics as nothing but the "continuation of war with other means", the difference between peace and a truce can only have rhetorical value.

Peace in the eyes of such a political realism is no more than the peace of calculation: a peace that does not "resist interests", a peace that transcends the present only in that parties of power abstain from war in order to gain a better position tomorrow. This peace is, as Levinas notes in *Otherwise than Being*, still better than war, but what makes it better than war is its relation to another notion of peace (AE 15-16; OB 4-5). In "Politics after!" it is spelled out more clearly: the alternative that Levinas entertains is not the possibility of reaching a utopian state of peace, not even as a regulative idea for actions; this idea he would describe, along with Nietzsche and Derrida, as an absolute violence. What he is talking about instead is a belief in the possibility of the "extraordinary" in politics, but without the appeal to the mystical that is otherwise associated with this concept.

"Politics after!" was inspired by Sadat's visit to Jerusalem in the year 1977 and the hope for peace which this visit stirred. Here, Levinas argues that "the human" is not merely a political concept; there is a notion of "the human" on this side of and beyond politics. This is also an attempt to gain another concept of politics, beyond that of political realism. As Levinas says in *Otherwise than Being*, it is not without importance

> to know if the egalitarian and just state in which man is fulfilled (and which is to be set up, and especially to be maintained) proceeds from a war of all against all, or from the irreducible responsibility of the one for all, and if it can do without friendships and faces (AE 249; OB 159).

Within this alternative, the former option is coincident with the dominant political view, namely egalitarianism born from a multiplicity of egoisms searching for mutual benefit from the rule of law. His own position is presented in the second option, describing justice as proceeding from the subject's irreducible responsibility. His reference to "friendship" is slightly misleading, since it might give rise to associations with communitarianism, a nostalgic dream of an Aristotelian-like politics predicated on a sense of community. This is far from Levinas's concern, he argues for a view of an "equality of all [...] borne by my inequality, the surplus of my duties over my rights" (AE 248; OB 159). As already noted, the argument presented in "Politics after!" appears against the backdrop of the protracted discussions surrounding the question of Israel and Palestine, a discussion which represents the conflict as a confrontation between different collective powers. In this discourse, the deployment of the word "human" by one side is seen by the other as but a rhetorical device in order to win compassion. According to the view against which Levinas positions himself, rational action is first and foremost political in the above sense, where all notions of the extraordinary are seen to be couched in religious and ideological terms. Against this, Levinas claims that the human relation, between peoples as well as between persons, goes "outside the order"; he claims that that which exceeds order can be described without denoting something supernatural or miraculous.

In light of these considerations, Levinas sees Sadat's decision, as the first Arab leader to go to Israel and talk before the Knesset, as recognition that the Israeli people are people to whom one can talk, and as an indication that peace is a notion that goes beyond the merely political. By this Levinas means that the notion of peace cannot be formulated strictly from the perspective of political realism, but only from the hope that the notion of the human has a signification beyond this. Of course one can and must interpret Sadat's act also from the view of a strict political realism. This is to say, the discourse of a peace beyond realist politics can and must be suspected of playing within the confines of a realist politics, as being guilty of hypocrisy, by constructing an ideological facade covering up the naked violence in which it is still engaged. Building on our discussion above, however, one could ask: is the notion of such a violence coherent without the sensibility for this violence, a sense that what is being violated ought to be treated in another way? When I say "ought" it should be thought in the subjunctive: this other way can of course always be suspect of violence, of hypocrisy.

The word hypocrisy comes from the Greek *hypokrinesthai* meaning "to play a theatrical part". But one could also, as a productive play on words—and as such, without claims of etymological fidelity—see hypo-crisy as a sub-critique, as the material which critique must work on, and to which critique must ceaselessly return. After all, is this not what Levinas meant when in *Totality and Infinity* he said (already quoted above, section 1.7): "It is perhaps time to see in hypocrisy not only a base contingent defect of man, but the underlying rending of a world attached both to the philosophers and the prophets" (TI 9; TaI 24). Critique is for Levinas dependent on a sensibility for the other, since this is the only hope that my position is indistinguishable from ideology. Maybe one could claim that there is no position from which I can justly claim to practice critique, and that any such claim will always show itself as hypocritical. Maybe hypocrisy is the only way to verbalise the ethical in the first person. Hegel describes this in the poignant narrative of the "Schöne Seele" in *Phänomenologie des Geistes.*[222] Here, Hegel tries to refute the possibility of a subjective account of morality by describ-

[222] Hegel, *Hauptwerke. Band 2. Phänomenologie des Geistes*, Wissenschaftliche Buchgesellschaft, Chapter VI C.c.: "Das Gewissen, die schöne Seele, das Böse und seine Verzeyhung", pp. 340-363.The relevance of this text for Levinas was pointed out by Bernasconi in his "Hegel and Levinas: The Possibility of Reconciliation and Forgiveness", *Archivio di Filosofia* 54, 1986, where he tries to show the workings of a Levinasian interruption in the system of Hegel.

ing the encounter of two minds. One of these minds claims a moral purity, a claim that would be but a pose, unless somehow it could be confirmed from the outside. This confirmation can only be valid when given by a critical mind. But the critical mind, Hegel shows, will always be able to deduce the claimed morality from a non-moral or egotistic point of view. One usually places the burden of proof with the moral agent, and since morality is not finally verifiable, his description of himself as ethical can and will always be deemed hypocritical. But what about me, the judge? If I judge the agent to be hypocritical, does this not mean that I am presupposing the possibility of true self-criticism, by which hypocrisy is to be compared and contrasted and thus only revealed as hypocrisy? Does not the hypocritical always imply the possibility of critique? And if this is so, how does this implication arise for me? Does it arise from my own actions, from self-observation? How can I claim this possibility of critique without regarding myself as a hypocrite, and without others seeing me as one?

Put otherwise, the question "Who is to say that this is not mere hypocrisy?" can be answered in the following way. In order to have meaning, the notion of hypocrisy as contrast presupposes the possibility of ethical justification. If we translate Levinas's speculations on hypocrisy (above) into the idiom of *Otherwise than Being*, hypocrisy is the expression of the split between the Saying and the Said, that which makes the very instance of critique possible. Critique in this sense cannot be understood apart from hypocrisy and vice versa. And since the very notion of hypocrisy presupposes critique, the cynical position exposing everything as hypocrisy cannot be consistently defended, without there being at least the idea of a meaningful critique, which already leads out of cynicism.

In order, then, for someone to denounce an attitude as hypocritical there must be some kind of measure that is not met. In the penultimate paragraph of *Otherwise than Being*, Levinas discusses his claim with the help of envisaging a utopian ethics from the viewpoint of the singular subject:

> "Here I am for the others",—an e-normous response, whose inordinateness is attenuated with hypocrisy as soon as it enters my ears [...] The hypocrisy is from the first denounced. But the norms to which the denunciation refers have been understood in the enormity of meaning and in the full resonance of their statement to be true like unrefrained witness. In any case nothing less was needed for the little humanity that adorns the world, if only with simple politeness or the pure polish of manners. A breakdown of essence is needed so that it not be repelled by violence. (AE 283; OB 185, translation slightly altered).

Thus the very accusation of hypocrisy presupposes what Levinas calls critique, a point outside of the economy of violence. Once this point is expressed, it takes part in the economy and is, as Derrida says, "involved in the war". But the involvement in the economy can only be visible as such with reference to an outside of the economy. There can be no taking part, without the perspective of not taking part; there can be no inside, without at least an imaginable outside: no immanence without transcendence.

For Levinas, one of the words for this transcendence is "the human". It is important to stress that the notion of the human does not denote something "real", or an ahistorical givenness. I see his recourse to this term instead as an attempt to reinscribe this notion in our language in a new way. He finds in language and in culture a trace of the notion of the human as the possibility of critique. This critical moment is not an ahistorical given, but is rather always threatened; it has to remain evasive and vulnerable. For Levinas, the role of philosophy is to make us aware of this precarious[223] nature of the human, forever recommencing its search at the borders of its disappearance (HAH 110; CPP 149). Philosophy tries in this sense to provide new possibilities for critique, as well as furnishing the grounds on which such critique is to be raised. Critique thus always presupposes a ground, a basis, if not a foundation. But since the human must, according to Levinas, be understood as restlessness—never to be founded in Being—these foundations will, if relied on, be seen as new layers of hypocrisy, which critique must in turn cut through. This need not negate the value of critique in the human sciences. What it does is to infinitise its task.

In the relation between hypocrisy and critique, we can find begin to construct a picture by which Levinas's philosophy of the human comes into view. If hypocrisy corresponds to the economy of violence, critique corresponds to the rupture, momentarily (as youth) transcending the violence.

---

[223] In *Precarious Life: The Power of Mourning and Violence*, Verso, 2004, Judith Butler makes an interesting reading of Levinas, where she shows how a Levinasian human science has a potential precisely in its insight into the precariousness of the human. Writing during the second Iraq war, she points to how the representations of the human in the media tends to hide this precariousness of the human: the woman in the burqa is represented as a Muslim woman in a burqa, the man with the long beard, represented as a terrorist—pictures that dehumanise people by this very categorisation.

2.4
On the Humanity and Inhumanity of Human Rights

Levinas's thought on the ethical has never been too far removed from a concern with the political, from his earliest works his philosophical itinerary was indelibly marked both by political events and by the need to formulate a thinking that moves from the ethical to the political. For this reason, it is not surprising that he found it necessary to write some essays on the topic of Human Rights. Human Rights constitute a discursive space within which ethics and politics co-appear, and where it becomes evident that they cannot be mutually independent. But, even so, the question remains: what is the precise character of this linkage between the ethical and the political? Is their encounter harmonious—a peaceful co-existence between complimentary discourses—or might their supposed encounter be conflictual, a putative relation that masks a fundamental incompatibility? To be more concrete here, we can point to a constitutive ambiguity that institutes itself at the very heart of the discourse on Human Rights. On the one hand, it can be said that the very existence of Human Rights expresses a moral distrust towards the political. Human Rights would not be necessary, were it not the case that the politics of the nation-state is considered insufficient for the protection of the people within its borders. After all, is this not what the UN declaration of Human Rights from 1948 attested to, a direct reaction as it was to the "barbarous" acts of World War II?[224] On the other hand, one could argue that the very notion of Human Rights relies on a trust in the political. They are an expression of the belief that one can legalise and institutionalise ethical values; as the preamble to the declaration of Human Rights prescribes, these values "should be protected by the rule of law". Whether, in the discourse of Human Rights, this relation between the ethical and the political is to be understood either in terms of a clash or an entreaty, a disjunction or conjunction is a question for which no immediate solution is to be offered. What I hope to show in this part of our inquiry is that Levinas can help us see the lineations of this dilemma more clearly. Here, the point is not to claim that the discourse of Human Rights is more important than other political discourses. It is my contention that Levinas's philosophy of the human opens up the possibility of

[224] *The Universal Declaration of Human Rights*, http://www.un.org/en/documents/udhr/ [Accessed Oct. 11, 2010].

reframing the way in which Human Rights can be defended without recourse to a self-complacent liberalism.

Levinas has written four short essays on Human Rights: "The Rights of Man and the Rights of the Other" (HS 157-170; OS 116-125); "The Prohibition against Representation and 'The Rights of Man'" (AT 127-135; AyT 121-130); "The Rights of the Other Man" (AT 149-156; AyT 145-150) "The Rights of Man and Good Will" in *Entre nous*. These texts, all written in the 1980s, argue for the necessity of Human Rights, with the important caveat attached that Human Rights must, unless they are to become mere instruments of political oppression, be justified from the viewpoint of the rights of the other. In many ways, they serve as an appropriate means of presenting the key features of his philosophy from the perspective of Human Rights, rather than to be considered as a distinct subset of his philosophy. Nevertheless, these essays are rather short and do not engage directly with other thinkers of Human Rights. Therefore, after a brief summary of Levinas's position, I shall present a contemporary debate on Human Rights, with the aim of shoring up what is to be learned from him in this field.

Levinas's central contention in all of the abovementioned essays is that Human Rights must be seen in terms of the rights of the other. This is summarised in the following way: "Their original manifestation as rights of the other person and as duty for an *I*, as my fraternal duty—that is the phenomenology of the rights of man (OS 125; HS 169). The rights, seen as rights of the other are explicated as the duty of an I. If one perceives the rights originally as the right of an I, the right of free will, one runs the risk of sanctioning a "war of each against all, based on the rights of man" (AT 151; AyT 147). The difference between a right as a justified demand and a demand that is without justification cannot be developed from the viewpoint of the subject claiming its right. Bernasconi has developed this point in "Toward a phenomenology of Human Rights",[225] arguing like this: "Rights do not become manifest when I make demands on my own behalf. Such demands are on the surface indistinguishable from egoism. The fact that I demand something for myself does not establish my right to it." The rights of the other always exist in conjunction with the duties of some I. This does not mean that Levinas refuses to see freedom as an original human right. The freedom is "invested" by the duty for the other, by the other's appeal to my responsibility (HS 169; OS 125). The notion of investiture suggests that it is on account of the subject's duty for the other that freedom rises to the dignity of an Idea that must be protected as a human right. Human Rights are, from the point of view that I am arguing in this book, not rights of Man in the sense of the rights of individuals belonging to category of the human (as pertaining to a defined enti-

[225] "Toward a Phenomenology of Human Rights", Revue internationale de philosophie moderne, Special Issue, 2008, p. 89. In this article, Bernasconi also notes, how the original drafts of the 1948 Declaration also stressed every human being's duty "to the common good", i.e. there was an attempt to understand Right from Duty, which was deleted in the final version.

ty, which in virtue of being the image of God or the rational animal, has a right to be protected). They cannot be anthropologically grounded, but rely on the generalisation of my (necessarily an-archic) responsibility for the other.

A common way to philosophically approach Human Rights has been to argue that since Human Rights have been threatened and questioned, and as such show themselves as in need of protecting, it is incumbent upon philosophy to provide them with the surety of a philosophical foundation. But how is this foundation to be furnished? If the Christian answer to this question was that human beings have a value since they are created in the image of God, the secularised answer has often been that since all human beings share the faculty of reason, they are to be valued, and protected by rights. After the critique of humanism, this way of reasoning seems less persuasive. We have already presented a summary of Levinas's answer to this modern predicament. But in order to better see how his approach to the problem of Human Rights can bear an impact on the contemporary debate, let us now attempt to give voice to some of the most significant positions staked out over recent years, and put them into dialogue with the Levinasian view on Human Rights.

One way to respond to the demise of Rationalism is to view Human Rights as founded in the "transcendental predicaments" of human society. One of the most well-known philosophers arguing for such a foundation today is Ottfried Höffe. His attempt is to found Human Rights on the "transcendental interest" in "life", which is common for all human beings transculturally.[226] Höffe reasons along the lines of the contractualist tradition: it is necessary that all parties agree not to threaten the lives of the others. The legitimacy of rights is founded in an original situation of "exchange" (p. 36). But it is by no means obvious that the interest of one's own survival exceeds that of all other interests for each and every one. There can be cultural, ideological and historical reasons for valuing many other things higher than life. Of course, one might, in turn, offer the rebuttal that this is merely evidence of the existence of differing opinions; it is not in itself an argument against this foundation of Human Rights. But the problem is that it is simply uncertain whether the interest of survival must surpass all other interests. The claim that survival is an interest transcending all others not only denies the possibility of self-sacrifice, but also the possibility of moral courage. A further problem with this contractualist approach is that it constructs law as the response to an original situation of *homo homini lupus*, where, in a conflict with all others every one cares for oneself. How can one understand the workings of present law from this fictional origin? Does it at all hold to ground a discourse of rights on such a basis? If the "original" situation of exchange would be such that the strengths are unequal, why would the stronger seek protection

[226] Ottfried Höffe "Transzendentaler Tausch. Eine Legitimationsfigur für Menschenrechte?" in Stefan Gosepath and Georg Lohmann (Eds), *Philosophie der Menschenrechte*, 1999, 31.

from the weaker, who surely could (from such a viewpoint that limits its scope to self-preservation) be merely excluded or annihilated? Höffe argues that the rights of the heavily handicapped can be founded on the fact that many of these disabilities are the consequences of specific risks belonging to our form of civilisation, risks before which we all are vulnerable (p. 42). It would therefore be in everyone's interest to preserve a State which protects the interests of the weak. But this reasoning would be logically binding out of necessity only if one were concerned for the fictional ego in the fictional state of nature. As for the well-being of one's actual self, concern for the weaker can of course lie in the interest of one's own self-preservation, but it is by no means necessarily so. As we know, different States and cultures have shown different sensibility to the needs of those who, in the eyes of those in power, contribute less to the general well-being. This is one of the many cases where we can see that the notion of transcendental exchange does not necessarily support Human Rights; the support would depend (if we insist on the jargon of transcendental exchange) on how the society chooses to value the risks and chances, profits and losses of the exchanges involved. This restriction does not seem to satisfy the idea of universality. For sure, the idea of exchange plays an important part in the formation of laws and conventions in a rationally ordered society. But it seems that one has to add many ad hoc premises in order to show how the rights after the transcendental exchange would cover also the weak. And is it at all sufficient to see Human Rights as means to an end? What is the final end? My survival? But is this story really about me? Is it not a story of some fictional protagonists in a fictitious state of nature, why would they matter to me? It would seem that Höffe first goes out of his way to show that one's concern for the other can be reduced to self-interest, but that on closer inspection this self-interest is not really is my concern for myself, but for a fictional self in a fictional world—thus implying a concern for an (albeit fictional) other.

Höffe is aware that the Levinasian position provides a threat to his own. This might be the reason why in his *Demokratie im Zeitalter der Globalisierung*[227] he claims that Levinas is unsuccessful in his attempt to understand Human Rights and human dignity starting from the face of the other, failing to found the dignity of the other in my moral effort. As we have seen, Höffe allows no other foundation than the self-interest of the subject, exchanged for the self-interest of the other. The implicit logic behind this reasoning is: if it is not reducible to an original egoism, it is not rational.

Levinas does not approach the matter of Human Rights by way of the construction of some fictional state of nature, or some other kind of metaphysical realm. His position, first and foremost, functions as a warning not to think the rights as belonging to subjects defending their own interests. Otherwise one risks

[227] C.H.Beck, 1999, p. 69.

ending up where Höffe claims to have started. One ends in the "war of each against all, based on the rights of man" as we already quoted Levinas saying (AT 151; AyT 147).

Höffe's final sentence of his article on transcendental exchange signals his difficulty of keeping track of this start and end: "wherever Human Rights cannot be legitimised with thoughts of reciprocity and balancing of injustices, one could ask oneself if it is possible that, perhaps, it is a case of human interests, and not really of Human Rights" (p. 46, my translation). Inversely, this would mean there is no such thing as a right other than as an interest anointed as a right through the process of the "original exchange". But since the original exchange was that which Höffe set out to make plausible, it appears that his argument has turned circular. Since, according to Höffe, the universality of rights must be reducible to the universality of interests; the interests that are only the interests of some (e.g. the disabled) cannot, if Höffe would be consistent in his argument, be the foundation of a right. Instead of universalising the *interest* of the I (in view of everyone being threatened by everyone else), with Levinas we can think Human Rights from the point of view of universalising *responsibility* (in view of the conflict between the responsibilities that I have for everyone). Höffe situates himself within a certain Kantian tradition. It is a tradition that, according to Höffe at least, understands rights as a protection from a state of nature in which human beings mutually recognise each other as posing a threat to their own existence. This is a tradition that Levinas does not shy away from engaging with. In his texts on Human Rights, he is in explicit dialogue with Kant's discussion of the limitation of the will. Levinas starts with a discussion of the Kantian concept of respect, *Achtung*, which Kant defines as a value, "der meiner Selbstliebe Abbruch tut", i.e. a value, which constitutes a break with my love for myself. What kind of value is this? Where does it come from? It is, Kant continues, a "durch einen Vernunftbegriff *selbstgewirktes* Gefühl"[228]—a feeling autoaffected through a concept of Reason. Levinas is more sceptical about the glories of auto-affective practical reason than Kant, and does not think that by itself a rational order is something to be trusted. The State develops its own rationality, and arguably a totalitarian state is such because it only recognises an auto-affective rationality. Of course, such a rationality is not worthy of its name. This applies as much to Kant as it does to Levinas. The limits lie especially in the believed self-sufficiency of reason. The rationality of Human Rights must therefore have a heteronomical justification:

---

[228] *Grundlegung zur Metaphysik der Sitten*, Sammlung Philosophie, Band 3, Vandenhoeck und Ruprecht, 2004 [1785], p. 401.

> The capacity to guarantee that extra-territoriality and that independence defines the liberal state and describes the modality according to which the conjunction of politics and ethics is intrinsically possible [...] The justice that is not to be circumvented requires a different "authority" than that of the harmonious relations established between wills that are initially opposed and opposable. These harmonious relations must be agreed upon by free wills on the basis of a prior peace that is not purely and simply non-aggression, but has, so to speak, its own positivity. Its dis-interestment is suggested by the idea of goodness, a dis-interestment emerging from love, for which the *unique* and *absolutely other* can only mean their meaning and in oneself (HS 167-168; OS 123-124).

This might sound dangerously close to building a politics on a religiously inspired love of humanity[229] But this is not Levinas's goal. When he speaks about love in this context, it is always a non-reciprocal, disinterested love, which he calls proximity. It is not a question of sympathy—the sympathy can be there or not, but the responsibility for the other is there regardless. Levinas performs a deduction of sorts from Human Rights to the rights of the other, and from the rights of the other to proximity, here laid out as the duty before the neighbour. This deduction he calls "the phenomenology of Human Rights" (HS 169; OS 125). Again, the opposite position is expressed by Kant: "Alle Achtung für eine Person ist eigentlich nur Achtung fürs Gesetz".[230] Respect for a person is in reality nothing but respect for the Law, which makes the law "the real object of respect."[231] But even if this seems to run counter-current to many of Levinas's formulations, Levinas sees himself as writing in the traces after Kant. Often he refers to himself not so much as a critic of Kant, but as an interlocutor and interpreter, or someone thinking in the spirit of Kant (cf. EN 22, HAH 90; ENO 10, CPP 138). As we saw, the relation to the other is for Levinas not a sentimentality (criticised by Kant) that can be satisfied by "good deeds", but the relation to the other is in a sense already law, in the sense that it is the measure of all law.

There are of course also theorists who argue in support of Human Rights without taking recourse to a language of foundation. One of the most famous and eloquent proponents of Human Rights today is the Canadian political theorist (and leader of the Canadian Liberal Party) Michael Ignatieff. Ignatieff does not try to defend Human Rights with an account of an ontological view of the human, nor by a transcendental exchange of interests. Rather, simply, Human Rights are good for pragmatic reasons. According to Ignatieff, Human Rights are

[229] Slavoj Žižek, who suspects this of Levinas, quotes the DDR Chief of Police as saying: "But I love you all", translating this very acutely as "I hate the enemies of socialism". ("Smashing the neighbour's face" http://www.lacan.com/zizsmash.htm [Accessed May 19, 2009].

[230] Immanuel Kant, *Grundlegung zur Metaphysik der Sitten*, Sammlung Philosophie, Band 3, Vandenhoeck und Ruprecht, 2004 [1785], p. 401n.

[231] Ibid.

effective in limiting political violence and reducing misery. He explicitly defends a minimalist account of Human Rights, which lays emphasis on the rights of the free individual to live and express herself freely. This is the basic prerequisite for struggling together with other individuals for social change: "Human Rights matter because they help people to help themselves".[232] The necessary prerequisite here is what Isiah Berlin—Ignatieff's constant point of reference—called "negative liberty". Ignatieff elaborates this as "the freedom to achieve rational intentions without let or hindrance" (ibid). In order for the culture of Human Rights to be efficient in communication with non-democratic culture, we must limit ourselves to a "defensible core" of Human Rights that promote this freedom, lest we are to risk a "rights inflation—the tendency to define anything desirable as a right" (p. 90). When he talks about what rights are needed for people to help themselves to social and economic security, he mentions "freedom to articulate and express political opinions [...] freedom of speech and assembly, together with freedom of property" (ibid). In so doing, Ignatieff draws the line at what he calls "collective rights", presumably, rights such as the rights to form trade unions, the right to a reasonable limitation of work hours, the right to equal maternal care.

In "Human Rights and the Politics of Fatalism",[233] the political theorist Wendy Brown convincingly shows Ignatieff to be less of a minimalist than he otherwise claims. According to Brown's reading, Ignatieff is actually arguing for Human Rights that function "as the essential precondition for a free-market order and for the market itself as the vehicle of individual social and economic security" (p. 458). Brown sees Ignatieff as representative of a certain type of politics of Human Rights, whose rhetoric typically stages itself as antipolitical, thereby hiding its political agenda—as in the Iraq war for example (which, as Brown reminds us, Ignatieff endorsed as a Human Rights effort (p. 455)). But this is not the all. Worst of all, Ignatieff forgets or, rather more strategically, conceals that it is itself a certain type of politics, presupposing a certain type of political subject, suitable for the Western liberal market economy. Brown does not speak out against Human Rights activism—instead she questions why it should be at the heart of politics today. Quoting Ignatieff directly, Brown's reticence is directed against his claim that "the reduction of suffering promised by human rights 'is the most we can hope for'" (p 461). Human Rights appear, thereby, as an alleviation to the cruelties which are thereby implied by Ignatieff to be necessities of society, a necessity which Brown would rightly question. She thereby repeats the gesture from Althusserian antihumanism, showing how humanism can function as an ideology in defence of capitalist society.

---

[232] *Human Rights as Politics and Idolatry*, Princeton University Press, 2001, p. 57.
[233] *The South Atlantic Quarterly* 103:2/3, Spring/summer 2004, 451-463.

The defence of Human Rights given by someone like Ignatieff is not only questionable for the reasons given by Brown, all of which I agree with. It has also the regretful internal effect of domesticating Human Rights discourse, reducing it to an apologia for the status quo. But the liberalist defence of Human Rights is not the only possible one. Levinas's take is however quite different. The strength of his view is precisely that Human Rights should be thought not so much as the Rights claimed by politically and morally isolated subjects pursuing their own freedom, but as the Rights of the other. This means that the rights are conceived firstly as duties, emanating from a responsibility for the other. This allows for a more extensive understanding of the limits of Human Rights, as Levinas argues:

> Behind the rights of life and security, to the free disposal of one's goods and the equality of all men before the law, to freedom of thought and its expression, to education and participation in political power—there are all the other rights that extend these, or make them, concretely possible: the right to health, happiness, work, rest, a place to live, freedom of movement, and so on. But also, beyond all that, the right to oppose exploitation by capital (the right to unionize) and even the right to social advancement (utopian or Messianic) to the refinement of the human condition, the right to ideology as well as the right to fight for the full rights of man, and the right to ensure the necessary political condition for that struggle. The modern conception of the rights surely extends that far! True, it is also necessary to ascertain the urgency, order and hierarchy of these various rights, and to enquire as to whether they compromise the fundamental rights, when all is required unreflectively. But that is not to recognise any limitation to the defense of these rights: it is not to oppose them, but to pose a new problem in connection with an unquestionable right, and, without pessimism, to devote necessary reflection to it. Thus the dynamic and ever-growing fullness of the rights of man appears inseparable from the very recognition of what are called the fundamental rights of man, from their requirement of transcendence [...]" (OS 120-121, HS 64)

When one starts out from the rights of the other, as Levinas does, the rights of freedom cannot have precedence over rights to life and security. Rather, these rights extend as a given society develops. The minimalist approach, to which a liberal like Ignatieff subscribes, is exposed as insufficient. As Levinas says here—and this point will be discussed further in connection with the work of Jacques Rancière—one can ascribe to Human Rights a certain dynamic, an "ever-growing fullness" (Ibid). This means that Human Rights never constitute a complete doctrine, a fixed and limited set of principles, prescriptions, and declarations, applicable for all time. The dynamic of Human Rights is a consequence of new principles and practices being grafted onto the existing set of rights. The discourse on human rights is subject to supplementation, to expansion, to rearticulations and otherwise unforeseen possibilities.

If Ignatieff's minimalism can be shown to be tied to a certain political subject, a thinker who attempted to entirely divorce the defence of Human rights culture from a rationalist and essentialist definition of the human being is the American philosopher Richard Rorty.[234] In his pragmatism, Rorty argues that since rationalist support for Human Rights does not seem to have anything to do with the Human Rights movement, there is no need to bother with Human Rights philosophically. What is needed is just a furthering of Human Rights culture, which means a sentimental education, a strengthened empathy with those who are "different" from us.

One might think that this critique of the rationalist defence of Human Rights is similar to that of Levinas. Rorty finds the strength in the Human Rights culture in it nurturing a sympathy for foreigners and strangers. But one must recall that Rorty defends Human Rights from a pragmatist view. From a Levinasian perspective his position is questionable for at least three reasons:

First, this defence of Human Rights relies on their usefulness, on Human Rights working for a (regrettably undefined) good. Even if this only remains implicit the corollary is that when Human Rights seem not to be working, they need not be defended. From the viewpoint of Levinas, Human Rights are, as the rights of the other, absolute, even if they might have to be refined and revised.

Secondly, Rorty leaves the question of the Good unclarified in a way that does not provide a position in which a radical self-critique is possible. How is this pragmatism to be evaluated? Rorty's refusal of rationalism becomes a refusal of justification altogether. He explicitly abdicates any philosopher's privilege, whereas for Levinas, Human Rights are part of the very justification for philosophy.

Thirdly, sympathy might seem close to what Levinas talks about when, for example, he speaks of the openness for the other as a passivity stronger than passivity. If one were to identify Levinas's position in that way, it would leave him open to the criticism of Slavoj Žižek, who comes close to arguing that the philosophy of the other is nothing more than a sentimentalism. Žižek, who worries about this being the consequence of Levinas's position, rightly answers that such sympathy only leads to charity, which may serve to soothe the conscience rather than provide the possibility for a serious critique. [235] But this is not

[234] Richard Rorty. "Human rights, rationality, and sentimentality". In S.Shute & S. Hurley (eds.) On Human Rights: the Oxford Amnesty Lectures 1993, Basic Books, 1993.

[235] This is how I read Žižek's critique of Levinas in "Neighbors and Other Monsters", *The Neighbor. Three Inquiries in Political Theology*, University of Chicago Press, 2006. Žižek mistakenly thinks that the relation to the other is a sentimentality that should lead the political reasoning, and instead pleads for an ethical violence, privileging the "coldness of the third" over the sympathy for the neighbour. For Levinas, this is not a choice to make; we are always forced standing in the relation to more than one, causing justice to be impersonal. Žižek reason as if Levinas were saying: help the one who appeals to you before responding to any political obligations.

Levinas's concern; he writes about a duty and a responsibility towards others, whether I am moved by them or not.[236]

The main problem with Rorty is that he does not clarify why sympathy is good, or why, for that matter, the Human Rights culture is good? Taking flight from the rationalist belief that knowing the good means being good, makes him retreat so far from the paradigm of understanding and justification that his descriptions boil down to common sense-assumptions, such as that "bad people [...] were deprived of [...] security and sympathy" (p. 128) in their upbringing. The surprising primitiveness of the way in which distinctions are drawn between "good" and "bad people", between "sentimental education" and "foundationalism", as well as the assertoric nature of his description that "Human Rights culture" is "morally superior to other cultures", ensures that one easily loses confidence in the genuineness of Rorty's anti-essentialism. Moreover, his unfounded certainty that the European and American cultures are better at bringing up people capable of sympathy (in the sense of being able more effectively to set oneself in the shoes of others) seems to be a performative self-refutation. If this self-righteousness were the inspiration for Human Rights activists, the critique of the imperialistic character of Western Human Rights, which is the charge often raised by post-colonial theory, would be justified even before the argument began. For many, the discourse on Human Rights is forever tainted by its association with Western liberal ideology. Rorty seems to provide an extreme case against which all of these accusations ring true.

A particularly potent critical examination of Human Rights is advanced by Giorgio Agamben. His central claim[237] is that Human Rights presently serve as the most fundamental example of how modern bio-power (his version of the Foucauldian concept, denoting the power over bodies, targeting people as specimens of bare life) operates. Agamben sometimes presents this claim as an interpretation of Hannah Arendt's descriptions of the plights of rightless refugees in *The Origins of Totalitarianism*, as if she had been demonstrating that Human Rights were the paradoxical cause of the absolute rightlessness of the refugees. Exciting as this claim might be, it does not quite seem to be Arendt's view. What

---

[236] An interpretation that seems to differ from mine in this respect is offered by Werner Stegmaier, "Die Bindung des Bindenden. Levinas' Konzeption des Politischen.", In: Alfred Hirsch und Pascal Delhom (Eds) *Im Angesicht der Anderen. Emmanuel Levinas's Philosophie des Politischen*, Diaphanes, 2005, pp. 25-44. Stegmaier finds that the "personalisation and moralisation of contemporary politics" actualises the Levinasian conception of the ethical in relation to the political: we are literally faced by the politicians and by victims dependent of the responsibility of politicians through our TV sets. The abstraction of political responsibility is thus concretised; we can literally *see* whether the politicians are taking their responsibility or not. But this assumes that the mediatisation of politics really produces a proximity in the Levinasian sense. In contrast to Stegmaier, a contrasting Levinasian interpretation of the media is given by Butler as described above, footnote 190.

[237] Cf. Giorgio Agamben, *Beyond Human Rights*. trans. Cesare Casarino, in Radical Thought in Italy, ed. Paolo Virno & Michael Hardt, University of Minnesota Press (Theory Out Of Bounds series), 2006.

Arendt shows, however, is how inefficacious Human Rights were when they were most needed. The millions of stateless refugees after World War I were never protected by them. As Arendt has become essential for almost all philosophical critiques of Human Rights today, let us note some of her observations:

> The Rights of Man, after all, had been defined as "inalienable" because they were supposed to be independent of all governments; but it turned out that the moment human beings lacked their own government and had to fall back upon their minimum rights, no authority was left to protect them and no institution was willing to guarantee them (p. 291-292).

Having no institutions to help them, the refugees were not protected by any civil law, and therefore were more than anyone else in need of Human Rights.

> The conception of human rights, based upon the assumed existence of a human being as such, broke down at the very moment when those who professed to believe in it were for the first time confronted with people who had indeed lost all other qualities and specific relationships—except that they were still human. The world found nothing sacred in the abstract nakedness of being human (p. 299).

And since Human Rights could never be applied in this environment,

> [t]he very phrase 'human rights' became for all concerned—victims, persecutors, and onlookers alike—the evidence of hopeless idealism or fumbling feeble-minded hypocrisy (p. 269).

The lesson that Arendt draws from this is that the nation-state and similar institutions are necessary for the protection of Human Rights, otherwise put, the sphere of Human Rights is dependent on the political sphere—what Arendt calls the "public space". Only in the plurality of the public space can one find the identity essential for human dignity.[238]

As we already noted, Agamben takes her claim of the futility of the bare humanity in another direction. Commenting on the title of Chapter Nine of her *Origins of Totalitarianism*, "The Decline of the Nation-State and the End of the Rights of Man" (the chapter from which the quotations above are taken), Agamben reads the causal relation between the terms in Arendt's title "such that the end of the latter necessarily implies the obsolescence of the former."[239] However Arendt reads the causal relation in the exact opposite direction. Thus she writes:

---

[238] Cf. *The Human Condition*, University of Chicago Press, 1998 [1958] p. 181.

[239] Giorgio Agamben *Beyond Human Rights*. trans. Cesare Casarino, in Radical Thought in Italy, ed. Paolo Virno & Michael Hardt, University of Minnesota Press (Theory Out Of Bounds series), Minneapolis, Minnesota, 2006, 18.9.

"not only did the loss of national rights in all instances entail the loss of Human Rights; the restoration of Human Rights as the recent example of the State of Israel proves, has been achieved so far only through the restoration or the establishment of national rights." (p. 295).

Why does Agamben force a change in direction between cause and effect here? Agamben has his own agenda: "the Rights of Man represent above all the original figure of the inscription of bare natural life in the legal-political order of the nation-state."[240] Agamben sees no hope emanating from within the present political order, but sets his hope on the figure of the refugee. The refugee is central in the theories of both thinkers. The precarious situation of the refugee, beyond the protection of any Human Rights, was for Arendt proof of the necessity of belonging to a polity, because in order to enjoy Human Rights, one must first be a citizen. For Agamben, the refugee becomes instead "the sole category in which it is possible today to perceive the forms and limits of a political community to come"[241], the way to envision a life liberated from the oppression of biopolitical power.

In a recent essay,[242] Jacques Rancière happily lumps Agamben and Arendt together, accusing both of holding a misconception about the limited political efficacy of Human Rights. What is problematic in their understanding is, according to Rancière, a too static conception. To demonstrate this, he switches example, replacing the figure of the refugee with that of the woman claiming equal (human) rights.

> Women could make a twofold demonstration. They could demonstrate that they were deprived of the rights that they had, thanks to the Declaration of Rights. And they could demonstrate, through their public action, that they had the rights that the constitution denied to them, that they could also enact those rights. So they could act as subjects of the Rights of Man [...] They acted as subjects that did not have the rights they had and had the rights that they had not (p. 304).

Rancière raises a riddle to the level of a formula: The Rights of Man opened up the possibility for the excluded to set up a two-fold demonstration, showing "the rights of those who have not the Rights that they have and have the rights that they have not" (p. 302). To a certain extent, with this formula Rancière confirms Agamben's view that the subject of Human Rights is rightless. At the same time, the formula challenges this view in the sense that it provides a more dynamic understanding of the procuring of Rights. Once the Rights of Man are put in circulation, they are open for all to claim and, in certain cases, when a society

[240] Ibid, 16.6.
[241] Ibid.
[242] "Who is the Subject of the Rights of Man?", *The South Atlantic Quarterly* 103: 2/3, Spring/Summer 2004, 297-309.

dismisses a particular subset of its population as incapable of acting as free and equal citizens, for those arbitrarily excluded elements to demonstrate their capacity to perform the content of the rights that they are otherwise deemed not to possess. The problem with Agamben's view, according to Rancière, is that an unchanging consensus is presupposed about both the content and the subjects of those rights, such that Agamben is inattentive to the ways in which disturbances and transformations are effected in political spaces, where such disruptions are the result of concrete struggles about what and who can procure rights in a given society. A risk with the claim that Human Rights are void, or merely a lofty reference to civic rights, is that one ends up in a vicious circle, emphasising and strengthening the division between those who have the right to enjoy rights and take part in politics, from those who cannot take part. Rather than "the original figure of the inscription of bare natural life in the legal-political order of the nation-state"[243] Human Rights can signify the possibility of previously excluded subjects acquiring civil rights. Politics "is not a sphere, but a process" (p. 305), conditioned by the unleashing of political dissensus. Rancière reads Agamben's/Arendt's understanding of Human Rights as symptomatic of a society where the political is stagnating into consensus, aiming for an "identity between law and fact", i.e., letting the political be handled by technocrats. In such an (a-)political environment, Human Rights may indeed seem void.

> They seem to be of no use. And when they are of no use, you do the same as charitable persons do with their old clothes. You give them to the poor. Those rights that appear to be useless in their place are sent abroad, along with medicine and clothes, to people deprived of medicine, clothes and rights. It is in this way, as the result of this process that the Rights of Man become the rights of those who have no rights, the rights of bare human beings subjected to inhuman repression and inhuman conditions of existence. They become humanitarian rights (p. 307).

What Rancière is saying here is that for a consensual political environment, where true critique is no longer possible, the political as such becomes invisible, and Human Rights seem to be needed only by those living at a distance from this society. The perceived misery of "the others", and the injustice apparent in their own society, becomes a way to establish the hegemony of liberal notions of justice and rule of law in consensual societies such as Western liberal democracies. The problem with these so-called "humanitarian" rights is that since they cannot be enacted by the "receivers", through an event of "return to sender" they become the "rights of humanitarian intervention" (pp. 308-309), allowing for a

[243] Agamben, "We refugees", http://www.egs.edu/faculty/agamben/agamben-we-refugees.-html, [accessed March 9, 2009].

humanitarian consensus on Good and Evil, for a drama of "Infinite justice against the Axis of Evil" to unfurl (p. 309).[244] Politics is replaceable with ethics.

In a critique similar to Badiou's, discussed in our introductory chapter, Rancière finds support for the recent emergence of this ethically inflected discourse in Jean-Francois Lyotard's "The Other's Rights"[245], and warns (as does Brown and Badiou) that this "reign of ethics" might lead to a "closure of all political intervals of dissensus." (p. 309).

Although Rancière does not like the idea of the Rights of the other, all the same it is with the help of his work that I wish to anchor Levinas's position in the contemporary debate. It is of urgency here to point to a difference between Lyotard's and Levinas's conceptions of the rights of the other. Even if he tries to claim Levinas for his cause,[246] Lyotard rather stands for an ethics of otherness in the sense of an "other than", i.e. a respect for everything that is different, the opaque otherness of that which we do not understand, and which cannot make itself heard. This is very close to the interpretation of Levinas from which, throughout this thesis, I am trying to disjoin him. The rights of the other as described by Rancière, mirroring Lyotard's understanding, might indeed be the consequence of a society of consensus. What Levinas means by the rights of the other is the first step from the singular responsibility for the other to the need for its universal expression. And the responsibility for the other is, as we have shown, the very point from which to think critique, the condition of possibility for political dissent.

Does not the dynamism of Human Rights Rancière describes hinge on those already having political rights coming to recognise their obligations to others formerly deemed rightless? Is this not what makes out the difference between a dissensus and a civil war? And does one not need what Robert Bernasconi called an "ethics of suspicion" (see above, section 1.12), i.e. an ethics suspicious towards ethics in order to break with a reign of ethics?

Answering these questions in the positive, I aim to show that Levinas's approach to Human Rights is complementary to Rancière's. Levinas's insistence on interpreting Human Rights as the rights of the other affords the possibility of describing how a *consensus* in a self-righteous liberal democracy can open up for acts of *dissensus*, for critique. With Levinas, the same sensibility for the other which necessitates Human Rights is the sensibility which is the condition of possibility of critique.

---

[244] Rancière is referring to the two more colourful expressions conjured up by the Bush administration in relation to the War on Terrorism: "Infinite Justice", the first name for the attack of retaliation on Afghanistan shortly after September 11 (soon to be renamed "Enduring Freedom"), and "The Axis of Evil" the expression naming the countries that, according to the US government, supported terrorism.

[245] "The Other's Rights", translated by Chris Miller and Robert Smith in In S.Shute & S. Hurley (eds.) *On Human Rights: the Oxford Amnesty Lectures 1993*, Basic Books, 1993.

[246] Ibid, p. 142.

Rather than providing a foundation for Human Rights, I read Levinas as rethinking what we mean by *human* rights, rethinking, as we have shown earlier, the notion of the human as for-the-other. By emphasising that Human Rights are first and foremost the rights of the other, Levinas is not justifying the "export" of rights, as Rancière described the Lyotardian conception of Human rights as rights of the other. Levinas's notion of the rights of the other implies a reflection on the sense in which a human being enjoys these rights. The reason that the classical liberalism of Ignatieff gives privilege to rights of expression over "collective" or "social" rights is perhaps linked to how liberalism views the subject—from the standpoint of an autonomous I, a subject of free will. Levinas thinks the rights from the subject's responsibility for the others who are vulnerable and in need of the defence of the laws. Rights are in this sense derivative from responsibilities.

As we can learn from our reading of Rancière, this can happen also if we export this notion of an I with rights to an other who is not empowered to make use of this right. As Rancière's example shows, this often results in the sender claiming to act in favour of the missing recipient. For Levinas, however, this is precisely not thinking the rights as rights of the other—it rather illustrates how one exports the image of the I to the others. From a Levinasian perspective this could be described as not letting the right of the other have precedence over the exercise of my right—sending the other a right such as I would have it, cannot satisfy the demands that my responsibility sets on me. In an earlier text, "Transcendence and Height", Levinas presented the following description of the problems of the modern so-called Socialist State:

> [its] central concern is how to confer on the Other (*Autrui*) the status of the I and how to liberate the I itself from the alienation that comes to it from the injustice that it commits. The right of man, which must be recognized, is the right of an I. Man is conceived of as an I or as a citizen—but never in the irreducible originality of his alterity, which one cannot have access to through reciprocity and symmetry [...] To contest that being is *for me*, not contest that being is for the sake of man; is not to give up on humanism, it is not to separate the absolute and humanity. It is simply to contest that the humanity of man resides in the positing of an I. Man par excellence—the source of humanity—is perhaps the Other (LC 71; BPW 14).

In order to adapt this early text to our purposes, we have to alter it to the later idiom where universalisation proceeds not by extending the *excellence* of the singular other to the many others, but by saying that the responsibility for the other must be universalised. Even so, this perspective does of course not lend itself to direct political application but it can add a further layer to Rancière's deliberation. The sender of "humanitarian rights" in Rancière's example inhabits a position to a certain extent corresponding to the Socialist State in Levinas's example, quoted above; when Rancière accuses the West of exporting "humanitarian rights" this is similar to the way in which the citizen is pre-shaped by the dictatorship in Levinas's example. When Levinas asserts that Human Rights are first and foremost the rights of the other, he wants to awaken an awareness of the asymmetrical situation of me being responsible for singular others, a constellation that the notion of Human Rights already distances itself from, in the sense that it is the universal right of each and every one. This distancing, on the other hand, is necessary for universalisation. The reference to the rights of the other is there to shed light on how this universalisation is produced and justified.

In the beginning of this section we presented positions in a debate, seemingly waged as it were between two extremes. On the one hand there is Höffe, understanding the state of nature as a Hobbesian state of war of all against all, which one can evade only with the help of Human Rights, as part of a rationally organised society. On the other hand, Agamben, who discovers that Human Rights are inextricably tied up with the violence of the History of Western metaphysics, repudiating both. Can we not, on both sides of this debate, find something like the belief in an escape from violence, which we discussed at the end of the first part?[247] These two positions are politically and philosophically far apart, but nonetheless they can be construed as sharing a belief in the escape from an economy of violence.

According to Derrida's "Violence and Metaphysics", violence is co-original with the face. If one assimilates this to the idiom of Levinas's "post-Derridean" writings, the said always has to be said, unsaid: every formulation of the human is a necessary betrayal. In order for Human Rights to be *human* rights, in the sense that Levinas gives the word, their application and place in discourse must correspond to a sense of the precariousness of the human, to an insight that the enforcement and even the discourse of Human Rights are a necessary violence, which must be met with constant critique. They can therefore not rely on a predetermined concept of the human, independent of the structure of responsibility, but must be thought as evental. Levinas describes this event as an

> [e]vent of sociality prior to all association in the name of an abstract and common 'humanity'. The right of man, absolutely and originally, takes on meaning only in the other, as the right of the other man. (AT 131, AyT 127).

It is from this discursive event, which we might call the event of the human, that we shall seek a meaning in the notion of Human Rights,[248] and it is also in this event that we locate the condition of possibility for a critique of consensus.

---

[247] Cf. above, section 1.11.

[248] In his Menschenrechten des Fremden inspired to a great extent by Emmanuel Levinas, Alfred Hirsch first beautifully summarises the point that I also am trying to make: "Mit den Menschenrechten hält sich die Einzigkeit und Freiheit des Menschen als Anderer wach gegenüber Anonymität und Symmetrie des Gesetzes und des Staates". This is the Levinasian

standpoint in the sense that we have sketched out here. But Hirsch continues: "Die Besonderheit und Vielzahl der Fremden spricht uns auch in Form der Menschenrechte an und verlangt nach einer eigentümlichen Universalität, die unabschließbar ist und immer wieder von Neuem benannt werden muß—einer ‚Universalität', die nur im ‚Anspruch' durch den Fremden und die Kultur der Anderen zu gewinnen ist." Of course, every notion of universality must be interculturally unfolded; the right of the other is only responded to by me if I respond to her in her particular sociocultural situation. Her culture will in some sense always be other than mine—but this is not the same otherness as that of the alterity of the event of sociality, where the alterity of the other is the very fact of not being me. In this sense one is not "more other" because one comes from further away. I think that Rancière and Badiou are right to criticise the idea of the rights of the other, if the other is taken in this understanding. It is one of the primary concerns of the dissertation to keep these two notions of otherness separate—we will discuss this further in the next section.

2.5
Tradition of the Universal

At this point we encounter a certain paradox in our discourse on the human. It can be phrased in the following way: if the notion of the human is the possibility of critique, now unfolding as the possibility of a critique of a consensus, how can this notion be carried within a tradition? If what is specific to the human is that it appears through events of dissensus, will this then not be detrimental to its own longevity? Even if the tradition of philosophy has not explicitly understood the notion of the human in the way Levinas advances it, is he not pointing towards a silent consensus that must hold for his understanding to gain plausibility? Does he not have to argue in some way that shows, even if against received opinion, that the concept of the human has already been understood in the way he solicits? Or if not, must not philosophers aim towards persuading others of the same understanding of a certain notion, i.e. must there not be, at least in the end, an aim towards consensus? Or does he claim his notion of the human to be independent of tradition?

It seems impossible to argue the latter. As with any philosophical concept or notion, "the human" draws its meaning from its inscription in a certain tradition. It takes its cue from a given tradition's view of what is human. Levinas draws on Biblical and Jewish sources in order to say what he is saying, and in interviews occasionally he goes so far as to venture that humanity is nothing but "the Bible and the Greeks".[249] The sensibility for the singular is, according to Levinas, the gift of the Bible, whereas the Greeks stand for the language of the universal. This oscillation between singularity and universality marks the Levinasian notion of the human, showing itself to be dependent on these two traditions. The question is whether Levinas saw himself as defending Civilisation against Barbarism (as in the Hitlerism text), even if, in his later writings, his philosophy was not couched explicitly in these terms. Another way to read such comments is as a way of showing the inextricability of the bond that ties what is avowed by Levinas together with his situatedness within a specific tradition. I have mentioned that the way in which Levinas develops the human is dependent on the Jewish and Greek traditions. But if it is thus dependent on tradition, is it then (like the view of man as an empirico-transcendental doublet that Foucault exposed) doomed to die

[249] Cf. "Intention, Ereignis und der Andere. Gespräch zwischen Emmanuel Levinas und Christoph von Wolzogen", *Humanismus des anderen Menschen*, Felix Meiner, 2005.

out? If it thus hinges on a certain tradition, can its message endure beyond the bounds of that understanding?

We must recognise that Levinas is not unambiguous on these questions. Firstly, Levinas does not always express his particular interpretation of the human in terms of a gift from a certain tradition. In "Politics After", discussed above, Levinas seems to put the point contrarily:

> "for men purely as men", independently of all religious consideration issuing from a denomination and a set of beliefs, the meaning of the human, between peoples as between persons, is not exhausted neither in the political necessities which hold it bound nor in the sentiments that release that hold. We believe that what escapes the order of things may impose itself upon the general picture without recourse to any supernatural or miraculous factor and, in demanding a behaviour that is irreducible to established precedents, may authorize its own projects and models to which, however, every mind—that is, every reason—can gain access (ADV 222; BV 189).

Here, there can be no doubt that Levinas expresses a belief in a universalism exceeding a certain cultural affiliation. Of course, this can be attributed to the specific circumstances—it may be considered unwise when applauding the peace effort of an Arab leader to say that humanity is nothing but the Bible and the Greeks. But in an interview from 1985 a similar universalism is argued for: "the calling of the holiness is recognised by all human beings and [...] this recognition defines the human" (AT 173; AyT 171).

Let us return to what Levinas says in *Totality and Infinity* as the face of the other as "the immediate". Even if he refrains from this terminology in the later work, the question is whether he relinquishes fully the notion of immediacy. It would seem unquestionable that the so-called immediacy of the face is mediated by tradition—for example the Jewish tradition. Does Levinas really need to claim that the human provides an access to the least conditioned or immediate? Can one not admit that the notion of the human is dependent not on one but several traditions, and is therefore all the more fragile and precarious?

How does all of this add up? How can Levinas claim on the one hand that the human is valid for all cultures at all times, and on the other offer the counter-claim that the notion of the human he is proposing hinges on one particular culture, deriving from a certain tradition? This aspect of Levinas has been critically addressed from different perspectives by both Robert Bernasconi (WN) and Rudi Visker.[250]

Before we turn to this criticism, let us first note that Levinas, the Holocaust survivor, is of course not ignorant of the guilt and responsibility of "the West".

---

[250] "Cf. Is Ethics Fundamental? Questioning Levinas on Irresponsibility", *Continental Philosophy Review* 36, 2003, pp. 263-302 and "Dis-possessed: How to remain silent 'after' Levinas", *Man and World*, 29, 1996, pp. 119-146.

Moreover, it is possible to claim that his whole oeuvre meditates upon this problem. In a text from 1972-73, devoted to Jacob Gordin, Levinas writes:

> Written by the victors, and meditating on the victories, our Western history and our philosophy of history announces the realization of a humanist ideal while ignoring the vanquished, the victims and the persecuted, as if they were of no significance. They denounce the violence through which this history was none the less achieved without being concerned by this contradiction. This is a humanism for the arrogant! (DL 257-258; DF 170).

Opposing this "humanism for the arrogant" (associated here with colonialism) Levinas believes in a "humanism of the suffering servant" (DL 258; DF 171), which can be learned from the Jewish tradition. And we must assume that he still (in 1972) persists in thinking his project in terms of this latter humanism. But this means that the West must learn above all from the Judaic tradition in order to amend the arrogance of its humanism. Is this not an arrogance redoubled?

With the trust that Levinas places in the Western tradition, it could be claimed that his moves are analogous to Husserl, whose attempt at leading reason to self-transparency in the *Krisis* was supplemented with a historical account of European man. In the *Krisis*, Husserl sketches out a history of science, from Greece to Galileo to the present. In it, he provides a genealogy of universalism, and shows how the notion of the universal, the idea of reason, and the emergence of the universal human being are part of a particular extended event. For Husserl, the advent of universality, of reason and Humanity coincides with the history of Europe. One can have different understandings about how widely one should search for these sources, as well as different views about whether "Europe" is a fitting term for the place of this development. Even so, it is difficult to contest the fact that the rise of the scientific world-view, which now dominates the globe, has a certain geographical locus. The problem with Husserl's view is not his ethnocentrism per se—it is difficult to conceive of such an account that would not be similarly ethnocentric. Rather, the problem lies in what can be termed a blindness—not only for this ethnocentricity, but the entire ipsocentricity, or self-centeredness of Husserlian thought. Husserl takes for granted that the *telos* of humanity is unfolded in "European humanity", and that the *telos* of European humanity lies in reason's self-transparency. Rationality is per definition that which leads to the good. It is therefore of course rational to desire rationality (Hu VI, §73, p.275). But since rationality has been shown to be rationality such as it has grown in the European tradition, it can only be our image or view of this rationality towards which we live. The rationality towards which we (we humans, Europeans, we scientists, we philosophers?) desire to live cannot, however, be limited to this view; it must be rationality as such. Every human being can take part in this adventure of reason, and can become European in this sense;[251] the focus on a European reason does not exclude other rational views. On the contrary, if another view is shown to be rational, it can serve to correct the view of rationality that functions as guide for the European adventure.

This still harbours a naïveté. The problem lies particularly in the identity that Husserl forges between humanity and rationality, between rationality and self-transparency. The philosopher is, as Husserl says, a functionary of humanity. For Husserlian ethics, developed in 1924-25 in the *Kaizo* articles, natural science operates an exemplar. Husserl writes: "We believe in a good humanity as an ideal possibility, a true and genuine possibility, as an objectively valid idea" (Hu XXVII, p. 10). The good comes from the true and the genuine. Husserl holds that since only something defined within limits can be good, the good humanity implies the true and genuine humanity as an objectively valid idea. Mathematics is here the model science. This does not mean that ethics should be subordinated to mathematics (Hu XXVII, p.17-18); assuming that a science of the lifeworld should be understood through mathematics is consonant with the reductionism that phenomenology has always criticised. What Husserl means is that ethics shall be an *a priori* science of the ideal. This science shall help us reach the goodness of humanity. And there is, according to Husserl, *one* good and authentic life form of humanity—"to live to become a genuine and true human being, or a man of reason [...]", for "to the extent that he is human, a human being has ideals" (Hu XXVII, p. 35) How do we know that this European philosophical way of life is the path to the human and to the good? The answer, from Husserl's viewpoint, seems to be self-given: this way of life desires to be rational, and the rational life is the life that desires the good. It is tautological. But the faculty of reason can never be fully developed, can never reach itself, which is its *telos*. It must always be in development. Every conception of rationality is thus provisional, i.e., potentially irrational. For the modus of theoretical language in which this is expressed, this might seem a paradox. But in aiming towards the good our lives are much wider than this intellectual theoretical discourse. Life includes our instincts, appetites, physical desires, and all other human abilities or faculties, of which the intellect is only one, and the power of theoretical discourse, only one focus of the intellect. Thus if rationality means pursuing the good, we must in our intellectual pursuit of this good give expression to the limits of our own view. And this is something for which Levinas did not find the tools in Husserl to argue; Husserl never wavered in his belief in the possible analogy between the theoretical and the practical-axiological. The risk with this belief is that the discrepancy between the proper view of the good and the good itself becomes blurred. This is the cause of the blindness for one's own ethnocentrism, one's own ipsocentrism, which ultimately is a blindness to the violence of one's own position as a subject. The fact that Husserl holds objectivity to be

[251] This is a view that is underscribed by Levinas in "Being a Westerner" (DL 79-84; DF 46-49).

intersubjectively constituted does not diminish, but possibly only serves to hide the problem. All problems of power relations, implicit in knowledge and its universalisation thereof, are obscured by Husserl's commitment to a universalism guided by the form of normality.[252]

Husserl can come to no other conclusion than that the philosophers are "the functionaries of humanity" (Hu VI, p. 17, 81), preserving the essence of the European spirit. European culture is on the one hand a culture among others, but it is also the culture of the universal, the culture of humanity. Human beings from other cultures all have the possibility of joining this culture, this project of universality, the possibility of Europeanising/humanising themselves. They are for Husserl of course already human in one sense, but can also become more human, by entering the culture of Europe. This is what made it possible for Husserl to speak of a Papuan as a human being "in a broad sense" (Hu VI, p. 321).[253]

It would not be right merely to isolate these views of Husserl, as one often does, by ascribing them only to their most specific cultural situation of Germany in the beginning of the 20th century. It is important to see how they are deeply anchored in the rationalism of Western philosophy as a whole. Husserlian phenomenology was, in this sense, a very consistent rationalism.

A self-glorification of the theoretical attitude will, in any culture, run the risk of a tautological self-confirmation and self-affirmation in discourse, which easily serves a cultural narcissism. Even if, in practice, Levinas showed his own weakness as a cultural narcissist, there is a potential in the Levinasian approach to found critical reason in ethical sensibility. This means that, since universalisation is both a violation of and a gift to the singular, it is intrinsic to the rational subject to be self-critical with respect to its very rationality. But how is this conflict between the universal and the singular played out concretely?

One event that motivated much criticism against Levinas was the radio discussion in which he took part shortly after the massacre of Palestinan refugees in Sabra and Shatila in 1982.[254] Levinas was asked by Shlomo Malka: "Emmanuel Levinas, you are the philosopher of the 'other'. Isn't history, isn't politics the very

---

252 Cf. *Krisis*, Husserliana Bd. 6, 1976, p. 181, according to which it is the "mature normal humanity", (not children and the insane) that partake in constituting a horizon of humanity. For Husserl, normality can of course be put into question by the confrontation with a foreign normality—but this is only if it turns out that this brings us closer to truth.

253 In a letter to Leo Strauss on September 17, 1943, Eric Voegelin draws a very harsh inference from Husserl's concept of humanity: "By thus confining humanity to the community of those who, in Husserl's sense, can philosophize with one another, the philosophical *telos* comes close to the particular, intra-mundane collectivities of the type of the Marxian proletariat, Hitler's German *Volk*, or Mussolini's *Italianità*)." *The Collected Works of Eric Voegelin. Volume 29, Selected* Correspondence, ed. Ellis Sandoz, University of Missoury Press, 2009, p. 367.

254 During the first Lebanese civil war, Israeli soldiers let armed Christian phalangists enter these two Palestine refugee camps. The phalangists attacked and killed over 2000 Palestinians, while Israeli soldiers stopped the Palestinians trying to escape the camp.

site of the encounter with the 'other', and for the Israeli, isn't the 'other' above all the Palestinian?' (IEP 5; LR 294). To this, Levinas answered:

> My definition of the other is completely different. The other is the neighbour, who is not necessarily kin, but who can be. And in that sense, if you're for the other, you're for the neighbour. But if your neighbour attacks another neighbour or treats him unjustly what can you do? Then alterity takes on another character, in alterity we can find an enemy or at least then we are faced with the problem of knowing who is right and who is wrong, who is just and who is unjust. There are people who are wrong [*Il y a des gens qui ont tort*] (Ibid).

Influential readers of Levinas[255] have taken this to mean that the Palestinians are dehumanised, that it is they who are "the enemy"; they are the people "who are wrong", and thus are disqualified as ethical others. My reading is entirely different. Even if he should have chosen his words more carefully, by reading the whole interview, one can see clearly he is not saying that the Palestinians are not ethical others for the Jews. What he is warning against is the reduction of "otherness" to cultural differentiation, a misunderstanding that Malka perpetuates in his very mode of questioning.

The problem Levinas wishes to focus on in the course of the radio discussion is the movement from the ethical to the political. If there were only one neighbour, my concern would be for that neighbour alone; there would only be the ethical unmixed with the political. But the fact is that there is not one but many and they can treat each other unjustly. As Levinas writes in *Otherwise than Being*, I have a responsibility also for the other's responsibility. Therefore, he asserts also in this interview, there is no way in which one can claim that a certain event (such as a massacre) is not our problem.[256] To paraphrase Dostoyevsky: Everything is everyone's problem, especially mine.

Some Jews in Israel had raised concern about this kind of criticism voiced from European shores. Since such critics had not taken part in building and defending Israel, they should now remain quiet on the question as to how Israel should conduct its domestic and foreign affairs. In this discussion, Levinas addresses this kind of defence of Israel, saying there is no way in which the Israelis can wave away the accusations from the Europeans by saying "You are beautiful souls". Levinas is alluding to Hegel's notion of "die schöne Seele",[257] such that the Israeli would hold the Europeans to be "beautiful souls", hypocrites, who should

[255] Cf. Howard Caygill, *Levinas and the Political*, Routledge, 2002, p. 193, according to which Levinas thereby suggests that "the Palestinians are not the others, are neighbours". Simon Critchley also agrees with Caygill, reading Levinas as not feeling able to condemn the murders (Critchley, "Five problems in Levinas's view of politics and the sketch of a solution to them", Political Theory, Vol. 32, No. 2, April 2004, p. 175.

[256] Levinas might be addressing Israeli Prime Minister Menachem Begin's famous statement after the massacre: "Goyim kill goyim and then they come to blame the Jews".

[257] Discussed above, section 2.3.2.

mind their own business and suspend judgement until such a time when the means have been justified by the ends. But Levinas replies: "Fearing to be beautiful souls, we decide to become villainous souls" (IEP 5; LR 294). Since my responsibility extends to the responsibility of others, I have not only the right, but the obligation to speak out against injustice. At the end of the interview he speaks out against the notion of "Zionism as a mystique of the earth" as a "calumny", a misuse of the biblical language. "The person is more holy than a land, even if it is a holy land, since before an injustice done to a person, this holy land appears in its nudity to be nothing but rocks and trees" (IEP 8; LR 296).

By reading the whole interview—and not only the excerpts that seem to be circulating among Levinas's critics—it becomes clear that the people "who are wrong" are the murderers, those assisting in the murder, and those who try to reduce this murder to political expediency for the sake of Israel. Why then can he not simply affirm that the Palestinian is the other of the Israeli? His point is that neither Palestinians nor Israelis are my neighbours *qua* Palestinians or Israeli; on the contrary, in my response to someone as my neighbour I cannot reduce him or her to their cultural identity.

Now, according to Robert Bernasconi, whose interpretation of Levinas's position in this matter (WN 6-7) I share, this unwillingness to give alterity a cultural content becomes precisely the sticking point with Levinas's position. Bernasconi writes:

> Has one welcomed the victim of colour prejudice when one still welcomes him or her only as human and without recognising the positivity of that which has previously been devalued? "Being human" is an idea with a content. Is it not imposed on the Other by an "imperialism and egoism" that "the humanism of the other man" is supposed to counteract? (WN 5).

Even if the theme is no longer about Israel and Palestine, nevertheless we find Bernasconi asking Malka's question all over again: is it not the very cultural difference, the fact of not being Jewish or Israeli, that constitutes the otherness of the Palestinians? Bernasconi asks, thus, that the other be viewed "in his or her particular cultural difference from me" (WN 26), "as ethnically Other" (WN 2). Elaborating on this, Bernasconi refers us to the preface from 1978 to *Time and the Other*, in which Levinas speaks of "alterity-content" (WN 8, 15, 24). This notion is used by Levinas by way of a justification for the somewhat bizarre conclusion reached during the 1946-47 lectures, where he claimed that the other is identified as the feminine. When, in the preface from 1978, he returns to this text, it is to salvage from this philosophical experiment the idea that otherness is more than a mere "other than", that there can be a proper content to alterity. This alterity-content is then filled with the domain of the ethical, later named proximity. Alterity is then never to be understood as "other than"—for example other than a particular culture. Of course, I never encounter the other outside of cultural contexts. However, the risk with saying that I always encounter the other in her cultural specificity is that I have already established "culture" as the system of coordinates in which the other can be encountered. The problem might become more clear if the claim were that we could encounter the other only in the specificity of his or her race. There is no such thing as race, one could protest. But is there, strictly speaking, any such thing as culture? There are always categories that affect the possibilities of encountering the other, but these categories are always in flux, and the concrete singularity of the other can never be reduced to them.

As I have argued earlier, Derrida's critique of Levinas's usage of the concept of alterity might be the reason that Levinas later prefers to talk about the proximity of the neighbour (*prochain*) rather than the alterity of the other, a concept that admittedly never leaves the foreground of his texts.

Levinas is consistent in saying how the proximity of the neighbour abstracts itself from his or her cultural origin. In the case of National Socialism, it seems evident that what transpired was a language and a pattern of behaviour that repeatedly managed to deny "the proximity" of the Jews. This was of course Levinas's most important example—so important that it almost ceased to be an example. In the dedication at the beginning of *Otherwise than Being* he identifies antisemitism with the hatred of the other man. This is his way of spanning the gap between particularism and universalism; in one breath Levinas claims to talk about one particular incomparable hatred, and the universal problem of the hatred against the other man. It is by "riveting" a person to her Jewishness (He 44), by disclaiming the way in which she disengages herself as an act of abstraction from culture, (HAH 60; CPP 101) that I am then in a position to commit crimes of racism and genocide. But of course, one could ask, as does Bernasconi, whether this "abstractness of the face mark[s] a certain continuity with abstract humanism and its complicity with homogenization?" (WN 5). To this we might answer yes, of course. There is no way in which it cannot. But a philosophy of the human must also aspire to include the capacity of self-reflexivity needed to discover itself as guilty of this homogenization. As an ever recurring task of fight this tendency, philosophy entails a practice of critique that never ceases to criticise its own hypocrisy—resaying the said.

The alternative, to let go of the concreteness of human proximity (which is, admittedly, also an abstraction), seems to me a more dangerous route. To claim that the other concerns me in his or her particular *cultural* difference from me, amounts to making the political practice of positive discrimination (affirmative action) the primary relation to the other. Politically, positive discrimination is often necessary, depending on the situation. Be this as it may, the critical question we might wish to raise to Bernasconi is whether, in his formulations, such a practice is to take prominence by default? If a person needs my help because she has been subjected to racism, then my help must of course take her cultural specificity into account; I cannot, as Levinas says, "approach the Other with empty hands" (TI 42; TaI 50). But this should not be confused with the question of *why* she is my concern. She is my concern simply because she is my neighbour. This is why I find the concept of proximity to be preferable to alterity. It is not because the other is *different* from me in any specific way that she concerns me, she simply does. This is the alterity-content of the other, that he or she is my concern! But, we could argue with Bernasconi that this very concern already has content. Indeed as Levinas describes it in biblical metaphors, the other is "the widow, the orphan and the stranger" (cf. DEE 162; EE 98). But these are also images of the other that are overrun, overdetermined by the ethical. Understanding proximity from a notion of ethnic or cultural alterity seems to carry the risk of what might brutally be called an ethical exoticism: the more different someone is, the more I should respond to her. To put it otherwise: by letting the cultural denominations be ethically overdetermined, we will contribute to solidifying racial and cultural hierarchies. Let us recall Beauvoir's criticisms regarding Levinas's exoticism of the woman as other (above, section 1.3), and ask: Was she not right to protest against his strategy of making the woman the other? Now, against the attempts to think the other in terms of the Palestinian, is not Levinas (this time wiser) equally right when he reacts in a similar way against this othering of the Palestinian? As soon as the framework for ethical otherness is given, the other is trapped in my scheme of reference. Frantz Fanon wrote of the dilemma that subtends a racialising scheme:

> As I begin to recognize that the Negro is the symbol of sin, I catch myself hating the Negro. But then I recognize that I am a Negro. There are two ways out of this conflict. Either I ask others to pay no attention to my skin, or else I want them to be aware of it.[258]

Either way, as soon as skin colour or culture is given a value, riveting the other to his or her culture will be just as violent as the abstraction from this culture. Then again, the other is always already placed and interpreted through my schemas. However, Levinas's notion of the proximity of the neighbour gives expression to an ethical concern that exceeds these schemas, and in doing so, serves both to problematise and challenge such categories. This does not mean that my hands are empty, only that it cannot be predetermined what I carry in these hands. The transcendence of the schemes such that they be replaced by other schemes that must be questioned anew—this is the interminable circle that both our ethical and critical tasks are bound by. I have discussed the same problem as the restlessness of the human, as youth, and (with the help of Bernasconi himself) as the non-violence never without violence yet irreducible to violence. In these formulations we come to an understanding of the human that opens up the possibil-

[258] Frantz Fanon, *Black Skin, White Masks*, Pluto Press, 1986, p. 197.

ity for enacting a dissensus against the culturalist discourse, which today has a monopoly on both the means and ends of ethically informed action. If Levinas sometimes highlights the figure of the stranger (in particular in the earlier texts) it is not because the stranger is more *worthy* of my concern. His reason for emphasising the stranger is that the concern for him is more *difficult* than for our close ones, because he is more likely to cause a disturbance in our economy of enjoyment than is our friend.

Rudi Visker shares a set of similar concerns with Bernasconi about Levinas's philosophy of the human. Through a close reading of *Totality and Infinity* (especially) and *Otherwise than being* (also), Visker delivers a complex argument, drawing the conclusion that Levinas ought to be less Platonist, his Other less abstract. Levinas is censured for placing too much emphasis on the other being above *culture*; the destitution of the other, so Visker claims, cannot be understood without seeing him as embedded in a culture he cannot rid himself of, although he does not have access to it. His destitution and otherness is then not only other in relation to me, but already other "to some 'Thing' which remains 'other' to him and yet singularizes him at the same time".[259] This does not mean that Visker seeks to refute Levinas's insight into the impossibility of reducing the Other to his cultural forms. The point is rather that the ethical other cannot be understood as being that which is principally outside of and above them. The destitution of the other would then have no meaning. According to Visker, the destitution thereby silently receives a theological meaning: ethics becomes a theology in disguise.

Visker's text is interesting in that it lays out certain aspects of the Levinasian structure in a new way. Nevertheless, Visker's main philosophical point can easily be posed within a Levinasian framework. The ethical relation to the other is always ontologically clothed, which is what Levinas means when he says that one cannot approach the other with empty hands. The "thing" which Visker wants us to understand the other as being defined by, corresponds to the necessity by which my response to the other must be given a particular content. It is important to uphold one distinction that becomes blurred in Visker's account (as well as in Bernasconi's): *that* the other might awaken my sensibility must be distinguished from the way her own situatedness might alter the way in which I need to respond. These two elements might in every case be inextricably intertwined: if a Muslim asks me to help her to defend her rights to wear the burka, I might end up in a dilemma of conflicting inclinations. I may be inclined both to help her defend her rights to wear what she chooses, as well as to persuade her to fight what I perceive as questionable patriarchal cultural practices which compel her to wear the burka. No matter how this is perceived by me, her appeal would not be transmissible if abstracted from cultural heritages (whether hers or mine),

[259] Visker, "Dis-possessed: How to remain silent 'after' Levinas", *Man and World*, 29, 1996, p. 140.

heritages which, Visker rightly argues, we are defined by in a way we cannot decide entirely on our own. What Levinas would emphasise is that ethical response cannot be pre-given by this cultural context alone—that the response as such exceeds this contextualism.

The problem remains, however: how shall we relate to the fact that the escape route for which Levinas opts is named and nurtured in the Western tradition? In a world so dominated by Western thinking, of technological, economic and political systems that derive from the West, what paths should "we" take in order to help the notion of the human remain an opening out of any systemic consensus? Is a philosophy of the human, in spite of it all, "our" discourse for this, and if so, can it nonetheless be a discourse open to other perspectives? The ideas that we have discussed in this section, and the position we have sought to develop throughout the whole of the investigation, can be pictured as offering a quite convenient solution, namely a notion of the human, around which a consensus of the dominant has often gathered, but which now, through a dialectical reversal, signifies the possibility of all dissensus, of all transcendence beyond a self-complacent consensus. The renewal of the notion seems to be a simple case of substituting one set of predicates (complacency, consensus, transcendental ego) with another set (dissensus, interruption, the other).

Here, the human seems to be both a formal cause of and an actual solution to the problem. In such a situation, how shall the concern be phrased? Levinas sees the threat in the historicity of the human. The human is a concept that was once found and might—as Foucault prophesied (even if his definition of the ending man was meant otherwise)—soon be no more. At the close of *Otherwise than Being*, Levinas asks himself if there is a risk that the meaning of the human he wishes to nurture, will end, will be no more. For Levinas, such a cessation would also entail the termination of critique, the end of philosophy. If most of the time, he dismisses all these "endings" as slogans from the Parisian intelligentsia (cf. HAH 95; CPP 141), here he seems to rather be expressing a true concern of this end of sense.

As its epigraph, the final chapter to *Otherwise than Being* commences with the following extract from Faust II:

Mephistopheles:	Willst du nur hören, was du schon gehört? Dich störe nichts wie es auch weiter klinge Schon längst gewohnt der wunderbarsten Dinge
Faust:	Doch im Erstarren such ich nicht mein Heil Das Schaudern ist der Menschheit bester Teil

(Goethe, Faust II, Act I)[260]

[260] English translation by George Madison Priest: "Mephistopheles: Will you but hear what you've already heard? / Let naught disturb you, though it strangely rings, / You! long since

Not immobilisation in a perfect state—no matter how beautiful the things Mephistopheles will show him—but "shuddering" is the best part of mankind, and it is the choice of Faust. As we saw in his very earliest texts, he associates humanity with restlessness and trembling. Levinas is not thinking of restlessness as the traditionally Faustian idea of constantly being in motion, on its way to better and newer goals. Nor does it only refer to the mere notion of being in constant change and flux. For Levinas, there can be no self-justification, neither movement nor rest are by themselves better, more justified; justification must be directed by the sensibility for the other. But on the other hand, in the notion of the human as critique lies a constant questioning of so-called foundations, showing a fundamental foundationlessness. In the penultimate paragraph of the final chapter of *Otherwise than Being*, the topic returns. It is a paragraph which functions as a meta-reflection on the scope of the book as a whole (AE 282-283, OB 184-185). Levinas starts:

> The book interprets the subject as a hostage and the subjectivity of the subject as a substitution breaking with being's essence (AE 282; OB 184).

Phrased in the terms we have become acquainted with in our investigation, we can say: the subject is a hostage, because it is defined as a transcendence from the economy of being; yet it is always drawn back in, violently captured by the very same economy. One must on the one hand conceive of the economy as violent; on the other hand, subjectivity—thought by Levinas as for-the-other or as he says here, substitution—allows one to break with the essence of Being. This rupture is analogous to what we have described in terms of one's irreducibility to an economy (the essence of being) in which one is nonetheless always-already inscribed. Levinas continues:

> The thesis is exposed imprudently to the reproach of utopianism in an opinion where modern man takes himself as a being among beings, whereas his modernity breaks up as an impossibility to remain at home. This book escapes the reproach of utopianism—if utopianism is a reproach, if any thought escapes utopianism—by recalling that what took place humanly has never been able to remain closed up in its site. (AE 282; OB 185)

What he construes is not utopianism in the sense of construing a place beyond places; it is utopian, however, if utopian means talking of that which goes beyond the topos, understood both as site and as theme. Somewhat further down he continues:

> Here I am for the others—an e-normous response, whose inordinateness is attenuated with hypocrisy as soon as it enters my ears forewarned of being's

wonted to most wondrous things. / Faust: And yet in torpor there's no gain for me; The thrill of awe is man's best quality.", Alfred A. Knopf, 1941.

> essence, that is, the way being carries on. The hypocrisy is from the first denounced. But the norms to which the denunciation refers have been understood in the enormity of meaning and in the full resonance of their statement to be true like an unrefrained witness. In any case nothing less was needed for the little humanity which adorns the world. (AE 283, OB 185).

With the idea of an e-normity of meaning we can perhaps find a protest against Husserl's notion of normality as constitutive of the human. Rather, the human can only be understood from out of the e-normity of a rupture, in the sense of the possibility of a rupture with the normal. This e-normity cannot be pronounced in a non-hypocritical way (let's face it: no-one is really there for the others in the radical way which Levinas bombastically pronounces it). Yet denouncing the norms as hypocritical means acknowledging them on a higher, "e-normous" (Ibid) level. It means that the sharpness of the critical glance discovering the hypocrisy of the moral claim is already part of the movement going beyond this hypocrisy. In order for there to be a meaning of a critique waged against hypocrisy at all, the e-normity of the human must be thought. The meaning of critique rests on this rupture, on this e-normity, on this "little humanity that adorns the world". It is neither "in" nor "beyond" the world, but it is the very quality of the rupture.

The little humanity that adorns the world wages "the just war waged against war" and trembles "because of this very justice"; it is thus not a shuddering before the immensity of harmonious being, but before the injustice of justice, the violence of non-violence. Its condition of possibility rests in youth, a youth that on the one hand per definition passes, but which in this passing makes possible the transcendence of the economy of violence. This transcendence cannot be a presence in which one can rest, it takes place as passing, unable "to remain closed up in its site".

This opens up our question about how Levinas views the stability of the very notion of the human. How can it, according to Levinas, be defended, how is it to live on? And in wanting it to live on, is one not asking it to do what precisely its definition proscribes? Did we not conceive of the human as a break with every consensus? I think it is in the answer to this question that we can most clearly detect a conservatism in the thought of Levinas. In his text from 1973, "Antihumanism and education" (DL 412-432; DF 277-288), he complains about the basic inability of Western liberalism to "guarantee the privileges of humanity of which humanism had considered itself the repository" (DL 418; DF 281). "The meaning of humanity", he says here, "is neither exhausted by the humanities; nor immune to a slippage that is at first imperceptible but can ultimately prove fatal" (Ibid). The antihumanists do a service to the Western tradition by questioning its self-congratulatory self-understanding. "Western Humanism has never managed to doubt triumph or understand failure or conceive of a history in which the vanquished and the persecuted might have some value" (DL 419;

DF 282). Levinas means that modern antihumanism therefore can play a part also in Jewish education, by "stripping certain commonplaces of their false foliage and putting an end to eloquence" (DL 421; DF 283).

Judaism has "the unique means to preserve the humanity and the personality of man. This agency teaches us true humanism... through the whole breadth of experience amassed over thousands of years, which has remained original throughout the course of history" (DL 425; DF 286). It would appear, then, that the notion of the human he wishes to introduce to philosophy rests, according to Levinas, on the Jewish traditions and practices that have developed over millennia: gestures and rituals, which have harnessed inspirations that would otherwise be lost. Like Nietzsche, Levinas believes that interiorisation and spiritualisation can lead to nihilism (DL 428; DF 288). But still, the practices have a purpose. He continues: "These are practices carried out to please God only to the extent that they allow one to safeguard the human in man" (DL 429; DF 288).

We find that, in consistence with his understanding of the human as the anarchic possibility of critique, Levinas welcomes the antihumanist criticism of humanist essentialism. But then, in a seemingly paradoxal way, Levinas shows that there is a particular understanding of humanity harboured in the practices of Judaism. If "the human" means restlessness, though, if it is an-archy, without foundation, is not this talk of safeguarding the human in man not a gesture that defeats its purpose, one that tries to permanently transcend the economy of violence? And do not his descriptions of the Jewish practices, supposedly "safeguard[ing] the human in man", repeat the eloquence that he commends antihumanism for dispelling? Even if they, as practices, have an existence beyond this discourse, it is through a discourse such as this that we are to be persuaded of their ability to "safeguard the human". The link between the practices and the discourse is silently assumed as a guarantee that the critique, made possible by these practices, is not itself hypocritical. But as we saw, the radical critique made possible by the notion of the human cannot claim to be untainted by hypocrisy. Hypocrisy is a human predicament, rather than a "base contingent defect of man" (Ti 9; TaI 24).

This talk of safeguarding the human has a parallel in the tendency of Levinas to let the ethical "outbid" the ontological, assuming and displacing thereby the foundationalist language of ontology. In fact, Levinas himself provides us with the tools for our criticism:

> The ethical (*l'éthique*) is before ontology. It is more ontological than ontology; an emphasis of ontology [...]. It is from there that a certain equivocation comes—whereby the ethical seems laid on top of ontology, whereas it is before ontology. It [his own philosophy] is thus a transcendentalism beginning with ethics (DVI 143; GCM 143).

By saying that ethics comes before ontology, or as elsewhere, that "ethics is first philosophy", Levinas repeats the gestures of ontologism. Of course, these are slogans and titles—but they are not unimportant. At the same time, he always warns against this interpretation. Such is the case when, for example, he asserts that ethics is nothing real (EDE 241), or in his most famous formula, naming the ethical the otherwise than being. Even so, these are negations which risk affirming the very paradigm he is criticising. Even in *Otherwise than Being,* he seems trapped in a set of problems the notions of the saying and the said were to protect him. This occurs for example, when he elaborates on the concept of proximity. First, Levinas convincingly shows, in a style similar to Husserl, Heidegger and Merleau-Ponty, that Euclidian geometry cannot have the exclusive right to the notion of proximity.

> If this geometry and physics were at the beginning, the signifying attributes would never have anything but a subjective existence in the heads of men, the customs and writings of peoples [...] The very presence of Man in these spaces, the alleged source of the signifying attributes, would be, outside of its strictly geometrical or physico-chemical sense, an interior fact of an absurd being cooked in its own juices (AE 130; OB 81).

This does not mean that space and proximity are to be associated with a state of consciousness, i.e. to the representations of the theorising subject. This understanding of proximity must, according to Levinas, via the notion of the third, refer back to proximity: "The representation of signification is itself born in the signifyingness of proximity in the measure that a third party is alongside the neighbour." (AE 132; OB 83).

Here, I think that Levinas has gone too far. He has already done enough when he shows that the proximity of the neighbour cannot be reduced to the proximity of two points in Euclidian space. When he tries to prove that the representation of space is "born" from the ethical proximity of more than one neighbour this is going too far. In fact, in his eagerness to show how the ethical proximity is beyond the geometrical or otherwise ontological space, he subsumes the ethical under an ontologist language.

Incidentally, this case of founding the geometrical proximity in the proximity of the neighbour replaces a movement in *Totality and infinity,* where the bizarre claim is raised that we can experience physical or spatial height only because of the asymmetrical relation to the other as higher than me.[261]

These are both examples of the suspicion towards metaphors that Derrida notes in Levinas (ED 210; WD 178); they are attempts to arrest the flux of lan-

---

[261] "Labor [...] already requires discourse and consequently the height of the other irreducible to the same, the presence of the Other. There is no natural religion; but already human egoism leaves nature *by virtue of the human body raised upwards,* committed *in the direction of height. This is not its empirical illusion but its ontological production and ineffaceable testimony.*" (TI 121; TaI 117; Levinas's emphasis).

guage by tying the notion of the human to an ontological structure. When Levinas does this it is with the same conservatism with which he claims that Judaism can "safeguard the human" in man. Did he not make this connection between ontologism and conservatism himself, when talking about "the essential conservatism" of the bourgeoisie and its philosophy? (DE 92; OE 50)[262]

However, if the notion of the human is used with this conservative tendency, maybe the consistent post-humanist Levinasian should just get rid of it altogether? Why does this interruption of the economy have to be connected to a sensibility for another person? Why could it not be sensibility for life itself in its non-unity, for anything other? This is an important question: on the one hand, the strength of the Levinasian approach is its insistence on understanding the ethical from out of its concretion. On the other, the concretion can be disturbing. Why this particular concretion, why stop at the human, why not the animal or life or Being as a whole? One attempt to deal with this problem is undertaken by Simon Critchley, in his recent work *Infinitely Demanding*.[263] Here, inspired by Levinas, he makes what I interpret as a very powerful and compelling attempt to dissociate ethics from humanism, indeed from any particular ethical content. Ethical experience, in the formal description that Critchley gives it, has two components: approval and demand. He remains a Levinasian in the sense of adhering to the notion of the ethical as an infinite demand on the subject. But it is not necessarily the face, the neighbour, the other that provokes this demand; Critchley wants to give a purely formal description of the ethical, abstracted from all content. The form that he arrives at is the ethical statement. In order for me to experience something as an ethical demand, I must first approve of a certain ethical statement, such as "love thy neighbour as thyself". Only those who approve of a certain ethical statement can experience it as a demand. This is an attempt to preserve the heteronomy of the Levinasian ethics whilst not specifying the object or the source of the ethical. Critchley is thus not here claiming to merely give an interpretation of Levinas, but developing the thought of Levinas in a less humanist way, in a way that is not dependent on a particular ontological description of what is ethically binding. In the way in which Critchley tries to avoid subordinating the ethical to the ontological, his line of argumentation is entirely consistent with Levinas. By letting the ethical appeal come from the statements of which the ethical subject itself approves, he is minimising the ontological account of a transcendent otherworldly, or something other which purportedly is the source of the ethical appeal.

One problem is that the approval must come from the approving subject itself. It seems that a truly heteronomous ethics, which Critchley still wants to defend, would have to be a demand on you before you approve of it; the approv-

[262] Discussed earlier, section 1.2.
[263] *Infinitely Demanding. Ethics of Commitment. Politics of Resistance*, Verso, 2007.

al could thus only be given ad hoc. Critchley could of course add that approving of a statement is not a matter of conscious choice: I cannot simply choose what statements I approve of, but they are somehow given to me by tradition and/or my previous reasoning; *hic et nunc* I might sense the demand as incumbent on me, from the outside. However, this privileging of the statement seems to amount to a logicisation of ethics, giving primacy of the said over saying in ethics; though not in the sense that it reduces the possibly paradoxical nature of ethical experience; this paradox could be accounted for by Critchley by demands from conflicting statements—such as "war is always evil", and "You have to fight against injustice". Even if we leave this aside, the question remains: can ethics really have its origin in an approval of a statement? How can statements be binding? Unfortunately we are led into a vicious circle. In order for moral statements to be binding, must not the subject approve of a statement saying that approved moral statements are binding? And so on, ad infinitum. Must we not first explain the subject's sensibility for moral statements? For Levinas, the moral statement can have its impact only because of the subject's vulnerability to a neighbour, or more simply put: only if others can be of my concern. In focusing on statements rather than vulnerability, Critchley seems to sacrifice the notion of sensibility, so central to Levinas. Of course, this might be countered by Critchley, who after all teaches us that the Levinasian subject is divided according to the formula the other-in-the-same, such that there is a heteroaffection within the subject. But still it seems to remain a relation between statements—one is not told why the statement as such affects me. Is it not because someone speaks them or writes them? Is not a statement a part of language, and is not the impact of language on me precisely the sensibility for the other? To summarise, Critchley switches the "ethical content" from the human to the statement, which in the end seems a deeply unsatisfying and non-intuitive source of our ethical affection. From a Levinasian point of view, the ethical source of the statement lies in it being spoken (or written) to and by the other, not in the content of the statement. This is how we are ethically implicated in language.

The location of Levinasian ethics is at the very intersection of the concrete and the abstract. Even if the notion of the human is an abstraction that does violence to our concrete ethical experiences, it is also the concrete form of a discourse in which, whether we like it or not, all of us are inscribed. Is it perhaps the case, therefore, that the notion of the human remains the ultimate form and content of political and ethical critique?

To my mind, this is an essential part of Levinas's insight. His philosophy is a meta-humanism: a philosophy that incorporates the movements of humanism and antihumanism in its philosophy, and which aims at a resaying of the human. Humanism has to be denounced for not caring enough for the notion of the human, (AE 203; OB 128) but antihumanism errs also, writes Levinas, by giving up the search in man for "the trace of this prehistorical and an-archical saying" (HaH 91; CPP 139).

As we have seen, the human is not at all a philosophical concept with a clear ontological content. But this does not mean that it is mere rhetoric. It has throughout the history of philosophy been tied to the structure of philosophy in its differing approaches and systems. Between eras of philosophy, the notion of the human has been understood differently. In humanism, the notion of the human was a "cosmic analogy" to which philosophy was the path[264]; antihumanism, on the other hand, is concerned with the theoretical destruction of a human subject constituting the world. Levinas shows how philosophy, already when it speaks, presupposes the notion of the human as critique, justification. This is the way in which Levinas can justly claim that ethics is first philosophy—philosophical justifications, even justifications of ontological claims are, finally, ethical. Levinas sees this as the ultimate meaning of the Copernican turn in philosophy, the reduction of content to communication, from the question 'what?' to the question 'who?', from the said to the saying.

The question of justification of philosophy cannot be given an ultimate answer; philosophy cannot be given a final foundation. But it is, on the other hand, not a question which philosophy, with peace of mind, can put to one side—if, that is, it harbours the hope of remaining a philosophy of radical questioning. Levinas, who thinks philosophy as critique, is not prepared to dispel such a hope.

264 "ein herzustellendes kosmisches Gleichnis", Eugen Fink, *Metaphysik der Erziehung im Weltverständnis von Plato und Aristoteles*, Kloterna, 1970.

Concluding Remarks

Where have we ended up? What is "the human" in the work of Levinas? This might seem to be the wrong way to pose the question. As we know, Levinas's own injunctive is that one should turn from the question 'what?' to the question 'who?', thus shifting from the thematic to the singular. One way of taking this objection into account would be to describe the notion precisely in this movement from the singular to the thematic, from the saying to the said. Levinas does not start from the notion of humankind, identifying certain characteristics shared by all human beings. Understanding the human as abstract humanity is for him secondary to the very social moment between the other and I, me and my neighbour, which makes possible a rupture with these abstract categories. And if in *Totality and Infinity* Levinas was dangerously close to reinventing a resting place in the surplus of experience—the *kath'auto* of the other—the social moment, in *Otherwise than Being*, is no longer understood from the category of an experience, or of a presence, not even as a transcendence beyond this experience. This emphasis on the rupture is thus not a blunt denial of the universal and the conceptual in favour of the singular and the experiential, a criticism, which, for example, both Žižek and Badiou raise at his thinking. On the contrary, the very path to the universal is initiated in the relation to the other, the neighbour. The rupture of the economy, which the opening to the neighbour signifies, is for Levinas the condition of possibility for the disinterested statement. This does not mean that the disinterested statement as such exists as an origin in itself. Doubtless this disinterested statement is a principle of science. But it is only as an intermittent rupture with interest that it receives its significance.

Another approach to the question of the thematisability of the notion of the human in Levinas would be to articulate this central idea in its relation to other terms. It is produced in a network of parallel concepts and notions, such as "obsession", "persecution", "substitution", "responsibility", and "proximity". It is a weaving together of this discourse which must at the same time provide an opening for that which it thematises, so that it can appear anew, always renewed, forever in its singularity. In the original French, Levinas does not define these concepts in terms of each other in the form of x is y, [265] but rather in the terms of impressionistically embroidered nominal phrases, continually varying similar themes, creating a wide parallelism of concepts. Levinas himself expresses the

[265] In the "Translator's Note" to *Otherwise than Being*, (OB xliv) Alphonso Lingis expresses his regret not being able to render this quality in the English translation.

suspicion that the copula is presupposed in these expressions, but nevertheless, in this way he shows the attempt of allowing the meaning to come from the movement to the beyond, rather than the horizontal significations in being. If in *Totality and Infinity* the human was the phenomenality that points beyond the phenomenon, the experience that points beyond the experience, in *Otherwise than Being* the notion of the human is the discursive structure that points beyond the discourse to the very opening of the discourse. It is therefore an opening that is not provided by a non-discursive givenness, be it the theological or phenomenological, exegetical or experiential. The opening is in this sense, as he says, an-archic. As is the case with Husserl and Hegel, Levinas inquires into the beginnings of rational discourse. Unlike Husserl, Levinas does not search for a foundation, but exactly for the an-archic, the non-principled beginning. From a Hegelian point of view this might be seen as the weakness of a non-dialectic movement. However, Levinas insists on such a weakness as the unavoidable heart of a philosophy examining its own premises, its own rationality. In *Totality and Infinity* this awareness of the necessary, and in a sense, aspired weakness of his own project was subdued by a fortification in a language he named metaphysics. In *Otherwise than Being* he would—for the most part—no longer rely on these foundations in language; instead he had found an appropriate language of weakness.

But is it a mere *pensiero debole*? A weakness to what end? Why privilege the weakness? If Derrida can be seen as a philosopher who deconstructs with the purpose of minimizing the violence within an economy of violence (Beardsley/Hägglund) or in privileging the margins (Critchley), one might ask what would be the reason for this privilege. When asking for a reason, what is the justification one is beseeching? For Levinas it has always been essential for philosophy to express a concrete direction—which in "Meaning and Sense" he expressed as a *sens unique*. During a period of time, this direction was provided by the notion of the face, designating an experience beyond experience. But after his implicit self-criticism in *Otherwise than Being*, rendered explicit in "Signature" and in interviews, Levinas is no longer satisfied with describing this weakness as an experience beyond experience. This reference to experience would still be an attempt to establish a secure point of reference outside of discourse, to another field than discourse, the *Hinterwelt*, the world beyond this world—a temptation which in *Totality and Infinity* Levinas tries to avoid.

Philosophy can, as Heidegger said, not justify itself with an external *Machtspruch*. Levinas would in the end not disagree with this. But this does not mean that the question of justification of philosophy (inherited from both Plato and Nietzsche) loses its urgency. For Levinas, the character of justification is irredeemably ethical, it presupposes the responsibility towards the other.

Let us briefly summarise the most important four points of our investigation:

I Our first point is exegetical: the notion of the human as transcendence (excendence) is always central for Levinas. He finds its point of anchorage in the asymmetric structure of responsibility to others.

II The relation of responsibility is the point which allows for an interruption of the ubiquity of the economy of violence, making critique possible.

III Levinas is neither a humanist nor an antihumanist, but he relates his philosophy intensely to this debate, making use of the antihumanist critique in order to chisel out a renewed notion of the human.

IV Universality can only be the goal and never the starting point for political thought.

I. From the start, Levinas was concerned with a philosophy of the human—the force (as weakness) to leave a situation where only force matters. As I hope to have shown, the structure of the social in the form of the relation to the other steps in so as to provide a meaning of the human as ethical transcendence, irreducible to the play of forces in immanent facticity. What Levinas found lacking in the contemporary understanding of the human (a problem which however seems present ever since the historical beginning of philosophy) was the possibility of conceiving of this transcendence apart from a philosophy of autonomy, which tended to create a new immanence as the subject conquers the world (philosophy of the same). With the notion of the human, an association is instead made with an economy of the subject which is transcended as rupture—indeed, this is what constitutes the very "subjectness" of the subject.

II. With the confrontation with the idea of justice as the lesser violence, I showed that the very concept of an economy of violence, as sketched out by Derrida in "Violence and Metaphysics", presupposes a perspective which transcends this economy in order for the economy at all to be visible as such. Thus, the hermeneutics of suspicion, showing ethics to be ideology, love to be violence, can never totalise itself—it must presuppose the limits of its own view. This does not take away the justification for such a perspective, which is necessary for a critique of power. Rather it strengthens it, making it visible as a method, rather than as an ontology. For Levinas, this critique is anchored in the subject's vulnerability to others: that the others concern me in spite of myself, whether I want it or not. This is not a statement on the goodness of human nature, but a reference to the conditions of discourse. In his earlier texts, this structure is shown in the notion of the human as a force of restlessness, which I laid out as the force to leave a situation where only force matters.

III. In the last period of his philosophy, Levinas no longer referred to his philosophy as a humanism. But neither was it antihumanist. In his mature thinking on this subject, we find out that both are integral moments in the movement in his thought. In this thought, neither humanism nor antihumanism are enough in themselves. Formulated dialectically: Antihumanism is a truer humanism.

Levinas would establish a certain distance to the idea of humanism, since it tends to presuppose a notion of the human in which one can rest—which, couched in the terms of this investigation, we can refer to as the *permanent* transcendence of the human from the economy of violence. Here, Levinas would have to agree with Heidegger, namely that the notion of humanism threatens not to be sufficiently sensitive to the "*Ereignis*" of the human. Nor would he call himself an antihumanist, which we now (seen undialectically) can define as the claim that the human is *permanently* inscribed in a general economy of violence. But if we understand transcendence from his idea of youth, we see that the notion of the human must, in order to justify itself, cut through and disturb any humanist formulation, and show how this formulation in itself already entails the establishment of an economy.

IV. Preserving a discourse on the human means preserving a discourse on universalism, but never as an order already established. Universalism must be understood from the viewpoint of the necessary yet infinitely incompletable task of universalising the singular relation of responsibility to the neighbour. This works as a reminder that neither democracy nor equal human rights are a reality, which can just be assumed. Human relations are unique and asymmetrical, not only because they are composed by individuals who always differ from each other, but because in each case they are someone's relation to another human being. In this relation I am me and the other is the other; these are not mere substitutable placeholders for the individual viewed from either a first or a second person perspective. There is an asymmetry in my relation to the other. Being me and being other are particular qualities which pertain to the intersubjective situation, exceeding the quality of being a certain individual as different from other individuals. There is no ethics of the other in Levinas, if by this one understands an ethics privileging those who are especially different from me culturally, socially or otherwise. Rather it is an ethics demanding a political universalism. It is primarily my responsibility for the singular other that needs to be universalised, not the subject as a pre-established individual taken in itself, with the categories and qualities that might define it.

The uniqueness of the being I or being you, in the sense that Levinas means, is thus a formal quality and not one of content. Being "you" for others, and being "me" for me (alterity and ipseity), are universals, which can apply to every individual, no matter how different or similar they are to me. Since the relation to the other always entails a responsibility, and since every other is an other for me, this responsibility *needs to be* universalised. This universalism will always transcend all formulations of it, since what it demands is a justice to every being in their singularity. But on the other hand, the universalist formulations can be brought alive by reading them as responding to this very injunction. As Levinas writes in “Toward the Other”: “Universalism has a greater weight than the particularist letter of the text; or, to be more precise, it bursts the letter apart, for it lay, like an explosive, within the letter” (QLT 61; NTR 28).

Key to Abbreviations

Texts by Emmanuel Levinas

TIPH	*Théorie de l'intuition tans la phénomenologie de Husserl*, Vrin, 2001 [1930].	TIHP	*The Theory of Intuition in Husserl's Phenomenology*, transl. André Orianne, 1995.
EDE	*En découvrant l'existence avec Husserl et Heidegger*, 2001 [1932-1967].	CPP	*Collected Philosophical Papers*, transl. Alphonso Lingis, Duquesne, 1998.
QRPH	*Quelques réflexions sur la philosophie de l'Hitlerisme*, Payot et Rivages, 1997 [1934].	RPH	"Reflections on the Philosophy of Hitlerism", transl. Sean Hand, *Critical inquiry* 17, 1990.
DE	*De l'évasion*, Le livre le poche, 1998 [1935].	OE	*On escape*, transl. Bettina Bergo, Stanford University Press, 2003.
He	*Cahiers de la Herne, Emmanuel Lévinas*, L'Herne, 1991[1935-1939].	BPW	*Basic philosophical writings*, ed. Adriaan Peperzak, Simon Critchley and Robert Bernasconi, Indiana University Press, 1987.
TA	*Le Temps et l'autre*, P.U.F., 1979 [1946/1947].	TO	*Time and the Other*, Duquesne University Press, transl. Richard Cohen, 1987.
DEE	*De l'existence à l'existant*, Vrin, 2004 [1947].	EE	*Existence and existents*, transl. Alphonso Lingis, Duquesne, 2008.
EN	*Entre nous: Essais sur le penser-à-l'autre*, Grasset, 1991 [1951-1990].	ENO	*Entre Nous. On Thinking-of-the-Other*, Columbia University Press, 1998.
TI	*Totalité et infini*, Le livre de poche, 1990 [1961].	TaI	*Totality and Infinity*, transl. Alphonso Lingis, Duquesne University Press, 2004.
HAH	*Humanisme de l'autre homme*, Le livre de poche, 1996 [1964-1972]	HO	*Humanism of the Other*, transl. Nidra Poller, University of Illinois, 2003.

QLT	*Quatre lectures talmudiques*, Les editions de minuit, 2005 [1968].		
DL	*Difficile Liberté*, Albin Michel, 1976.	DF	*Difficult Freedom*, transl. Sean Hand, John Hopkins University Press, 1990.
NP	*Noms propres*, Fata Morgana, 1976	PN	*Proper Names*, transl. Michael B. Smith, Stanford University Press, 1996.
ADV	*L'au-déla du verset*, Les éditions du Minuit, 1982 [1969-1980]	BV	*Beyond the Verse*, transl. Gary D. Mole, Indiana University Press, 1994.
ADV	*L'au-delà du verset*, Les éditions de Minuit, 1982		
AE	*Autrement qu'être*, Le livre de poche, 1990 [1974].	OB	*Otherwise than Being*, trans. Alphonso Lingis, Duquesne University Press, 2004.
IEP	"Israël : éthique et politique, entretiens avec S. Malka (avec Alain Finkielkraut)" in *Les Nouveaux Cahiers*, vol. 18, n°71, hiver, 1983, p. 1-8	LR	*The Levinas Reader*, ed. S. Hand, Blackwell, 1989.
DVI	*De Dieu qui vient à l'idée*, Vrin, 1982.	GCM	*Of God Who Comes to Mind*, transl. Bettina Bergo, Stanford University Press, 1998.
		PM	"The Paradox of Morality", an interview by Tamra Wright, Peter Hughes, Alison Ainley, transl. Andrew Benjamin and Tamra Wright, in Bernasconi, Robert and Wood, David (eds), *The provocation of Levinas*, Routledge, 1988.
EI	*Éthique et Infini. Dialogues avec Philippe Nemo.*, Livre de poche, 2002 [1982].		
HS	*Hors sujet*, Fata Morgana, 1987.	OS	*Outside the Subject*, transl. Michael B. Smith, Stanford University Press, 1993.
LC	*Liberté et Commandement*,		

Fata Morgana, 1994.

AT	*Altérité et transcendance*, Livre de poche, 2006 [1995].	AyT	*Alterity and Transcendence*, transl. Michael B. Smith, Athlone Press, 1999.
IEA	"Intention, Ereignis und der Andere", Interview with Christoph von Wolzogen in *Humanismus des anderen Menschen*, Felix Meiner, 2005, pp. 131-150.		

Texts by Other Writers

EA De Beauvoir, Simone, *The Ethics of Ambiguity*, transl. Bernhard Frechtman, Kensington, 1976.

ED Derrida, Jacques, *L'écriture et la difference*, Èditions du Seuil, 1967.

ES Bernasconi, Robert, "The Ethics of Suspicion", *Research in Phenomenology*, 20, 1990, pp. 3-18.

Hu Husserl, Edmund, *Husserliana*, Martinus Nijhoff.

KSA Nietzsche, Friedrich, *Kritische Studienausgabe*, 15 Bände (eds. Colli and Montinari), de Gruyter, München, 1999.

MC Foucault, *Les mots et les choses*, Gallimard, 1966.

OT Foucault, Michel, *The Order of Things*, Routledge 2008 [1966]

PM Heidegger, Martin, *Pathmarks*, Cambridge University Press, 1998.

PMA De Beauvoir, Simone, *Pour une Morale de l'ambiguité*, Folio, 2008 [1947]

WD Derrida, Jacques, *Writing and Difference*, Routledge, 1978.

WM Heidegger, Martin, *Wegmarken*, Klostermann, 1997.

WN Bernasconi, Robert, "Who is my neighbour? Who is the Other? Questioning 'the Generosity of Western Thought'" in *Ethics and responsibility in the phenomenological tradition*, Pittsburgh 1992, pp. 1-31.

List of References

Abensour, Miguel, "Anarchy between Metapolitics and Politics", *Parallax* vol. 8, nr.3 2002, pp. 5-18.

Abensour, Miguel, "Le Mal élémental", in *Quelques réflexions sur la philosophie de l'Hitlerisme*, Payot et Rivages, 1997 [1934].

Agamben, Giorgio, "Beyond Human Rights", transl. Cesare Casarino, in Radical Thought in Italy, ed. Paolo Virno & Michael Hardt, University of Minnesota Press, 2006.

Agamben, Giorgio, *Homo Sacer*, Stanford University Press, 1998

Agamben, Giorgio, "Introduzione", in: Emmanuel Levinas's, *Alcune riflessioni sulla filosofia dell'hitlerismo*, transl. Andrea Cavalletti and Stefano Chiodi. Macerata: Quodlibet, 1996, pp. 7-17.

Agamben, "We refugees", http://www.egs.edu/faculty/agamben/agamben-we-refugees.html, [accessed March 9, 2009].

Althusser, *Pour Marx*, La Découverte, 2005 [1965].

Arendt, Hannah, *Der Liebesbegriff bei Augustin: Versuch einer philosophischen Interpretation*, J. Springer, 1928.

Arendt, Hannah, *The Human Condition*, University of Chicago Press, 1998 [1958].

Arendt, Hannah, *The Origins of Totalitarianism*, Harcourt, 1976 [1948].

Backström, Joel, *The Fear of Openness. An Essay on Friendship and the Roots of Morality*, Åbo akademi, 2007.

Badiou, Alain, *Ethics. An Essay on the Understanding of Evil*, Verso 2001 [1998].

Bataille, Georges, "De l'existentialisme au primat de l'économie" in Critique, 19, 1947, pp. 127-141.

Bataille, Georges *The Accursed Share, Volume 1: Consumption*, transl. Robert Hurley, Zone Books 1991.

Beardsworth, Richard, *Derrida and the Political*, Routledge, 1996.

Beauvoir, Simone de, *Pyrrhus et Cinéas*, Gallimard 1944.

Beauvoir, Simone de, *The Second Sex*, Penguin, 1986.

Beistegui, Miguel de, *Truth and Genesis. Philosophy as Differential ontology*, Indiana University Press, 2004.

Bergson, Henri, *Creative Evolution*, transl. Arthur Mitchell, University Press of America, 1983,

Bersgson, Henri, *L'évolution créatrice*, P.U.F., 1959 [1907].

Bernasconi, Robert, Wood, David (Ed.), *Derrida and Difference*, Northwestern University Press 1988.

Bernasconi, Robert, "Heidegger's Alleged Challenge to the Nazi concepts of Race", in Faulconer, James (ed.), *Appropriating Heidegger*, Cambridge University Press, 2000. pp. 50-68.

Bernasconi, Robert, "Hegel and Levinas: The Possibility of Reconciliation and Forgiveness", *Archivio di Filosofia* 54, 1986, pp. 325-346.

Bernasconi, Robert, "No Exit. Levinas' Aporetic Account of Transcendence, in: *Research in Phenomenology*, 35, 2005, pp. 101-117.

Bernasconi, Robert, "Strangers and Slaves in the land of Egypt: Levinas and the Politics of Otherness", in *Levinas and Justice: Commentaries on Levinas and Politics*, eds. Asher Horowitz and Gad Horowitz, University of Toronto Press, 2006, pp. 246-261.

Bernasconi, Robert, "Toward a Phenomenology of Human Rights", Revue Internationale de Philosophie Moderne, Special Issue, 2008, pp. 83-96.

Bernet, Rudolf, "Levinas's Critique of Husserl", in: Critchley, Simon and Bernasconi, Robert (eds), In: *The Cambridge Companion to Levinas*, Cambridge University Press 2002, pp. 82-99.

Birnbaum, Daniel, "Den andre och tiden—om alteritet och närvaro i Husserls filosofi", in: Alexander Orlowski and Hans Ruin (eds), *Fenomenologiska perspektiv. Studier i Husserls och Heideggers filosofi*, Stockholm: Thales 1997, pp. 95-111.

Birnbaum, Daniel and Wallenstein, Sven-Olov, *Heideggers väg*, Thales, 1999.

Björk, Ulrika, *Poetics of Subjectivity*, Filosofisia tutkimuksia Helsingin yliopistosta 21, 2008.

Blanchot, Maurice, *The Infinite Conversation*, University of Minnesota Press, 1992.

Brown, Wendy, "Human Rights and the Politics of Fatalism", *The South Atlantic Quarterly* 103:2/3, Spring/summer 2004, pp. 451-463.

Bruaire, Claude, *Pour la métaphysique*, Fayard, 1980.

Butler, Judith, *Precarious Life: The Power of Mourning and Violence*, Verso, 2004.

Cairns, Dorion, Review of Emmanuel Levinas, *Théorie de l'intuition dans la phénoménologie de Husserl*, Paris: Librairie Philosophique J. Vrin, 1930; transl. Fred Kersten, 2007 (www.dorioncairns.net/levinasreview.htm. [Accessed February 26, 2010]).

Calin, Rodolphe, *Levinas et l'exception du soi*, P.U.F., 2005.

Cairo Declaration on Human Rights in Islam, Aug. 5, 1990, U.N. GAOR World Conf. on Hum. Rts., 4th Sess., Agenda Item 5, U.N. Doc. A/CONF.157/PC/62/Add.18 (1993). http://www1.umn.edu/humanrts/instree/cairodeclaration.html [Accessed April 12, 2009]

Caygill, Howard, *Levinas and the Political*, Routledge, 2002.

Chalier, Catherine, "Introductions aux texts de Lévinas (1935-1939)", in Emmanuel Levinas, *Cahiers de l'Herne*, 1991, pp. 139-141.

Chalier, Catherine, *Lévinas. L'utopie de l'humain*, Albin Michel, 1993.

Chalier, Catherine, *What Ought I to Do? Morality in Kant and Levinas*, transl. Jane Marie Todd. Ithaca: Cornell University Press, 2002.

Comte, Auguste, *Système de politique positive ou traité de sociologie instituant la religion de humanité*, Thunot, 1851-1854.

Courtine, Jean-François, "Fundamentalontologin hos Levinas", translated by Jim Jakobsson, in: Bornemark, Jonna (ed.) *Det främmande i det egna*, Huddinge: Södertörn Philosophical Studies, 2007, pp. 125-145.

Critchley, Simon, *Ethics of Deconstruction*, Edinburgh University Press, 1999.

Critchley, Simon, "Introduction", in: Critchley, Simon and Bernasconi, Robert (Eds), *The Cambridge Philosophy to Levinas*, Cambridge University Press, 2002.

Critchley, Simon, "Five problems in Levinas's view of Politics and the Sketch of a Solution to them", *Political Theory*, Vol. 32, No. 2, April 2004, pp. 172-185.

Critchley, Simon, *Infinitely Demanding: Ethics of Commitment, Politics of Resistance*, Verso, 2007.

Deleuze, Gilles, *Nietzsche and Philosophy*, Continuum, 2006.

Delhom, Pascal, *Der Dritte. Lévinas' philosophie zwischen Verantwortung und Gerechtigkeit*, Fink, 2000.

Derrida, Jacques, *Adieu*, Galilee, 1997.

Derrida, Jacques, "Derrida avec Lévinas: « entre lui et moi dans l'affection et la confiance partagée »", Interview with Alain David in *Magazine littéraire*, no 419, April 2003.
Derrida, Jacques, "Force of law: the 'mystical foundation of authority'", translated by M. Quaintance in *Deconstruction and the Possibility of Justice*, ed. D. Cornell and D. G. Carlson, Routledge, 1992, pp. 3-67.
Derrida, Jacques, *Lagens kraft*, Symposion, 2005.
Derrida, Jacques, "Letter to a Japanese Friend" in *Derrida and Difference*, ed. Robert Bernasconi and David Wood, Northwestern University Press, 1988. pp. 1-5.
Derrida, Jacques, *Limited Inc*, translated by S. Weber, Northwestern University, Evanston, 1988.
Derrida, Jacques, *Margins of Philosophy*, translated by A. Bass, University of Chicago Press, 1982.
Derrida, Jacques, *Marges de la philosophie*, Minuit, 1972,
Derrida, Jacques, *Of Grammatology*, Translated by Gayatri Chakravorty Spivak, Johns Hopkins University Press, 1974.
Derrida, Jacques, *Passions, 'L'offrande oblique'*, Galilée, 1993.
Derrida, Jacques, "Passions. 'An oblique Offering'", tr. D. Wood, in *Derrida: A Critical Reader*, ed. D. Wood, Blackwell, 1992, pp. 5-35.
Diels, Hermann Alexander, *Die Fragmente der Vorsokratiker*, rev. by Walther Kranz, Weidmann, 1952.
Drabinski, John E., *Sensibility and Singularity. The Problem of Phenomenology in Levinas*, State University of New York Press, 2001.
Fanon, Frantz, *Black Skin, White Masks*, Pluto Press, 1986
Farías, Victor, *Heidegger et le nazisme*, Verdier 1987.
Feuerbach, Ludwig, *Das Wesen des Christentums*, Akadmie-Verlag, 1984 [1841].
Fink, Eugen, *Metaphysik der Erziehung im Weltverständnis von Plato und Aristoteles*, Kloterna, 1970.
Finkielkraut, Alain, *In the Name of Humanity*, Columbia University Press, 2000
Foucault, Michel, *History of Sexuality*, 3 Volumes, Penguin, 1988-1992 [1976-1982].
Foucault, Michel. *Introduction to Kant's Anthropology*, Semiotexte, 2008.
Foucault, Michel, "La torture, c'est la raison", Interview with K. Boesers, December 1977, *Dits et écrits III*, Gallimard 1994, pp. 397-8
Foucault, Michel, *Madness and civilisation: A History of Insanity in the Age of Reason*, Vintage Books, 1988.
Foucault, Michel, "The Subject and Power", in Dreyfus, Hubert and Rabinow, Paul, *Michel Foucault: Beyond Structuralism and Hermeneutics*, University of Chicago Press, 1982.
Foucault, Michel, "What is Critique?", in *The Politics of Truth*, eds. Sylvère Lotringer and Lysa Hochroth, Semiotexte, transl. Lysa Hochroth, 1997 [1978].
Freud, Sigmund, "Das ökonomische Problem des Masochismus", *Studienausgabe*, Bd. III, Fischer, 1982 [1915], pp. 339-354.
Freud, Sigmund, "Das Unbewusste", *Studienausgabe*, Bd. III, Fischer, 1982 [1915] pp. 119-154.
Freud, Sigmund, *Jenseits des Lustprinzips*, Internationaler psychoanalytischer Verlag, 1921.
Goethe, Johann Wolfgang Friedrich von, *Faust II*, Reclam, 1999 [1832].
Goethe, Johann Wolfgang Friedrich von, *Faust*, transl. George Madison Priest, Alfred A. Knopf, 1941.
Hägglund, Martin, *Radical Atheism. Derrida and the Time of Life*, Stanford University Press, 2008.

Hägglund, Martin, "The necessity of discrimination", Diacritics 34.1, spring 2004, pp. 47-48.
Hegel, Georg Wilhelm Friedrich, *Phänomenologie des Geistes*, Felix Meiner, 1980 [1807].
Hegel, Georg Wilhelm Friedrich, *Hauptwerke in sechs Bänden*, Wissenschaftliche Buchgesellschaft, 1999.
Heidegger, Martin, *Die Selbstbehauptung der Deutschen Universität*, Korn, 1933.
Heidegger, Martin, *Einführung in die Metaphysik*, Niemeyer, 1953.
Heidegger, Martin, *Sein und Zeit*, Niemeyer, 1993 [1927].
Hirsch, Alfred, "Menschenrechte des Fremden", in: *INEF Report* Heft 76, 2005.
Höffe, Ottfried, *Demokratie im Zeitalter der Menschenrechte*, C.H.Beck, 1999
Höffe, Ottfried, "Transzendentaler Tausch. Eine Legitimationsfigur für Menschenrechte?", in Stefan Gosepath and Georg Lohmann (Eds), *Philosophie der Menschenrechte*, 1999, pp. 241-274.
Husserl, Edmund, *Formale und transzendentale Logik*, Martinus Nijhoff, 1974.
Husserl, Edmund, *Ideas Pertaining to a Pure Phenomenology and to a Phenomenological Philosophy, First Book, General Introduction to a Pure Phenomenology*, trans. F. Kersten, Martinus Nijhoff, 1982
Husserl, Edmund, *Méditations cartésiennes: Introduction à la phénoménologie*, translated by Emmanuel Levinas and Gabrielle Pfeiffer, Vrin, 1966 [1929].
Husserl, Edmund, *The Phenomenology of Internal Time Consciousness*, trans. James S. Churchill, Indiana University Press, 1964.
Ignatieff, Michael, *Human Rights as Politics and Idolatry*, Princeton University Press, 2001.
Janicaud, Domninique, "L'humanisme: des malentendus aux enjeux", *Revue philosophique de Louvain*, Vol. 99, no 2, May 2001, pp. 183-200
Kant, Immanuel, *Grundlegung zur Metaphysik der Sitten*, Sammlung Philosophie, Band 3, Vandenhoeck und Ruprecht, 2004 [1785].
Kant, Immanuel, *Kritik der reinen Vernunft*, Felix Meiner, 1998 [1781]
Kant, Immaunel, *Political Writings*, Cambridge University Press, 1991.
Kant, Immanuel, *Schriften zur Anthropologie, Geschichtsphilosophie, Politik und Pädagogik*, Werkausgabe in 12 Bänden. Band XI:1, Suhrkamp, 2006.
Kierkegaard, Søren, *Book on Adler, Kierkegaard's Writings*, Vol. 24, Princeton University Press, 1998.
Kojève, Alexandre, *Introduction à la lecture de Hegel*, Gallimard, 1968 [1947].
Lee, Mara, *Hennes vård*, Vertigo, 2004.
Llewelyn, John, "Levinas's Critical and Hypocritical Diction", *Philosophy Today*, Supplement 1997, 28-40.
Lévi-Strauss, Claude, *Anthropologie structurale*, Plon, 1958
Lévi-Strauss, Claude, *La pensée sauvage*, Agora, 2009 [1962]
Lévi-Strauss, Claude, *Tristes tropiques*, Plon, 1955
Löwith, Karl, *Das Individuum in der Rolle des Mitmenschen: Ein Beitrag zur anthropologischen Grundlegung der ethischen Probleme*, Drei Masken Verlag, 1928.
Loidolt, Sophie, *Anspruch und Rechtfertigung: eine Theorie des rechtlichen Denkens im Anschluss an die Phänomenologie Edmund Husserls*, Phaenomenologica, Band 191, 2009.
Lyotard, Jean-François, *Libidinal Economy*, Continuum, 1993.
Lyotard, Jean-François, "The Other's Rights", translated by Chris Miller and Robert Smith in S.Shute & S. Hurley (eds.) *On Human Rights: the Oxford Amnesty Lectures 1993*, Basic Books, 1993.
Marion, Jean-Luc, *L'idole et la distance* B. Grasset, 1977.
Marion, Jean-Luc, *Sur le prisme métaphysique de Descartes*, PUF Épiméthée 1986.

Marx, Karl, *Marx-Engels-Werke, Bd. I, Kritik der Hegelschen Rechtsphilosophie*, Dietz Verlag, 1976 [1843].

Marx, Karl and Engels, Friedrich, *On Religion*, (ed. Reinhold Niehbuhr), Scholars, 1982.

Merleau-Ponty, Maurice, *Signs*, Northwestern University Press, 1964

Milbank, John, *The Shares of Being or Gift, Relation and Participation: an Essay on the Metaphysics of Emmanuel Levinas and Alain Badiou* (http://www.theologyphilosophycentre.co.uk/papers/Milbank_Metaphysics-LevinasBadiou.doc [Accessed 15 dec. 2009]

Moyn, Samuel, *Origins of the Other, Emmanuel Lévinas between Revelation and Ethics,* Cornell University Press 2005.

Nietzsche, Friedrich, *Beyond Good and Evil*, transl. Helen Zimmern, Plain Label Books, 1917.

Niettzsche, Friedrich, *Kritische Studienausgabe* (KSA), 15 Volumes, edited by Colli und Montinari, DeGruyter, 1999.

Nietzsche, Friedrich, *On the Genealogy of Morals*, translated by Douglas Smith, Oxford University Press, 1996

Nolte, Ernst, *Three Faces of Fascism: Action Française, Italian Fascism, National Socialism*, trans. Leila Vennewitz, Holt Rinehart, 1966.

Ott, Hugo, *Martin Heidegger, Unterwegs zu seiner Biographie*, Frankfurt a. M.: Campus, 1988

Overgaard, Søren, "On Levinas's Critique of Husserl" in Dan Zahavi et al (eds), *Metaphysics, Facticity and Interpretation*, Dortrecht: Kluwer, 2003, pp. 115-138

Rancière, Jacques, "Who is the Subject of the Rights of Man?", *The South Atlantic Quarterly* 103: 2/3, Spring/Summer 2004, 297-309

Ramshaw, Sara, "Monstrous Inventions: The Ethics and Trauma of Scientific Discovery", In: *Thinking Through Gender and Science Workshop*, Queen's University, http://www.qub.ac.uk/sites/QUEST/FileStore/Issue3GRFSpecial/Filetoupload,55420,en.pdf [accessed 30 september 2010].

Ricoeur, Paul, *Freud and Philosophy: An Essay on Interpretation*, Yale University Press, 1970.

Robbins, Jill (Ed.), *Is it Righteous to be? Interviews with Emmanuel Levinas*, Stanford University Press, 2001

Rockmore, Tom, *Heidegger and French Humanism*, Routledge, 1995.

Rorty, Richard. "Human rights, Rationality, and Sentimentality". In S.Shute & S. Hurley (eds.) *On Human Rights: the Oxford Amnesty Lectures 1993*, Basic Books, 1993.

Rosmarin, Leonard, *Emmanuel Lévinas, humaniste de l'autre homme*, Éditions du Gref, Collections L'un pour l'autre, no 1, 1991.

Safranski, Rüdiger, *Heidegger, Between Good and Evil*, Harvard University Press, 1998

Sandford, Stella, "Plato and Levinas: The Same and the Other," *Journal of the British Society for Phenomenology*, 1999, 30(2), pp. 131-150.

Sartre, Jean-Paul, *Cahiers pour une morale*, Gallimard, 1983.

Sartre, Jean-Paul, *Écrits posthumes de Sartre, II* (ed. Juliette Simont), Vrin, 2001, pp. 27-59.

Sartre, Jean-Paul, "La liberté cartesienne", *Situations 1*, Gallimard, 1947, pp. 314-335.

Sartre, Jean-Paul, *La Nausée*, Gallimard, 1938.

Sartre, Jean-Paul, *L'Être et le néant,* Gallimard, 2006 [1943]

Sartre, Jean-Paul, *L'existentialisme est un humanisme*, Gallimard, 1996 [1945],

Simont, Juliette, “La morale de Sartre, entre humanisme et anti-humanisme”, *Daimon, Revista de Filosofia*, no 35, 2004, pp. 23-24.

Søltoft, Pia *Svimmelhedens Etik—om forholdet mellem den enkelte og den anden hos Buber, Lévinas og især Kierkegaard*, Gads forlag, 2000.

Stegmaier, Werner, “Die Bindung des Bindenden. Levinas‘ Konzeption des Politischen.”, In: Hirsch, Alfred and Delhom, Pascal (Eds) *Im Angesicht der Anderen. Emmanuel Levinas's Philosophie des Politischen*, Diaphanes, 2005, pp. 25-44

Ten Hoor, Marten, The Nazis purge philosophy, in *The Kenyan Review*, vol. 3, nr. 3 1941, http://www.kenyonreview.org/issues/archives/tenhoorS1941.php [accessed 15. 2. 2007]

Universal Declaration of Human Rights, http://www.un.org/en/documents/udhr/ [Accessed Oct. 11, 2010]

Vietta, Silvio, *Heideggers Kritik am Nationalsozialismus und der Technik*. Niemeyer, 1989.

Visker, Rudi, “Dis-possessed: How to remain silent ‘after’ Levinas”, *Man and World*, 29, 1996, pp. 119-146.

Visker, Rudi, “Is ethics fundamental? Questioning Levinas on irresponsibility”, *Continental Philosophy Review* 36, 2003, pp. 263-302.

Voegelin, Eric, *The Collected Works of Eric Voegelin. Volume 29, Selected Correspondence*, edited by Ellis Sandoz, University of Missoury Press, 2009.

Voegelin, Eric, “The Origins of Totalitarianism”, In: *Published Essays: 1953-1965*, Volume 11, University of Missouri 2000, pp. 15-23

Wahl, Jean, *Vers le concret: Études de histoire de la philosophie contemporaine*, Vrin, 1932.

Zahavi, Dan, *Self-Awareness and Alterity, A phenomenological Investigation*, Northwestern University Press, 1999.

Žižek, Slavoj, *Smashing the neighbour's face*, http://www.lacan.com/zizsmash.htm [accessed 19 May 2009].

Žižek, Slavoj, *The Neighbor. Three Inquiries in Political Theology*, University of Chicago Press, 2006.

Södertörn Doctoral Dissertations

1. Jolanta Aidukaite, *The Emergence of the Post-Socialist Welfare State: The case of the Baltic States: Estonia, Latvia and Lithuania*, 2004
2. Xavier Fraudet, *Politique étrangère française en mer Baltique (1871–1914): de l'exclusion à l'affirmation*, 2005
3. Piotr Wawrzeniuk, *Confessional Civilising in Ukraine: The Bishop Iosyf Shumliansky and the Introduction of Reforms in the Diocese of Lviv 1668–1708*, 2005
4. Andrej Kotljarchuk, *In the Shadows of Poland and Russia: The Grand Duchy of Lithuania and Sweden in the European Crisis of the mid-17th Century*, 2006
5. Håkan Blomqvist, *Nation, ras och civilisation i svensk arbetarrörelse före nazismen*, 2006
6. Karin S Lindelöf, *Om vi nu ska bli som Europa: Könsskapande och normalitet bland unga kvinnor i transitionens Polen*, 2006
7. Andrew Stickley. *On Interpersonal Violence in Russia in the Present and the Past: A Sociological Study*, 2006
8. Arne Ek, *Att konstruera en uppslutning kring den enda vägen: Om folkrörelsers modernisering i skuggan av det Östeuropeiska systemskiftet*, 2006
9. Agnes Ers, *I mänsklighetens namn: En etnologisk studie av ett svenskt biståndsprojekt i Rumänien*, 2006
10. Johnny Rodin, *Rethinking Russian Federalism: The Politics of Intergovernmental Relations and Federal Reforms at the Turn of the Millennium*, 2006
11. Kristian Petrov, *Tillbaka till framtiden: Modernitet, postmodernitet och generationsidentitet i Gorbačevs glasnost' och perestrojka*, 2006
12. Sophie Söderholm Werkö, *Patient patients?: Achieving Patient Empowerment through Active Participation, Increased Knowledge and Organisation*, 2008
13. Peter Bötker, *Leviatan i arkipelagen: Staten, förvaltningen och samhället. Fallet Estland*, 2007
14. Matilda Dahl, *States under scrutiny: International organizations, transformation and the construction of progress*, 2007
15. Margrethe B. Søvik, *Support, resistance and pragmatism: An examination of motivation in language policy in Kharkiv*, Ukraine, 2007
16. Yulia Gradskova, *Soviet People with female Bodies: Performing beauty and maternity in Soviet Russia in the mid 1930–1960s*, 2007
17. Renata Ingbrant, *From Her Point of View: Woman's Anti-World in the Poetry of Anna Świrszczyńska*, 2007
18. Johan Eellend, *Cultivating the Rural Citizen: Modernity, Agrarianism and Citizenship in Late Tsarist Estonia*, 2007
19. Petra Garberding, *Musik och politik i skuggan av nazismen: Kurt Atterberg och de svensk-tyska musikrelationerna*, 2007
20. Aleksei Semenenko, *Hamlet the Sign: Russian Translations of Hamlet and Literary Canon Formation*, 2007
21. Vytautas Petronis, *Constructing Lithuania: Ethnic Mapping in the Tsarist Russia, ca. 1800–1914*, 2007

22. Akvile Motiejunaite, *Female employment, gender roles, and attitudes: the Baltic countries in a broader context*, 2008
23. Tove Lindén, *Explaining Civil Society Core Activism in Post-Soviet Latvia*, 2008
24. Pelle Åberg, *Translating Popular Education: Civil Society Cooperation between Sweden and Estonia*, 2008
25. Anders Nordström, *The Interactive Dynamics of Regulation: Exploring the Council of Europe's monitoring of Ukraine*, 2008
26. Fredrik Doeser, *In Search of Security After the Collapse of the Soviet Union: Foreign Policy Change in Denmark, Finland and Sweden, 1988–1993*, 2008
27. Zhanna Kravchenko. *Family (versus) Policy: Combining Work and Care in Russia and Sweden*, 2008
28. Rein Jüriado, *Learning within and between public-private partnerships*, 2008
29. Elin Boalt, *Ecology and evolution of tolerance in two cruciferous species*, 2008
30. Lars Forsberg, *Genetic Aspects of Sexual Selection and Mate Choice in Salmonids*, 2008
31. Eglė Rindzevičiūtė, *Constructing Soviet Cultural Policy: Cybernetics and Governance in Lithuania after World War II*, 2008
32. Joakim Philipson, *The Purpose of Evolution: 'struggle for existence' in the Russian-Jewish press 1860–1900*, 2008
33. Sofie Bedford, *Islamic activism in Azerbaijan: Repression and mobilization in a post-Soviet context*, 2009
34. Tommy Larsson Segerlind, *Team Entrepreneurship: A process analysis of the venture team and the venture team roles in relation to the innovation process*, 2009
35. Jenny Svensson, *The Regulation of Rule-Following: Imitation and Soft Regulation in the European Union*, 2009
36. Stefan Hallgren, *Brain Aromatase in the guppy, Poecilia reticulate: Distribution, control and role in behavior*, 2009
37. Karin Ellencrona, *Functional characterization of interactions between the flavivirus NS5 protein and PDZ proteins of the mammalian host*, 2009
38. Makiko Kanematsu, *Saga och verklighet: Barnboksproduktion i det postsovjetiska Lettland*, 2009
39. Daniel Lindvall, *The Limits of the European Vision in Bosnia and Herzegovina: An Analysis of the Police Reform Negotiations*, 2009
40. Charlotta Hillerdal, *People in Between – Ethnicity and Material Identity: A New Approach to Deconstructed Concepts*, 2009
41. Jonna Bornemark, *Kunskapens gräns – gränsens vetande*, 2009
42. Adolphine G. Kateka, *Co-Management Challenges in the Lake Victoria Fisheries: A Context Approach*, 2010
43. René León Rosales, *Vid framtidens hitersta gräns: Om pojkar och elevpositioner i en multietnisk skola*, 2010
44. Simon Larsson, *Intelligensaristokrater och arkivmartyrer: Normerna för vetenskaplig skicklighet i svensk historieforskning 1900–1945*, 2010
45. Håkan Lättman, *Studies on spatial and temporal distributions of epiphytic lichens*, 2010
46. Alia Jaensson, *Pheromonal mediated behaviour and endocrine response in salmonids: The impact of cypermethrin, copper, and glyphosate*, 2010
47. Michael Wigerius, *Roles of mammalian Scribble in polarity signaling, virus offense and cell-fate determination*, 2010
48. Anna Hedtjärn Wester, *Män i kostym: Prinsar, konstnärer och tegelbärare vid sekelskiftet 1900*, 2010
49. Magnus Linnarsson, *Postgång på växlande villkor: Det svenska postväsendets organisation under stormaktstiden*, 2010

50. Barbara Kunz, *Kind words, cruise missiles and everything in between: A neoclassical realist study of the use of power resources in U.S. policies towards Poland, Ukraine and Belarus 1989–2008*, 2010
51. Anders Bartonek, *Philosophie im Konjunktiv: Nichtidentität als Ort der Möglichkeit des Utopischen in der negativen Dialektik Theodor W. Adornos*, 2010
52. Carl Cederberg, *Resaying the Human: Levinas Beyond Humanism and Antihumanism*, 2010
53. Johanna Ringarp, *Professionens problematik: Lärarkårens kommunalisering och välfärdsstatens förvandling*, 2011
54. Sofi Gerber, *Öst är Väst men Väst är bäst: Östtysk identitetsformering i det förenade Tyskland*, 2011
55. Susanna Sjödin Lindenskoug, *Manlighetens bortre gräns: Tidelagsrättegångar i Livland åren 1685–1709*, 2011
56. Dominika Polanska, *The emergence of enclaves of wealth and poverty: A sociological study of residential differentiation in post-communist Poland*, 2011
57. Christina Douglas, *Kärlek per korrespondens: Två förlovade par under andra hälften av 1800-talet*, 2011
58. Fred Saunders, *The Politics of People - Not just Mangroves and Monkeys: A study of the theory and practice of community-based management of natural resources in Zanzibar*, 2011
59. Anna Rosengren, *Åldrandet och språket: En språkhistorisk analys av hög ålder och åldrande i Sverige cirka 1875–1975*, 2011
60. Emelie Lilliefeldt, *European Party Politics and Gender: Configuring Gender-Balanced Parliamentary Presence*, 2011
61. Ola Svenonius, *Sensitising Urban Transport Security: Surveillance and Policing in Berlin, Stockholm, and Warsaw*, 2011
62. Andreas Johansson, *Dissenting Democrats: Nation and Democracy in the Republic of Moldova*, 2011
63. Wessam Melik, *Molecular characterization of the Tick-borne encephalitis virus: Environments and replication*, 2012
64. Steffen Werther, *SS-Vision und Grenzland-Realität: Vom Umgang dänischer und „volksdeutscher" Nationalsozialisten in Sønderjylland mit der „großgermanischen“ Ideologie der SS*, 2012
65. Peter Jakobsson, *Öppenhetsindustrin*, 2012
66. Kristin Ilves, *Seaward Landward: Investigations on the archaeological source value of the landing site category in the Baltic Sea region*, 2012
67. Anne Kaun, *Civic Experiences and Public Connection: Media and Young People in Estonia*, 2012
68. Anna Tessmann, *On the Good Faith: A Fourfold Discursive Construction of Zoroastripanism in Contemporary Russia*, 2012
69. Jonas Lindström, *Drömmen om den nya staden: stadsförnyelse i det postsovjetisk Riga*, 2012
70. Maria Wolrath Söderberg, *Topos som meningsskapare: retorikens topiska perspektiv på tänkande och lärande genom argumentation*, 2012
71. Linus Andersson, *Alternativ television: former av kritik i konstnärlig TV-produktion*, 2012
72. Håkan Lättman, *Studies on spatial and temporal distributions of epiphytic lichens*, 2012
73. Fredrik Stiernstedt, Mediearbete i mediehuset: produktion i förändring på MTG-radio, 2013
74. Jessica Moberg, *Piety, Intimacy and Mobility: A Case Study of Charismatic Christianity in Present-day Stockholm*, 2013
75. Elisabeth Hemby, *Historiemåleri och bilder av vardag: Tatjana Nazarenkos konstnärskap i 1970-talets Sovjet*, 2013

76. Tanya Jukkala, *Suicide in Russia: A macro-sociological study*, 2013
77. Maria Nyman, *Resandets gränser: svenska resenärers skildringar av Ryssland under 1700-talet*, 2013
78. Beate Feldmann Eellend, *Visionära planer och vardagliga praktiker: postmilitära landskap i Östersjöområdet*, 2013
79. Emma Lind, *Genetic response to pollution in sticklebacks: natural selection in the wild*, 2013
80. Anne Ross Solberg, *The Mahdi wears Armani: An analysis of the Harun Yahya enterprise*, 2013
81. Nikolay Zakharov, *Attaining Whiteness: A Sociological Study of Race and Racialization in Russia*, 2013
82. Anna Kharkina, *From Kinship to Global Brand: the Discourse on Culture in Nordic Cooperation after World War II*, 2013
83. Florence Fröhlig, *A painful legacy of World War II: Nazi forced enlistment: Alsatian/Mosellan Prisoners of war and the Soviet Prison Camp of Tambov*, 2013
84. Oskar Henriksson, *Genetic connectivity of fish in the Western Indian Ocean*, 2013
85. Hans Geir Aasmundsen, *Pentecostalism, Globalisation and Society in Contemporary Argentina*, 2013
86. Anna McWilliams, *An Archaeology of the Iron Curtain: Material and Metaphor*, 2013
87. Anna Danielsson, *On the power of informal economies and the informal economies of power: rethinking informality, resilience and violence in Kosovo*, 2014
88. Carina Guyard, *Kommunikationsarbete på distans*, 2014
89. Sofia Norling, *Mot "väst": om vetenskap, politik och transformation i Polen 1989–2011*, 2014
90. Markus Huss, *Motståndets akustik: språk och (o)ljud hos Peter Weiss 1946–1960*, 2014
91. Ann-Christin Randahl, *Strategiska skribenter: skrivprocesser i fysik och svenska*, 2014
92. Péter Balogh, *Perpetual borders: German-Polish cross-border contacts in the Szczecin area*, 2014
93. Erika Lundell, *Förkroppsligad fiktion och fiktionaliserade kroppar: levande rollspel i Östersjöregionen*, 2014
94. Henriette Cederlöf, *Alien Places in Late Soviet Science Fiction: The "Unexpected Encounters" of Arkady and Boris Strugatsky as Novels and Films*, 2014
95. Niklas Eriksson, *Urbanism Under Sail: An archaeology of fluit ships in early modern everyday life*, 2014
96. Signe Opermann, *Generational Use of News Media in Estonia: Media Access, Spatial Orientations and Discursive Characteristics of the News Media*, 2014
97. Liudmila Voronova, *Gendering in political journalism: A comparative study of Russia and Sweden*, 2014
98. Ekaterina Kalinina, *Mediated Post-Soviet Nostalgia*, 2014
99. Anders E. B. Blomqvist, *Economic Natonalizing in the Ethnic Borderlands of Hungary and Romania: Inclusion, Exclusion and Annihilation in Szatmár/Satu-Mare, 1867–1944*, 2014
100. Ann-Judith Rabenschlag, *Völkerfreundschaft nach Bedarf: Ausländische Arbeitskräfte in der Wahrnehmung von Staat und Bevölkerung der DDR*, 2014
101. Yuliya Yurchuck, *Ukrainian Nationalists and the Ukrainian Insurgent Army in Post-Soviet Ukraine*, 2014
102. Hanna Sofia Rehnberg, *Organisationer berättar: narrativitet som resurs i strategisk kommunikation*, 2014
103. Jaakko Turunen, *Semiotics of Politics: Dialogicality of Parliamentary Talk*, 2015
104. Iveta Jurkane-Hobein, *I Imagine You Here Now: Relationship Maintenance Strategies in Long-Distance Intimate Relationships*, 2015
105. Katharina Wesolowski, *Maybe baby? Reproductive behaviour, fertility intentions, and family policies in post-communist countries, with a special focus on Ukraine*, 2015

106. Ann af Burén, *Living Simultaneity: On religion among semi-secular Swedes*, 2015
107. Larissa Mickwitz, *En reformerad lärare: konstruktionen av en professionell och betygssättande lärare i skolpolitik och skolpraktik*, 2015
108. Daniel Wojahn, *Språkaktivism: diskussioner om feministiska språkförändringar i Sverige från 1960-talet till 2015*, 2015
109. Hélène Edberg, *Kreativt skrivande för kritiskt tänkande: en fallstudie av studenters arbete med kritisk metareflektion*, 2015
110. Kristina Volkova, *Fishy Behavior: Persistent effects of early-life exposure to 17α-ethinylestradiol*, 2015
111. Björn Sjöstrand, *Att tänka det tekniska: en studie i Derridas teknikfilosofi*, 2015
112. Håkan Forsberg, *Kampen om eleverna: gymnasiefältet och skolmarknadens framväxt i Stockholm, 1987–2011*, 2015
113. Johan Stake, *Essays on quality evaluation and bidding behavior in public procurement auctions*, 2015
114. Martin Gunnarson, *Please Be Patient: A Cultural Phenomenological Study of Haemodialysis and Kidney Transplantation Care*, 2016
115. Nasim Reyhanian Caspillo, *Studies of alterations in behavior and fertility in ethinyl estradiol-exposed zebrafish and search for related biomarkers*, 2016
116. Pernilla Andersson, *The Responsible Business Person: Studies of Business Education for Sustainability*, 2016
117. Kim Silow Kallenberg, *Gränsland: svensk ungdomsvård mellan vård och straff*, 2016
118. Sari Vuorenpää, *Literacitet genom interaction*, 2016
119. Francesco Zavatti, *Writing History in a Propaganda Institute: Political Power and Network Dynamics in Communist Romania*, 2016
120. Cecilia Annell, *Begärets politiska potential: Feministiska motståndsstrategier i Elin Wägners 'Pennskaftet', Gabriele Reuters 'Aus guter Familie', Hilma Angered-Strandbergs 'Lydia Vik' och Grete Meisel-Hess 'Die Intellektuellen'*, 2016
121. Marco Nase, *Academics and Politics: Northern European Area Studies at Greifswald University, 1917–1992*, 2016
122. Jenni Rinne, *Searching for Authentic Living Through Native Faith – The Maausk movement in Estonia*, 2016
123. Petra Werner, *Ett medialt museum: lärandets estetik i svensk television 1956–1969*, 2016
124. Ramona Rat, *Un-common Sociality: Thinking sociality with Levinas*, 2016
125. Petter Thureborn, *Microbial ecosystem functions along the steep oxygen gradient of the Landsort Deep, Baltic Sea*, 2016
126. Kajsa-Stina Benulic, *A Beef with Meat – Media and audience framings of environmentally unsustainable production and consumption*, 2016
127. Naveed Asghar, *Ticks and Tick-borne Encephalitis Virus – From nature to infection*, 2016

www.ingramcontent.com/pod-product-compliance
Lightning Source LLC
Chambersburg PA
CBHW080439170426
43195CB00017B/2826
9789186069216